Finding the River

AN ENVIRONMENTAL HISTORY OF THE ELWHA

JEFF CRANE

Oregon State University Press • Corvallis

Library of Congress Cataloging-in-Publication Data

Finding the river : an environmental history of the Elwha / Jeff Crane.
    p. cm.
 Includes bibliographical references and index.
 ISBN 978-0-87071-607-2 (alk. paper)
 ISBN 978-0-87071-646-1 (e-book)
 1. Elwha River (Wash.)--History. 2. Elwha River (Wash)--Environmental conditions. 3. Water--Pollution--Washington (State)--Elwha River. 4. Dams--Environmental aspects--Washington (State)--Elwha River. 5. Dam retirement--Washington (State)--Elwha River. I. Title.
 GB1227.E58C73 2011
 333.91'621530979798--dc23
                    2011019518

Oregon State University Press
121 The Valley Library
Corvallis OR 97331-4501
541-737-3166 • fax 541-737-3170
http://osupress.oregonstate.edu

Finding the River

Table of Contents

For Jennine, Chloe, and Ella

Introduction

Find the River

THE PRESENT AND HISTORICAL ELWHA

The ocean is the river's goal
from "Find the River"
REM

To hikers moving up the Elwha River from the Whiskey Bend trailhead, the river is a teasing presence, lying far below, with the trail providing occasional glimpses. But upon reaching Hume's Ranch and breaking from the trail down to the river itself, the sound gathers up, compelling an increase in gait as the river draws near. And what you see is worth the sweat you have produced by this point. The Elwha's beauty could serve as a model, an icon, of Pacific Northwest rivers. The deep green pools; the wide gravel beds with rich, aerated riffles; the variety of cobble and larger rocks in the riverbed—all suggest a perfect Pacific Northwest river, one that should roil with bright red and green-hued spawning salmon. The fog coiling down from the mountainsides and the bent branch of a hemlock or cedar dipping in a quiet pool, being tugged by the river, seemingly forever without end, create an image and place of Zen-like solace and beauty. In these moments and places, contemplation leads one to wonder at the past of this river and its inhabitants, and at possibilities.

The section of river described here is located within the Olympic National Park and was upstream of two aging dams. The Elwha Dam was built in 1913 and the Glines Canyon Dam, in 1927. Approximately five miles upstream of the river mouth on the Strait of Juan de Fuca, the Elwha Dam was remarkably primitive looking, nothing like the monolithic Grand Coulee Dam on the Columbia

River or Hoover Dam on the Colorado River. Squat, covered in moss, and leaking in multiple locations, the Elwha Dam looked its age, like an antique of early Pacific Northwest industrialization. The Glines Canyon Dam was built eight and a half miles upstream of the first dam, and was more elegant in construction, reflecting improvements in dam engineering.

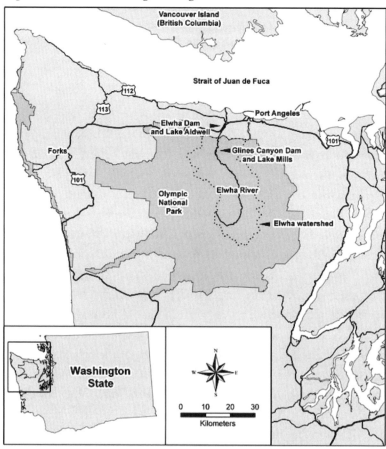

Olympic Peninsula and Elwha River watershed. Map is courtesy of the U.S. Department of Commerce, National Oceanic and Atmospheric Administration, and National Marine Fisheries Service, "NOAA Technical Memorandum NMFSNWFSC-90, Elwha River Fish Restoration Plan, Developed Pursuant to the Elwha River, Ecosystem and Fisheries Restoration Act, Public Law 102-495," April 2008.

The lower dam immediately blocked the spawning migrations of salmon and steelhead. As one wades the riffles, fishes the pools, and explores the Elwha and its tributaries above the dams, it becomes clear that the salmon and steelhead are absent. Biologically speaking, the river is a shadow of its former self. Before the Elwha Dam was built, the river produced approximately 400,000 salmon and steelhead a year, with some chinook weighing over 100 pounds. It is an odd experience to be deep in the Elwha River valley, surrounded by healthy forest, viewing a clean and healthy river ecosystem, and comprehend the diminished river.[1] While magnificent, beautiful, and even transcendent, the river exudes a fundamental emptiness that is the legacy of settlement and development—a legacy specifically due to the two aging dams and the historical and economic processes that culminated in their construction, blocking determined salmon from moving further upstream into healthy and available salmon habitat.

Hope among environmentalists for the restoration of the Elwha's native runs was kindled in the early 1990s, when President George H. W. Bush signed landmark legislation to restore the Elwha River and its salmon fisheries, including removal of the Elwha and Glines Canyon Dams if necessary. The legislation was unprecedented; the political dissonance that accompanied it was not. Conflict and resistance derailed the river restoration effort, and appropriations were dispensed slowly. In spite of all this, the dams began to come down in September 2011.

What sort of river is this now? More important, what is the "best" Elwha River? One that resembles its historical self, rolling free with potential prolific salmon runs, or an organic machine, providing necessary power for economic development and jobs? How is it possible that a dam constructed in 1913 to bring "civilization" and wealth to the Olympic Peninsula could be slated for removal a mere 80 years later, after only two generations? What drove American environmental attitudes to change dramatically between the time when the first dam was built, and when dam removal legislation was passed? These forces, and the prevailing opinions and sensibilities behind them, will be explored here.

Many Americans struggle to understand and negotiate the role of nature in their lives. The story of the Elwha River reveals a great deal about this relationship, tying together river ecosystems and human communities and fueling discourse over environmental issues, economics, and government power. Our evolving views and uses of the Elwha River reflect the very values and debates that define our culture.

Removing human monuments to progress in order to improve nature, advocates of Elwha River and fisheries restoration prove that competing constituencies and interest groups can negotiate a new ethical and ecological middle ground. Aldo Leopold wrote, "We shall hardly relinquish the shovel." On the Elwha River it was put to good use more than once.

Chapter 1

Strong River, Strong People

THE EARLY HISTORY OF THE ELWHA RIVER
AND THE LOWER ELWHA KLALLAM INDIANS

Give me a shovel and I'll take that dam down myself.

Jim Crane[1]

The Elwha River is located on the northern edge of the Olympic Peninsula, on the southern shore of the Strait of Juan de Fuca, nestled under the shadows and dark forests of the Olympic Mountains. On this far northwestern corner of the continental United States, storms roll in off the Pacific drenching the range's western side, depositing lesser amounts of rain on the eastern edge and in the rainshadow on the northeast slope. The geologically young Olympic Mountains dominating the peninsula originate from the action of plate tectonics. The collision of the oceanic Juan de Fuca plate against the North American continental plate produces an uplift. This created the Olympic Mountains and still forces the mountains skyward. Thick with river-borne sediments layered on top of a platform of basalt, the Juan de Fuca plate is denser and heavier than—and therefore forced under—the continental plate. Throughout this process the edge of the continental plate scrapes off river-deposited sediments from the top of the Juan de Fuca plate and these sedimentary rocks pile up against the leading edge of the continent to form the Olympic Mountains.[2]

Glacial and river erosion produced the jagged profile of the Olympics, the series of steep peaks and precipitous ridges that constitute the range. Unlike the Cascades, where drainages generally flow either east or west, the rivers of the Olympics all flow outward from the center, forming a radial pattern running north, east, south, and west. An abundance of rivers carrying the heavy rains or snowmelt dumped on these mountains by Pacific storms cut deep valleys throughout the Olympics. Over time, salmon migrated into and filled these rivers and their tributaries.[3] Where these rivers cut through basalt they formed narrow gorges; where they cut through sedimentary rock they created wide meandering paths with gravel bars covered by alder. Both of these types of riverbeds are present on the Elwha River. The erosional process continues today; the cutting action of the rivers and their tributaries carry the soil of the Olympics to the sea, even as the movement of the tectonic plates still pushes the mountains ever skyward; uplift and erosion is the continual process of this dynamic range and continues as it has for hundreds of thousands of years. One key element of this natural cycle was interrupted for almost a century; salmon and steelhead no longer followed the Elwha River back into the heart of the mountains.

While rivers have played an important role in sculpting the geography of the Olympics, glaciation, too, has worked significant changes on the mountain landscape. During a series of ice ages, beginning in the Pleistocene Epoch approximately 2 million years ago and ending about 12,000 years ago, the Olympics were covered by alpine glaciers and surrounded by the Cordilleran ice sheet. The massive glacier extended south from Canada to what is now the southern end of Puget Sound in the vicinity of Olympia. Glaciers are slow-moving rivers of ice forced into movement downhill from the accumulated weight of snow. As they grind downhill they greatly erode the landscape, cutting U-shaped valleys and scraping away rock and soil along the sides and bottom of the glacier. Glaciation during the Pleistocene era resulted in more than the carving of rock, however. The southern extension of the Cordilleran ice sheet blocked the migration of numerous species such as mountain goats, coyotes, wolverine, lynx, pica, porcupines, and grizzly bears from the mainland onto the peninsula. In the 20th century, mountain goats were introduced into the Olympic Mountains. Coyotes and porcupines have also made their way to the peninsula, and flourished in the predator void created by the extermination of wolves when the peninsula was settled. In some cases, what many might think of as natural to the Olympic Peninsula actually reflects human manipulation and interference.[4]

The Elwha penetrates the Olympics farther than most rivers in this range and originates from deep in the heart of the mountains—approximately in the middle of the Olympics, where the Bailey Range, the Mount Olympus Range, and the Elwha Basin Range come together. From there, the river drops quickly to its mouth at the Strait of Juan de Fuca, the wide body of saltwater connecting the Pacific Ocean to Puget Sound and separating the northern edge of the Olympic Peninsula from Vancouver Island. The river descends 45 miles to the sea and drains an area of approximately 321 square miles. Because most of the Elwha River watershed is located within Olympic National Park, it has mostly escaped the development and environmental deterioration of most rivers in the Pacific Northwest. Upper regions of the Elwha River Basin, in fact, have never been logged. The major environmental impact on the river has arisen from the construction of two dams, the Elwha Dam in 1913 and the Glines Canyon Dam in 1927.[5]

SALMON HEAVEN

Slicing its path down the glacier-carved valley, cutting deep and narrow through basalt and meandering through sedimentary rock, the Elwha River varies in its 45-mile length—from quiet sections of small, sinuous stream to loud, thunderous canyons of water blasting and roaring through narrow, glistening black basalt chutes to lower stretches where the river runs shallow and broad, eddying around boulders and riffling over gravel and cobble. This was and still is good habitat for the salmon redds (nest-like beds in the river floor, dug and covered by spawning salmon) where eggs are deposited, fertilized, and then hatched. Deep pools shadowed by the overhanging branches of alder and western red cedar break the movement of the river, offering a moment of quiet contemplation for

Asahel Curtis photograph of a forest outside of Port Angeles, 1911. Western red cedar and ferns are visible in this photo. Courtesy of Washington State Historical Society

travelers and respite to spawning salmon, a place to rest and marshal strength before continuing again upstream.

Below the alpine zone the climate is quite moderate; winters are mild and wet with summers relatively cool and dry. The average rainfall is approximately 60 to 80 inches a year along the lower reaches, more in the higher elevations of the river's course. The flanks of the mountains and the valley bottoms are draped in forests of western red cedar, Douglas fir, and hemlock with swordfern, madrone, and moss growing in the shadows. Douglas fir is the primary tree of the lowland forest, and the poet, environmental activist, and author Tim McNulty describes it thus: "The deeply furrowed, rust brown, often fire-charred bark of ancient Doug-firs always catches my eye in the shade of a mixed forest. As early morning or evening light threads its way through the columns of the forest, an old Douglas-fir can seem as luminous as a softly glowing lamp. Its coarse-textured, moss- and lichen-flaked bark seems to invite the hand, and a few old giants alongside popular trails show evidence of years of 'hugging.'"[6]

Pacific yews are interspersed in the forest and along the river, and on gravel bars, maples and alders thrive. This mixed forest bottomland is important wintering and reproduction ground for elk. The grown-over meadows of homesteads harbor gnarled old apple trees and large alders. Except for periodic fires and logging on the lower parts of the river, the forest vegetation along the Elwha River has changed little since before construction of the dams. The inclusion of much of this land within the Olympic National Park in 1938 and 1940 limited logging in the watershed and kept salmon-free habitat relatively healthy for possible future salmon. This is a unique situation; rarely has a river ecosystem remained so ecologically healthy in American history.[7]

Prior to the building of the first dam, the Elwha River was the home of year-round, bountiful runs of salmon and steelhead and gained a reputation as one of the most productive rivers in the Pacific Northwest. Five types of Pacific salmon as well as multiple steelhead and sea-run cutthroats thrived here. Chinook salmon, also known as king and tyee, are the best known of the Pacific salmon species. True to their majestic moniker, they can reach 130 pounds and chinooks of over 100 pounds have been reported on the Elwha River. Salmon are anadromous fish, meaning that they are born and spend their early lives in freshwater, migrate to the ocean where they live for varying amounts of time depending on the species, and then return to the river to spawn and die. This complex and highly developed life cycle has led to magnificent species of fish that thrive in the right conditions, but are also vulnerable to threats at multiple points in their life stages. One of the remarkable qualities of Pacific salmon is their almost flawless ability to find their home stream and return there to spawn.

Eleanor Chittenden with a steelhead, 1907. Photograph taken by Asahel Curtis. Courtesy of Washington State Historical Society

THE LIVES OF SALMON

The life of an Elwha River salmon is one that begins and ends in the river and its tributaries. Born in redds, salmon fry (baby salmon) emerge from their eggs and spend anywhere from a few days up to a year, depending on the species, in their birth streams, before smolting[8] and being washed downstream to the Strait of Juan de Fuca and eventually the Pacific Ocean in most cases. The quality of the habitat of the natal or birth stream is important. An appropriate blend of gravel and cobble of different sizes is required so oxygenated water can flow through to the hidden eggs. The gravel and cobble, as well as woody debris such as logs, stumps, and branches in the streams and rivers, also provide hiding places for the smolts (young salmon), which are natural prey for trout, sculpin, mergansers, kingfishers, and other predators. Salmon species follow different patterns and spend varying amounts of time at sea, but in the end they return to their birth streams. Salmon follow the earth's magnetic field, which brings them close to their streams when it is time to spawn. At that point, each fish is drawn to a particular river, and into the waterway's mouth. The salmon then follows the tributary stream to its birth site to spawn and continue the cycle. Interestingly, a certain percentage of salmon do stray, meaning they migrate to and spawn in streams other than the ones in which they were born. The number of straying salmon can be based on external factors such as low water levels or high turbidity[9] in the stream. This behavior is functional in that it has allowed salmon to expand their range over time. It was central to the process by which salmon colonized empty rivers and streams after the last period of glaciation on the Olympic Peninsula, approximately 12,000 years ago. The salmon of the Elwha River are relatively young in historical terms, arriving in the area as the river was exposed by the retreating ice sheet, and making their evolutionary adaptations to the river since then.[10]

While smolts are born in streams, lakes, and rivers, their destiny is to seek the sea and their journey downstream is the first arduous step in their lives. Even while they are flushed to the sea, smolts' bodies change, their physiology adjusting from freshwater conditions to life in saltwater. When they begin their migrations back upstream for spawning purposes, the fish are actually beginning to die, steadfastly moving upstream to reproduce without eating, living off the fat they have accumulated in the ocean. When they approach the rivers, salmon also undergo a stunning transformation of their physical features. Sockeye salmon develop hooked jaws that extend down over the front of their mouths. Their bright silver changes into stunning shades of red and green. The pink salmon sprouts a huge hump and a slightly hooked jaw as well. Spawning salmon become both beautiful and fearsome as they begin their last journey. It is a perilous odyssey, as they overcome rapids and waterfalls on a steady upstream ascent to their birth stream. Besides these inanimate barriers, many living creatures seek to stop the salmon from completing their trip. Bald eagles, bears, and other species are eager to consume the protein- and fat-rich salmon flesh. Historically, Indians on the Elwha and other rivers throughout the region also harvested salmon as they made the dangerous journey.

When the female arrives at the spawning site, having survived the challenges of the journey, much of her labor still lies before her. First, she needs to find a suitable site for the redd. In doing so, she assesses water flow for the right speed, the appropriate water depth, the size of gravel and cobble, and limited amounts of sand and silt.[11]

Once she has determined the ideal site, she must defend it from later-arriving female salmon and begin digging her redd. The stronger, fitter females who arrive first claim the best sites; weaker, later ones are pushed to the margins of the premium spawning habitat. The female salmon begins preparing the redd, using her tail to sweep dirt and sand and create a hole in the gravel and cobble. During this labor, other female salmon will attack and try to seize the site. Once the site is complete she prepares for male suitors; not a long wait. The male salmon compete for the right to fertilize the eggs, using attacks and slashing bites to establish their dominance. Crossing over, back and forth, behind the female, the male will determine when she is ready and "signal his readiness by repeatedly crossing over and by quivering alongside her body."[12] She releases her eggs and the dominant male discharges his milt (seminal fluid of the male fish) to quickly fertilize the eggs as they drop into the redd. In many cases, subordinate male salmon will dash in from the edges and release their milt into the eggs as well. These competitive efforts to ensure propagation contribute to the success of the species, by creating more genetic diversity within a single redd. The female salmon then uses her tail to cover the eggs with gravel and cobble, and proceeds to repeat the process several times before using up all of her eggs. Once she has dropped all of her eggs and the male salmon have spent themselves, they finish dying, gasping in the shallows and on the sides of the streams, their flesh rotting in gray chunks and strips even as they still live, easy prey for bears, ravens, raccoons, eagles, and numerous other species.[13]

Bruce Brown, the author of *Mountain in the Clouds: A Search for the Wild Salmon*, describes the frenzy of activity in a pink salmon run on the Graywolf River. The Graywolf is only approximately 30 miles from the Elwha as the raven flies and once hosted mighty pink runs like the Elwha's. Brown's poetic description reflects the beauty of salmon in this landscape: "On the heart of the glide a mass of salmon was wheeling in an endless circuit, drifting sideways to expose their broad sides when hostile, and gliding past each other like fingers into a glove when not. Viewed from the shore, the pinks appeared as a shifting lavender stain on the sunny riverbottom."[14]

A healthy river and riverbed are critical factors in any salmon river at this juncture in the salmon life cycle. Such a river includes a number of features like deep pools, riffles, and a variety of bottoms including spawning sites with gravel and cobble. While these features are critical elements in any productive salmon river, a particular combination of genetics and topography produced exceptional salmon on the Elwha, as well as stunningly large runs. Genetically, Elwha chinook salmon are programmed to stay at sea a year longer than fish in other streams, a habit that allows them to grow to enormous size before spawning. The need to pass through a steep, narrow canyon like Goblins Gate in Rica Canyon selects for stronger, more powerful fish. Geographically, the Elwha's unusual northward drainage and the protection from Pacific storms provided by the Olympic Mountains make it a remarkably stable river. Rarely hit by winter flooding, the river, which is fed predominantly by mountain snowmelt, maintains consistent levels all summer. That makes the Elwha a superb river for both spawning and habitat.[15]

SALMON AND NATURE

Western Europeans and Americans have known about the remarkable king salmon of the Elwha ever since Spanish explorer Manuel Quimper purchased several chinooks, each weighing 100 pounds, from Indians who were most likely Lower Elwha Klallam, near the Elwha in 1790. The anadromous fish of the Elwha played an integral role in the Elwha River ecosystem. Besides the wildlife that preyed on fish struggling up the river to spawn, the dying and dead salmon (steelhead, otherwise known as sea-run rainbow trout and sea-run cutthroat, return to the sea after spawning) also served as an important food source for a variety of animals. The rotting flesh of the dead fish served to enrich the soils along the Elwha and its tributaries, as well as providing carbon, phosphorus, and nitrogen for the aquatic biotic community.[16]

The salmon runs moving out into the Pacific and returning to the Elwha, as in other river systems, are described by fishery biologists as an energy system. The salmon and steelhead, traveling through the waters of the Pacific, gather up energy from the sea and carry that energy with them into the river ecosystem. Some energy is transferred to predators such as humans, eagles, and bears that eat the salmon flesh. The process is complicated by carcasses being partially eaten and dragged away from the river and its tributaries, improving the soil and the growth of trees and other plants as well as feeding more bugs like stoneflies and caddis flies. This is a long chain; more bugs mean more food for salmon smolts and for birds. Not only did the characteristics of the Elwha River contribute to the evolution of the river's salmon and steelhead, but the fish themselves (and later their eradication from the ecosystem) have influenced the Elwha River ecosystem in turn. By contributing their nutrients and energysalmon strengthened various animals, birds, bugs, and even plants in the river watershed. Removing the salmon from the Elwha weakened its overall health in myriad ways that are sometimes difficult to see. This seemingly healthy ecosystem was diminished because of the loss of the salmon runs.[17]

Before the Elwha was degraded as a salmon river, these fish were a central part of the local ecosystem and Indian culture. The abundance of salmon historically, and the critical role they played in Pacific Northwest coastal Indian cultures, can scarcely be overstated. James G. Swan, one of a handful of white settlers in the Northwest coastal region, made his home along the shoreline of western Washington on the edges of the Pacific in 1852.[18] He reveled in the abundance of the region. In tones reminiscent of John J. Audubon's bird-hunting accounts, Swan described the abounding plethora of birds: "As far as the eye could reach might be seen immense flocks of gulls, plovers, curlew, snipe, crows, ravens, and eagles. We amused ourselves as we went along shooting these birds, and soon had enough for dinner."[19] Swan waxes rhapsodic in describing the feasts of plenitude laid before him by nature and local Quinault Indians (located on the western side of the Olympic Peninsula), with a few of his own provisions mixed in:

> [We] soon had a fine supper cooking for the whole party. There was boiled rice and boiled salmon, boiled and roast potatoes, roast salmon, roasted crabs and clams, cold raccoon, dried salmon, seal oil and whale oil, to say nothing of hard bread, a pudding made from boiled flour, and tea made from a species of huckleberry leaves.[20]

Swan wrote of salmon runs as well. The tenor of his prose is matter-of-fact, even careless, in the face of such plenty. The language and description reinforces the impression of overwhelming abundance.

> Although the river was filled with salmon, and the banks literally piled with the dead fish killed in attempting to go over the falls, yet, the season being so far advanced, there were comparatively

*few really prime ones. The salmon, after casting its spawn, grows
thin, and the flesh loses its bright pink color. The fish then is of
little value either to the whites or Indians.*

Swan then explained how the Quinaults harvested the worn-out
salmon.

*Our Indians, who were well skilled, started up stream to
commence, as their custom always is to go up the stream, and
then letting the canoe float down, catch the fish as they pass. As
the tide fell, the Indians left their canoes and waded in the stream.
We joined them, and such a splashing and dashing I never before
witnessed.*

His account of this fish frenzy, where he managed to grab seven, is
followed by a description of him amusing himself by shooting ducks
and the returning of the Quinaults to camp with over a "hundred
fine salmon."[21]

THE STRONG PEOPLE

Swan experienced the Pacific Northwest and salmon at a time of
overwhelming, even incomprehensible, natural abundance, when the
ecosystem and the Indians were enriched and defined by the plentiful
salmon resource. Prior to contact with Europeans and devastation
by disease and conquest, the Pacific Northwest coastal Indians
constituted some of the most complex and richest Indian cultures
on the North American continent. They thrived on an abundance
of nature that was primarily focused on the harvest of salmon,
whale, shellfish, elk, and of course numerous berry and root plants.
From this wealth of natural abundance, coastal Indians produced a
splendid material culture of hand-crafted goods and artwork, as well
as an intricate and vast body of oral literature. The Lower Elwha
Klallam Indians were part of this broader culture and lived along
the lower Elwha River on the banks of the Strait of Juan de Fuca.
As Colleen Elizabeth Boyd writes, "The story of the Elwha River
begins with Klallam people. They provide the common thread that

weaves human history to the physical environment."[22] Indians like the Elwha Klallam occupied the coast of the Pacific Northwest, as well as living on the islands and the shores of the Strait of Juan de Fuca and Puget Sound.

Tapping the resources of rivers, ocean, forests, and even prairies like those on Whidbey Island and on the northern Olympic Peninsula, they probably experienced less famine and hard times than many interior peoples. These Indians crafted a rich culture reflecting their interdependence with the various organisms of the world around them. Spruce, western red cedar, seals, halibut, deer, trout, salmonberries, blackberries, and thimbleberries all constituted important parts of their culture and economy. The Elwha River salmon occupied a place of greater dietary and cultural significance than anything else. The Lower Elwha Klallam creatively pursued and harvested salmon while celebrating them, propitiating the fish and preserving their own culture and continuity in the process. In so doing, they found a way to live sustainably for at least several centuries along the banks of the Elwha without destroying the river or its salmon resource.[23]

The Lower Elwha were part of the broader Klallam Indian group situated along the southern shoreline of the Strait of Juan de Fuca from the mouth of the Hoko River to Discovery Bay, and across the Strait of Juan de Fuca on the western coast of Vancouver Island, around the present-day city of Victoria, British Columbia. The Lower Elwha Klallam shared similarities with other Salish coastal peoples in both culture and resource use and were particularly fortunate to be based on a river so rich in fish that they could ground much of their culture and economy on the multiple runs of salmon in the river. The Lower Elwha Klallam believed they were brought into existence on the river by a creator who "bathed and blessed them."[24] Trusting that they had been born from dirt scooped out of deep holes in rocks in the river, they would return to that sacred site to gain information on their future by pulling objects from the holes.

Rooted in the river, these Indians believed—and continue to believe—themselves a strong people and tell a story denoting that essential truth. In this story they tell of a large assembly of Klallam eating and participating in the building of a longhouse by the Elwha River. When someone asked who could lift a big log to the roof of the building, all of the other tribes attempted to lift it with brute force but were not able to. The Klallam showed that strength is at least partially a function of careful thought. They floated the log in the water and the strongest men then stood in deep water so the log would float onto their shoulders. They then walked out of the water carrying the log. "Upon reaching the long house, everyone shouted at the same time, 'Shashume, Shashume, Shashume,' and on the third 'Shashume' they all lifted the log to the top. The other tribes thought that the mighty Klallams must be very strong to put the log up so high and also so smart to use the water to first get the log onto their shoulders. They all shouted, 'Klallam, Klallam!' which means Strong People! That was how our tribe received its name so long ago."[25]

The Strong People occupied as many as 12 residential and camping sites located on the lower river and coast of the strait, including a major village on the west bank at the confluence of the Elwha with Indian Creek and Little River.[26] This pattern of one major village surrounded by multiple satellite sites was typical of coastal Indians in this region. The Lower Elwha Klallam made their homes along the lower reaches of the Elwha where the river split the village in half as it reached the Strait of Juan de Fuca and at the base of Ediz Hook. They were active in and dependent upon the ecosystem of the Elwha River and the surrounding environment in myriad ways, and were one of the more powerful Indian groups in the region. Myron Eells wrote of a belief that the Lower Elwha Klallam had control of a mysterious power to summon a person from as far as 50 miles away by merely muttering the individual's name in a low voice. According to Eells, in addition to that power it was also believed that if a Lower Elwha Klallam talked badly about a person, "his heart was in a complete whirl, and that if they talked ill and wished to do evil to any one thus distant, his eyes were made to whirl and the evil wish came to pass."[27] This power was supposed to originate from basins in river rocks high in the headwaters of the Elwha River. One of the basins remained full of black water, regardless of drought or rain, and the Lower Elwha Klallam washed their hands and arms in this basin of dark water, accruing magical power.[28]

Klallam villages were typically located in coves that offered some protection from weather, where freshwater streams and rivers drained into the Strait of Juan de Fuca and associated bodies of saltwater. Located next to a wide beach, fish would be cleaned where the canoes were pulled out of the water, and pits for cooking shellfish lined the beach. The houses were laid out in a single row with the doors facing the water. Generally 20 by 30 feet in size and rectangular in shape, the houses were constructed of wooden planks that were 16 to 18 inches wide and 2 inches thick. The planks were grooved together and the roofs gabled. Cedar shakes were used for the roofs of homes while grooved planks were employed on longhouses. A few shakes were always left loose so they could be removed to create smoke holes.[29]

Nature in the Elwha River valley and surrounding countryside offered numerous resources, and the Lower Elwha Klallam showed ingenuity, creativity, and a long tradition of accumulated and stored knowledge in their use of plants, animals, and fish. The heavy forests of this Douglas fir bioregion provided several types of trees important to them. For example, the western yew was crucial to the Elwha economy. Its needles were dried and ground up as a substitute for tobacco. The strong and tough wood of the yew was crafted into bows and arrows by the Natives of this area. The yew's wood was also used for canoe paddles and the leaves could be crushed, boiled, and drunk as a tea for internal injuries or pain. The western hemlock grew in forests from the water's edge to an elevation of approximately 3,000 feet. This tree was used by the Lower Elwha Klallam in numerous ways. The bark was boiled for a dye of red-brown color, the saplings of the tree used for fish traps in streams, the bark combined with licorice ferns to stop hemorrhages, and the tips of young hemlocks were boiled by the Klallam and consumed to help stimulate appetite and cure tuberculosis. The Douglas fir, the most abundant tree in this region, provided fewer uses for these Indians. The pitch was chewed as a gum, probably for medicinal reasons, and the wood supplied an important source of firewood. Also, spear and harpoon shafts were made from this tree.[30]

With such a rich environment and a large number of personal goods, the Klallam required ways to store their items. Cedar boxes for storage of salmon, water, and personal goods were made from the strong and water-resistant western red cedar. The boxes, with their intricate, colored designs and their careful construction, demonstrate the sophistication of this Indian culture. The labor put into converting wood to usable objects was sometimes complicated and rigorous. Anthropologist Erna Gunther described the complex construction of a cedar water bucket, noting that the sides are cut from a single piece, which is "bent three times at kerts cut at intervals equal to the length of the sides. The joint is pegged together and pitched. A handle is attached across the top. It is tied to each side with twisted cedar limbs through holes bored in the sides. The handle is bent slightly upward in the middle."[31]

The Lower Elwha Klallam Indians were endlessly creative in crafting cultural items and tools from the resources surrounding them. They carved dishes from the wood of alder and maple, and spoons from Pacific madrone. Mussel and clam shells were used for spoons as well. The Lower Elwha Klallam not only produced buckets from the wood of the western red cedar but also manufactured other items such as towels, capes, and dance headdresses from shredded cedar bark. The oils in cedar rendered it more resistant to moisture and rot than other woods, thereby making it a critical resource in the wet climate.[32]

From childbirth on, the Klallam forged a close and intricate relationship with nature—from the foods they ate, and the tools and other devices created from shells and wood, to the parts of the natural world they incorporated into daily routines of hygiene and decoration. While the Klallam did not commodify nature in the way later settlers did, they understood the ways in which almost every organism in that greater ecosystem could be used. When a baby was born, the body received a great deal of loving touch, being washed daily with the limbs massaged to help render them straight and slender. As the children grew older they were taught to rub their skin with rotting hemlock or cedar bark after bathing in order to keep the skin soft. Facial skin was kept pliable with deer tallow that also functioned as a foundation for face paint for men and women. Red clay burnt in a fire resulted in the favorite face paint of the Klallam. Children started painting their faces at age six and both men and women decorated their faces. According to Gunther, the designs applied by the Klallam were simple, with some use of diagonal lines. Secret society rituals required male members to paint their faces black with charcoal; they had to maintain a serious demeanor while wearing this black paint.[33]

Of course, the stomach is a demanding master and food could be found from multiple sources throughout the region. While salmon constituted the largest portion of their diet, the Indians on the Elwha did not live on salmon alone. Men occasionally hunted for deer and elk in the mountain interior; however, the hunting of such game was typically limited to one hunter per tribe. And while bears were killed and eaten if found close to camp, they were not actively pursued.[34] Whales were hunted by some Klallam in the Clallam Bay area, the westernmost range of these Indians, but theirs was not a whaling culture like the Makah on Cape Flattery to the west, and whales were pursued only when spotted from shore. The Lower Elwha Klallam were active sealers, using their meat, fat, and oil. Smaller fish that schooled and spawned in great numbers also proved valuable. Herring were an important food source and swarmed in great numbers in shallow water. They were usually harvested by means of a rake with teeth made from sharpened elk bones, the rake employed to lift the herring into a canoe. The Klallam showed particular ingenuity in crafting a way to harvest herring eggs, a favored delicacy. When the tide was low they laid hemlock twigs on spawning sites on the beach. Later, they collected the twigs covered with eggs, allowed them to dry, then shook the dried eggs off the twigs into baskets for later consumption.[35]

The resourcefulness of the Klallam is particularly marked in their pursuit of waterfowl. To hunt these species they erected large poles, typically 40 feet high, but sometimes as high as 80 or 100 feet, as British explorer George Vancouver recorded. Nets lay on the ground as Indians on each side of the poles waited in hiding. When the flocks took off to fly between the poles, the Klallam would pull on ropes, thus lifting the nets 40 to 80 or even 100 feet, catching the birds in the air like fish trapped in nets.[36]

Women played a pivotal role in this economy and while they did some fishing—sometimes assisting in catching halibut, an important food source, or rainbow trout, a small part of the Indians' diet— the larger part of their activities was geared towards gathering wild plants. With the help of their children and female slaves, Klallam women gathered huckleberries, elderberries, blackberries, camas, salal, Oregon grape, strawberries, wild carrots, and the roots and bulbs of various ferns, along with many other plants. They also harvested clams, mussels, and other seafood. Although the Lower Elwha Klallam spent most of their time in their primary camps, they maintained several additional sites, depending on the season and resources available for harvest. Fishing, berrying, and hunting activities took place at various times of the year and in a variety of locations. Burnt-over patches where berries are abundant likely indicate their use of fire, as has been established for many other Native American peoples.[37] In addition to harvesting locally, they also traveled seasonally in pursuit of different commodities. They made multi-family trips to the Hood Canal in pursuit of dog salmon or to the head of Sequim Bay for berrying on a large burnt-over prairie. Women would travel considerable distances in pursuit of plant products, generally in groups due to fear of raiding enemy tribes.[38]

The abundance of resources available to them resulted in a broad array of harvesting and gathering methods and a fair amount of travel. The flexibility of Indian cultures seems to be a constant that is easily applied to the Lower Elwha Klallam because they and other Indians of the region were constantly on the move in order to hunt, harvest, or fish as well as to visit and participate in important events such as potlatches and marriages. For the Klallam, salmon were their most important resource and they actively pursued and harvested the plentiful fish, including chinook, chum, pink, sockeye, and silver salmon. In saltwater, they employed numerous methods to harvest salmon, as well as many other fish species, and when the salmon entered the rivers to spawn, the Indians harvested them with traps, spears, or gill nets. In the early part of the 20th century Erna Gunther observed that "every river and creek has at least one salmon trap across it."[39]

Salmon were at the very heart of the Lower Elwha Klallam economy even as they constituted the vital core of the Elwha River ecosystem. Much of what we know of the fishing, harvesting, and storage of salmon comes from the prodigious and thorough work of Gunther. The richness of her research and writing was in the detail provided. In describing the methodology of harvesting salmon, for example, Gunther attained a level of specificity that seemingly does not miss a single facet or feature. She explained that a weir extending across the river was the most significant trap used by the Klallam. Two rows of fir trees, 10 feet tall and 4 inches in diameter, were driven into the river bottom in two rows so that they slanted and crossed at the top. Gunther further explained the weir construction:

They are placed at intervals of twelve feet across the stream. The crossed tops which extend above the water are tied with stripped cedar limbs. Poles are laid in the crotch of these tied trees. Then two parallel poles are tied to the upstream side of the slanting poles; one just below the water, the other just above the river bed. Now a webbing is made of little fir trees about one inch in diameter. These trees are taken from a place where there is a thick growth so that there are no limbs on the lower part of the trunks. The tops are cut off so that they measure six feet long. The webbing is made by tying these small trees together with twined cedar limbs and it is then laid against the parallel poles that were tied to the upstream side of the weir.[40]

The river's current held this webbing in place and a door was placed in the center of the webbing, which could then be opened and closed as necessary to gather fish. Gunther went on to explain the construction in enough detail that a committed Indian, historian, or historical preservationist could use her description to rebuild the weir. A platform was built onto this structure that the Indian fishermen would sleep on, feel the salmon beat against the weir, and then remove the fish. This intricately designed trap, using a great amount of wood and requiring extensive labor and craft, serves as a reminder of the amount of time and energy dedicated to harvesting salmon by the Lower Elwha Klallam. It is clear also that they demonstrated the mechanical aptitude to consume the salmon resource in its entirety, if they so chose.[41]

The best traps, meaning the ones closest to the mouth of the river or at the narrowest points, were normally controlled by more powerful members of the village. Typically the owner would use the trap at night during the best fishing, but then allow other members of the village, often from within his extended family, to harvest from the trap during the day. While intent is hard to determine, the river current and the natural irregularity of the stream bottoms created holes under the traps allowing some fish to pass and spawn, thereby ensuring the return of salmon in the future. It is problematic to argue for conservation management of resources by Indians, although limited examples exist, but it is not a stretch to argue that these holes were observed and allowed to exist in an acknowledgment of the need for fish to spawn and reproduce. Certainly, Gunther believed that the holes were left intentionally to allow some fish to move past the traps: "There is always a hole left under each trap so some of the salmon can go up the river."[42]

With salmon and steelhead swarming through the ocean to the Elwha almost every month of the year, the Klallam were almost always in pursuit of the fish so central to their economy and culture. In so doing, they employed a variety of harvesting methods besides traps. Spring chinooks were trolled for from canoes, using hooks made from elk bones affixed at the end of a kelp line. Also, when there was abundant herring for the salmon to feed on, gill nets made of nettle twine were used to harvest spring chinooks that were close to shore prior to entering the river. Fishing for salmon could be as simple as spearing them in rivers or from shore at night by torchlight. During the months that salmon were not spawning, sea-run trout, both rainbow and cutthroat, were making their way up the river.

The Elwha, like other rivers on the Olympic Peninsula and in the coastal and Puget Sound region, served as a primary resource base, which could be depended upon during a large part of the year as a food supply anchor for the Indians. Not only did they harvest vast amounts of salmon from their home streams, the Klallam traveled to other productive rivers like the Hamma Hamma on the eastern side of the Olympic Peninsula, or the Dungeness River about 20 miles away, to harvest from other large runs.[43]

Following harvest, preservation of the catch was the primary order of business. Salmon were cut in strips with the bones removed. Fern leaves were used to wipe the flesh clean. Hanging in a smokehouse overnight with an alderwood fire burning imparted a pleasant taste and kept the flesh soft. The salmon was then cut into smaller pieces, spread on crossed sticks, and hung for a week to dry. Important taboos were heeded with salmon preparation. Bones with the head attached had to be cooked and eaten the day the fish was caught because keeping the head and bones in the house overnight would bring bad luck. Similarly, it was believed that fishermen lost their spearing and trolling skills if the head of a spring salmon was dried. "The intestines are cooked and fed to the dogs. The heads, after boiling, are roasted by being stuck on a split stick with the backbone running parallel to the stick. The stomach is washed out and with the eggs and milt is laid on sticks and roasted."[44] Gunther also pointed out that the Klallam never dried the eggs of spring salmon but provided no explanation. They did dry and consume other salmon eggs, so it is clear that the spring salmon held special significance and power for the Klallam Indians.

Even after the initial drying, there was still much labor to be performed in preserving the salmon. During drying, women would take each strip down at least every two days and render it soft through twisting and bending. This allows air to get inside the flesh and helps prevent rotting. Also, every salmon harvest required the parallel harvest of new poles for drying. According to Gunther, "It is believed that the salmon play on these poles while they are drying and the new poles make them happy. They are always treated as though they were alive. Fish are never wantonly wasted."[45] After the fish were dried, they were folded and stored in cedar baskets over beds in tribal homes.[46]

While this food kept their bodies nourished, a complex and voluminous oral history helped the Lower Elwha Klallam situate themselves within their ecosystem and understand their place in the world in both a material and spiritual sense. The material and spiritual were intertwined for the Klallam. Stories provided the mythic and historical basis for this culture. As Boyd explains, the Klallam organized stories between "mythic" and "real," with mythic stories generally explaining events prior to humans or very early in their history as well as introducing certain key ceremonies and cultural practices. The "real" stories dealt with human history, although Boyd reminds the reader that this does not construe a simple fiction/non-fiction dichotomy. Also, it does not suggest a fantastic versus mundane bifurcation. Spiritual elements and events and powers associated with the "mythic" are often present in the stories of the "real" as well.[47]

The Klallam took great care when killing animals and gathering plants, avoiding waste or disrespect in order to maintain a harmonious relationship with the other beings of their world. They also followed a strict set of rules and obeyed taboos to maintain this healthy relationship. For example, their oral tradition warned of ridiculing or denigrating other creatures. The key lesson in most stories is to not mock the fish or play with them as they are waiting to be cleaned. In one story, "A girl of about ten was swimming in the Dungeness River and made fun of an old salmon. Soon after, she became ill. Her eyes began to look like salmon eyes and her actions were just like the movements of the fish as they swim. Her people asked her if she had played with a salmon. She admitted that she had. The shaman could do nothing for her and she soon died."[48] In another Klallam story, some bold young men questioned the validity of the first salmon ceremony, deriding the idea of an old salmon leading back the young salmon. As a test they attached parts of their ceremonial headdresses to the tails and fins of the old salmon, then released him to see whether the stories were true and he would bring back another run of fish. Shocked when this salmon did return the following year with remnants of the headdress still attached to his body, they died soon afterward, thrashing like dying salmon.

Not all stories in the vast oral literature were morbid cautionary tales. In fact there is much humor in their oral tradition as well. The Klallam related a large collection of stories about their ecosystem and their culture, explaining their history and their role in the environment. Many stories proscribed certain behaviors toward other species, particularly salmon, in order to avoid offending them and to assure their return in the future. Others warned of greed or laziness, and many were just funny.

The Strong People lived in a land and along a sea abundant with power and life, in a manner that reflected their dependence on the nature around them and their respect for the creatures with which they shared the world. Their beliefs showed how the denizens of nature protected them as well. For example, the Orca whale is considered a protector of the tribe because of an incident in their early history. Returning from a trading trip in the area of Victoria, a long canoe was crossing the Strait of Juan de Fuca when a sudden squall blew in, creating choppy, dangerous seas. A Klallam woman in the boat who could call the Orca began chanting and praying for their assistance. Several of the killer whales appeared, surrounded and protected the canoe from the waves, and escorted the Klallam home. While it is simplistic to portray the Klallam and other Indians as native environmentalists living in pastoral harmony with nature, their spiritual and religious system did not prize human domination of nature as European and American culture did and does. They sought to maintain a balance between themselves and the many other creatures and plants inhabiting their world, which they believed held value besides as simply resources for human use and consumption.[49]

Because of the salmon's deep value, it could become the source of conflict. A traveler's account from 1859, during which the writer was traveling by canoe with Makah Indians, spoke of an encounter between the Lower Elwha Klallam and Makahs several years earlier: "He then related to me that a few years before, he had come up with a party of Mackahs [*sic*] to catch salmon at this place. He was a mere boy and accompanied his father and uncle. The Elwhas were very insolent and refused to let them catch fish in their river. The Mackahs left but during the night they returned, and while the Elwhas were asleep they attacked them, killing twelve men and taking prisoners of all the women."[50]

Recognizing the importance of salmon to their way of life and survival, and in an effort to maintain a harmonious relationship with the salmon, the Klallam practiced the first salmon ceremony like most coastal Indians in the region. While the practice varies between Indian groups and even villages, the basic approach was fairly consistent. Generally, the lead salmon in a run, considered a chief of those salmon, would be harvested and cooked in a traditional ceremony run by the village shaman. Then, depending on taboos, the various members of the tribe would eat the flesh of the salmon and the bones would be placed back in the river, always handled with reverence and care, so that the chief might return to the salmon people in their villages at the bottom of the ocean and bring them back again for the next spawning run. The Klallam on the southern coast of the Strait of Juan de Fuca cut the lead salmon into two pieces and then joined the fish together again and hung it with its head up. It was then boiled into a soup, from which everyone partook except the host. The remains were placed in the river to bring the fish back again the next year.[51]

Imbued with great spiritual power, certain salmon could lead to problems for the Klallam. For example, a salmon with a crooked mouth foretold disaster. To prevent a calamitous event, the crooked-mouthed salmon was boiled and all of the children of the village partook of it. After the ceremonial consumption of this fish, the backbone was carried to the end of the village where it was placed on a pole facing the water.[52]

Taboos applied not only to hunting and handling of salmon but to many other aspects of tribal life as well. During pregnancy, the expectant mother could not eat any animal that suffered while being killed. If a pregnant mother ate the meat of a deer that had tried to escape into water while being hunted, and frothed at the mouth in fear while being pursued and killed, it was believed the woman's baby would froth at the mouth as well. Moreover, the partner of a pregnant woman could not hunt wildcats or raccoons because the child would become sick and act like these animals.[53]

The Klallam used their local resources well but also traveled a great deal in pursuit of food, sometimes great distances. Travel was conducted in large canoes because it was easier to travel by water than through the deep forests and through the ramparts of mountains that filled the peninsula. Practically the whole Klallam community, from Clallam Bay to Port Townsend, broke camp to head to Hood Canal for dog salmon, leaving only the old behind in the permanent villages. Hood Canal drops south from the Strait of Juan de Fuca, east of the Olympic Mountains and west of the Kitsap Peninsula. Numerous rivers follow sharp gradients quickly down the steep east slope of the Olympics to the deep, protected waters of the canal, home territory of the Skokomish Indians. Paddling their canoes along the northern rim of the Olympic Peninsula in the Strait of Juan de Fuca, then taking a sharp right and heading south into the Hood Canal, the Klallam would head for the salmon rivers of this area. There are many rivers that were profligate with dog salmon, including the Dosewallips, Hamma Hamma (which means stinky, stinky for the smell created by the thousands of spawned-out salmon rotting on its banks), Skokomish, and the Duckabush.

The favored sites of the Klallam were the Hamma Hamma and the Dosewallips. Both areas host extensive clam and oyster grounds, so it is likely that the opportunity to pursue those resources in addition to salmon made these locations attractive. Another reason for the popularity of the Dosewallips site, today located close to the town of Brinnon, Washington, was the vast amount of huckleberries ripe and ready for plucking at the same time as the dog salmon runs. While the Dosewallips and Hamma Hamma sites were the favorites of the Klallam and were located at the northern end of the canal, many would also travel to the southernmost part of the canal for salmon. They set up camps close to permanent Skokomish villages, allowing for a great deal of socializing and cultural exchange.

Trade was always an important part of Klallam life and these trips provided tribal members the opportunity for commerce with the Skokomish. Because of their heavier dependence on game like deer, the Skokomish desired the dried clams and salmon of the Klallam, exchanging baskets for these commodities. Located on the western side of the Olympic Peninsula and Klallam territory, the Makah also traded with them for dried clams, a commodity for which the Klallam were famous. They continued to use dried shellfish as the basis for barter after white settlement, even as the Indians traveled to the hop fields for wage labor. For example, the Yakama Indians from the eastern side of the Cascade Mountains were known to have traded with the Klallam for dried clam in the hop fields.[54]

These travels for food, trade, and socializing were not short trips, usually lasting from August until late November or December; clearly the dog salmon and barter of the Hood Canal represented an important part of their seasonal round. Generally, they returned to their permanent villages in time for winter celebrations and dances. However, some Klallam families would remain at the sites on Hood Canal through the winter.[55]

The creativity of the coastal tribes was not limited to their various uses of nature, but was also revealed in the strategies of consolidating power and distributing resources, facilitated through the famous potlatch ceremonies. The potlatch is well known to Pacific Northwesterners and is typically described as a ceremony in which one successful member of an Indian group distributes food and goods to other members until he is left with nothing. In fact, this culturally important event is more complex than is generally understood. The potlatch was a large event involving numerous communities and even different Indian groups. It lasted days at least, sometimes weeks, with hundreds of guests to be fed and entertained. While the potlatch is best recognized as a way to achieve higher status within the community and to build reciprocal relationships to enhance political power, it also served a principal purpose of redistributing resources to maintain relative balance within Indian communities and across the region. According to anthropologist Wayne Suttles, "The potlatch is part of a larger socioeconomic system that enables the whole social network, consisting of a number of communities, to maintain a high level of food production and to equalize its consumption both within and among communities."[56]

The preparation for a potlatch could take years, as community members used a variety of means to accumulate the food and wealth (masks, clothing, tools, etc.) necessary for the event. Going to war, trading, gambling, and providing services for trade were ways to accrue the necessary wealth and food. Suttles explains a particularly innovative way of storing goods in a pre-capitalist economy when the Indians had limited space. They used a "put-away" system where objects and food would be given to a relative, friend, or person of equal status with the understanding they would be returned when needed. This was often done years in advance of the potlatch. These steps were required to prepare for an event that mandated feeding hundreds of people for several days or weeks and distributing wealth to all of them.[57] Suttles provides a concise description of the flow of events in the potlatch:

The potlatch itself consisted of a fixed sequence of events. On the first day, relatives and affinals paid their debts to the hosts. This greatly increased the hosts' already large accumulations of wealth and gave them the food with which to support the guests during their stay. During the next several days the hosts celebrated various life crises, changes of status, memorials to the dead, all events being enhanced by the display of hereditary masks and other privileges insofar as possible. Persons other than the principal potlatchers took advantage of the occasion to seek similar recognition. [58]

Upon reaching the final day of the ceremony, the potlatch hosts would stand on a platform extending from the roof of their house and hand out expensive gifts, calling the names of invited guests to give them a valuable item such as a blanket, and then finally tossing the last pieces of property to the crowd.[59]

SACRED NATURE, SACRED SALMON

Trade, travel, and potlatch ceremonies all marked the passage of the year for the Elwha Klallam, but it was the Elwha River that proved to be the most consistent thread through their lives. A rich, complex culture was predicated on resource wealth—the most important resource being salmon. The river itself was probably valued for its beauty and clean water, along with its provision of abundant natural food resources for the Indians. They did not seek to transform or harness the river but to harvest necessary resources from it. But mere subsistence does not do justice to the role of the Elwha River and its salmon, as well as other species and stock, in the Klallam culture and worldview. Nature was not commodified as it would be in the arriving capitalist economy. Wildlife such as salmon, deer, raven, and others held a spiritual significance and the Strong People treated their landscape and its denizens with great respect. While it is anachronistic to portray Indians as environmentalists in modern terms (there are many examples of Indian peoples damaging ecosystems and certain species like the beaver during the beaver fur trade), in the case of the Klallam, we see a system of use and respect that worked for at least several centuries, was clearly sustainable, and preserved a healthy river and fisheries into the late 19th century.

Those who are strongest critics of the idea of Indians practicing a more restrained, sensible form of resource use assert that the limited impact of Indians on the landscape is simply a function of low population numbers. Historian Joseph Taylor takes this issue on in his first chapter of *Making Salmon*. Noting the dominant assumption that Indians in the Pacific Northwest (his focus is Oregon but also deals with interior as well as coastal Indians) did not destroy their salmon resource simply because they lacked the numbers to do so or the market motivations to overharvest salmon, Taylor effectively renders these points meaningless, demonstrating that the Indians created a mastery of fishing technology that gave them the capacity to harvest far beyond their need.[60] In fact, their harvests in some years are estimated to have equaled peak years of harvest on the Columbia River. In addition, the salmon-harvesting Natives of the Northwest did indeed trap, hook, spear, net, and smoke salmon for trade locally and in extended markets reaching all the way to the Great Plains. Granted, this is not the same market system that arose later when salmon were canned and shipped to Chicago, New York, London, and India but it reveals a more complex Indian economy than is generally supposed, while showing that the Indians had the technology and the motivation to harvest far beyond their own needs for consumption. So, what stopped them from doing so? As Taylor points out, and is clear from my discussion of Klallam Indian culture, a spiritual and taboo system emphasizing respect, propitiation, fear, and balance limited salmon harvest and destruction. While there is some evidence for active conservation measures, the respect and the practice of ceremonies restricted consumption of salmon in one very tangible way: the first-salmon ceremonies and others consumed so much time, required such deliberation and careful consideration, that they in effect guaranteed the passage of large numbers of salmon upstream. The fact that these ceremonies were practiced in one form or another along the coast from Alaska to northern California resulted in a wide-scale form of conservation preventing the eradication of total runs and allowing enough fish for continual reproduction.[61]

CHANGING FACE OF THE LAND

Taboos and respect were no match for the pathogens that wrought destruction on Pacific Northwest Indians. Disease foretold the arrival of the white traders and settlers who would eventually force the Klallam and other tribes away from their rich homeland onto restricted and smaller fragments of land. Smallpox and other diseases, likely introduced by Spanish explorers in the late 18th century, reduced Northwest coastal Indian populations from an estimated high of 180,000 to somewhere between 30,000 and 40,000 by 1800. Not having antibodies to Old World afflictions like smallpox, influenza, measles, and others, the Indians suffered a virgin soil epidemic. Whole villages were destroyed. The British explorer George Vancouver described abandoned villages littered with bones in 1792. Turned into a vast killing field, the region was destabilized by this brutal and ongoing pathogenic catastrophe. Indian nations, villages, and families were undermined by sudden and unpredictable deaths; traditional beliefs, rules, and religious systems shattered by events far beyond their experience and control. The Klallam population, estimated at over 3,000 in 1770, dropped to 485 in 1880. The Lower Elwha Klallam were reduced to 67 people. As late as 1853, a brutal smallpox epidemic devastated the Klallam, even as an increasing wave of "newcomers" washed up on their shores and began occupying land that was seemingly vacant.[62] Indians grappled with a spiritual crisis, questioning their own faith as they died off in the face of the seemingly stalwart Europeans and Americans, who thrived. Many Indians questioned their traditional beliefs and the efficacy of their faith and gods, making them more amenable to conversion and welcoming of white missionaries.[63] As had happened across the North American continent, the depredations of disease made it that much easier for the new white arrivals to gain control over the Indians' traditional lands and resources.

The Klallam Indians lost their homelands in the 1855 Point No Point Treaty with Washington Territory Governor Isaac Stevens, just one of the several treaties he crafted on his barnstorming tour across the region, in which he argued, bullied, begged, and bribed numerous

Indian tribes off large parts of their most desirable lands, while guaranteeing continued access to customary fishing and hunting sites. The Lower Elwha Klallam contractually gave up much of their land for cash and goods, a reservation on Hood Canal with the Skokomish, and continued access to their main livelihood of fishing. However, they refused to move to the Skokomish Reservation. Typically, none of the promises to the Indians in the treaty were fully met. Nevertheless, the way was cleared for white settlers and exploitation of resources for profit.[64]

The previous sentence would serve as a useful ending to the chapter, except that it would then contribute to one of the great flaws in American historiography and popular culture—that is, writing the Indians out of the picture as soon as white development begins and Indians are pushed to the margins, economically, politically, and culturally. However, most of the Lower Elwha Klallam chose to remain in their traditional territory (and remain a part of the historical narrative of the region), continuing to forge an existence from the land and resources around them, even while losing land and witnessing the natural environment begin its decline under the twin pressures of American settlement and capitalist development. They attempted to purchase their lands, but because they were not U.S. citizens, were unable to obtain legal title. Furthermore, while the passage of the Indian Homestead Act allowed them to purchase and gain title to land, with about ten Klallam families gaining ownership of approximately 1,300 acres by 1884, the Indians who purchased land were forced to sever ties with their tribe. This was consistent with government and reform efforts in this era to compel assimilation of Indians into American culture through land distribution schemes. Because the leaders of white communities marginalized Indians socially, even while stripping them of their lands and resources, little is available in the written records of these native people in the late 19th century. Port Angeles newspapers of the time indicated that they sold fruit in town as well as salmon that had been harvested from the Elwha River. The papers also reveal the continued harvesting of trout, halibut, and crabs by the Indians.[65]

During this same period, however, the Lower Elwha Klallam suffered increasing land pressure from settlers moving into the area, undermining the Indians' ability to make a living from the land. 1887 saw a number of settlers moving into land west of the Elwha River and beef, plums, eggs, and vegetables were produced there for the Port Angeles market. Much of this land had been opened by the impact of disease and abandoned by Indians not able to gain title without breaking ties with the tribe, something many were unwilling to do. They moved to the area west of the river and onto Ediz Hook, abandoning better land to Americans moving into the area. The lands in this area were fertile enough to support productive yields of oats, barley, wheat, and potatoes. Such a subtle form of conquest, startlingly similar to the process of settlement employed by the Puritans in New England in the early 17th century, converted the landscape to a European-American tableau, while also extending a capitalist market economy. This biological and economic conquest weakened the Klallam by taking needed land and resources, marginalizing them culturally and financially in the process. Little did they know that their key source of sustenance and the heart of their culture would be radically transformed to their detriment under the ideology of settlement, development, and industrial capitalism.[66]

Chapter 2

"And What Would Be the Possibilities of That Power?"

THE DAMMING OF THE ELWHA RIVER

The more thou damm'st it up, the more it burns.
The current that with gentle murmur glides,
Thou know'st, being stopp'd, impatiently doth rage;
But when his fair course is not hindered,
He makes sweet music with the enamell'ed stones
       from *Two Gentlemen of Verona*
          William Shakespeare

The Americans migrating into the Elwha River and Port Angeles area carried a complex set of ideas about nature, land, and resource use. Nevertheless, in the early stages of settlement, new arrivals were compelled to eke out an existence highly dependent on the natural resources of the land, much like the Lower Elwha Klallam that they were squeezing out and pushing to the margins of traditional Native territory. Prior to 1860, little non-Indian development or settlement occurred in this part of the Olympic Peninsula; the closest thriving community was Port Townsend, located about 50 miles northeast of the mouth of the Elwha River. However, early boosters with excited imaginations and visions of the pastoral ideal painted a portrait of the settlement they dreamed would surely emerge upon this last, far-flung corner of the continental United States. The description in the following passage, written in 1860, just as the region was being settled, reveals a great deal about the aspirations for the domestication of this landscape.

The great Sierra of the Olympic range appears to come down quite to the water's edge, and presents a wild and forbidding aspect. But as the land is neared we see the line of foot-hills, before dimly visible through the mist, now assume their proper form, and disclosing deep ravines, with fertile valleys lying between them, and reaching quite to the base of the great mountains of the coast range . . . gently undulating ground bearing the sturdy giants of the forest, offering inducements of various kinds to settlers to come and locate, and build up the towns and villages that are destined . . . to line the shores of the bays and coves . . . with the pleasant sight of white cottages sending up blue clouds of smoke from hospitable hearths.[1]

Many migrating Americans shared the impulse to tame and convert this landscape, and during the 1850s and 1860s settlement increased on the Sequim prairie about 20 miles east of the Elwha River, where farmers grew potatoes and raised cattle, sheep, and hogs. The Sequim prairie had been a site of intensive use by the Klallam. They burned on a regular basis to keep the forests at bay and reinvigorate the grasses, berries, and other key plants used for food and other purposes, on land that appeared to settlers as natural prairie. Not only did the firing of the prairie allow these Indians to grow approximately 80 plants critical to their economy, but they also grew camas, a plant brought over from the eastern, drier side of the Cascade Mountains and planted by Indians throughout the region. Camas was popular for its root, which was used and consumed like potatoes. (Appropriately enough, when potatoes were introduced into the region by the Hudson's Bay Company in 1821, the Klallam began raising those on the Sequim prairie.) Indeed, many of the Klallam were practicing limited forms of agriculture when Americans took the land from them. In addition, the use of fire to manage the Sequim prairie, as practiced on Whidbey Island to the north and in prairies south around Olympia (all, incidentally, the first areas of settlement for non-Indians migrating into the region), provided forage for numerous game species important to the Indians, particularly elk, deer, and various birds.

Replicating the patterns of the Indians, even while forcing them off the land and away from their resources, settlers supplemented agriculture and husbandry by hunting the plentiful game and fowl. They gathered fish and shellfish from the Dungeness and Elwha rivers and the beaches of the Strait of Juan de Fuca. Settlers cut trees from the forests to build homes and fences and, like the Klallam, supplemented their diets by picking wild berries. Indeed, blackberry gathering parties, like those of the Indians, constituted not only a means of harvesting an important food source, but also an activity of social significance in the community. These white settlers were highly dependent on the land for sustenance but expressed confidence that subsistence would soon be replaced by industry, wealth, and new opportunities. Through the end of the 19th century until the boom of the World War I years, inhabitants of the Port Angeles and Sequim areas continued to rely on the natural products of the ecosystem even as the economy grew increasingly market-oriented and driven by logging and salmon canning.[2]

IF YOU BUILD IT THEY WILL COME

For the next twenty years, Port Angeles experienced little development from its meager beginnings and did not appear destined for explosive growth. However, with the completion in 1883 of the Northern Pacific Railroad to Tacoma, the flow of settlers to the Northwest increased substantially. During the 1880s, the Pacific Northwest population increased by 165 percent. Not only did the completion of the transcontinental railroad and connecting railroads open the Northwest to a flood of new arrivals seeking opportunity in the area, railroads also transported Northwest products to eastern markets. The flow of investments, commodities, and new settlers facilitated by the expansion of railway systems to the West contributed significantly to the development and growth of Port Angeles. As historian William Cronon argues in *Nature's Metropolis:*

The Great City and the American West, the forests north of Chicago and the grasslands of the Great Plains to the west of that city were fundamentally transformed by the reach of America's second city into the countryside. The railroads, enabling the flow of credit and capital into the hinterlands, including the Pacific Northwest, and facilitating the conversion of the landscape to a commercialized economy serving and served by urban centers, wrought great changes on the land. Such was the case for the Port Angeles region as well as the Pacific Northwest in general. The welcoming hand of urban capitalism extended its reach a little later there in the far northwestern corner of the United States.[3]

Ironically then, a group of idealists troubled by the power of unbridled capitalism provided Port Angeles its first major growth spurt in the late 1880s. The Puget Sound Cooperative Colony was a utopian society organized in 1887 and situated in Port Angeles at the mouth of Ennis Creek. Historian Murray Morgan described the creation of the colony. "The Puget Sound Cooperative Colony, which was capitalized for one million mostly theoretical dollars, was thought up by a New York State judge, Peter Peyto Good, who wanted it to be the forerunner of a society untainted by capitalism. Good died before the colony got out of the dream stage, but his work was carried on by a friend, George Venable Smith, another lawyer deeply troubled by social injustice." According to Morgan, these men had met in Seattle while organizing anti-Chinese riots, which, from their perspective was consistent with improving conditions and opportunities for the working man—as long as he wasn't from Asia.[4]

Having purchased land at the mouth of the creek, they built a sawmill and used it to produce lumber for the colonists' cabins. The additional construction of a store, a 60-ton sloop, and a meeting house, either respectfully or jokingly named Potlatch House, provided a figurative nod to the important Native ceremony that had happened at that site before disease, settlement, and displacement ended the practice there. It marked an auspicious start for this idealistic community. They would be the ones to domesticate this landscape, with cabins huddling under the snow-capped mountains, close to shore, comfort and success signified by gray smoke curling upward from the chimneys of hardworking yeomen. In so doing, they would also introduce and nurture a more moderate and less selfish form of capitalism on the shores of the Strait of Juan de Fuca. They sought to domesticate the landscape and capitalism; they shared the confidence of all boosters, town founders, and utopian leaders.[5]

With a newspaper articulating the ideas of the colony while providing steady criticism of the industrial capitalism of the Gilded Age, the community abandoned the dollar for its own currency, which was awarded on the basis of labor performed. The colony peaked at around 1,000 members by 1888, but the departure of Smith and the onset of economic difficulties brought the utopian experiment to an end. Most of these colonists stayed, due to the ties of friendship and community and their love of the location. They remained also because rumors of a transcontinental railroad making Port Angeles its western terminus foretold a prosperous future of economic growth.[6]

THOMAS THE CONQUEROR

An idealist of the industrial capitalist stripe, a young Canadian emigrant named Thomas T. Aldwell disembarked from the *George E. Starr* in 1890 and cast his ambitious eyes upon the muddy but growing town of Port Angeles. In his autobiography *Conquering the Last Frontier*, Aldwell in hindsight described his original vision of the potential metropolis, the "harbor rimmed with vital industry with payrolls expanding, houses being built, and streets being laid. The raw material was here; raw materials that called for the minds and hands of builders who would think of this as a home to make for their children and their grandchildren and their great grandchildren." It is hard to know Aldwell's original feelings (as compared to how he described those feelings from the perspective of age and having played a major role in the development of Port Angeles), but he is clearly indicating in this passage that he would be one of those who would take the raw materials of the muddy, waterfront town and surrounding landscape and build something he perceived as better. "I felt I had met a challenge to help build a happy and prosperous community, and I decided to accept it. Whatever I would do in life was now tied to a ragged, sprawling, ambitious little town called Port Angeles."[7] He also noted the 200 to 300 Lower Elwha Klallam living and camped on the beach of Port Angeles, their large canoes pulled onto the shore and in constant use. But they disappear from his narrative after that point, echoing the physical diminishment of the Klallam because of the "newcomers,"[8] as well as Aldwell's contribution to the decline of the Strong People.[9]

Casting himself in the image of the heroic pioneer, he saw or portrayed himself as playing a critical role in transforming raw wilderness, as he understood it, into a thriving urban community, not merely a domesticated landscape of welcoming hearths but one of production and wealth. With this vision in mind, Aldwell began a career that would enable him to work his changes upon the landscape and harness it for industrial development.[10]

This booster and self-named "conqueror" of the wilderness had chosen a propitious year for emigration to Port Angeles. Due to recent population growth, a land boom starting in 1889, and speculation surrounding the eager anticipation of a railroad being built to Port Angeles, the town's future was brushed with a roseate bloom as residents expected industry, development, and prosperity.[11] This excitement and sense of impending growth and prosperity was furthered by another event occurring soon after Aldwell's arrival. Led by lawyer and Olympia legislative clerk John Murphy, residents of Port Angeles embarked on a campaign to pry loose 3,100 acres from the federal reserve designated at the original townsite. Residents resented the land being controlled by the federal government and argued that the reserve was blocking the town's natural growth; a later booster pamphlet published by the Clallam County Immigration Association in 1898 referred to the federal land as "locked up," foreshadowing later wise use movement rhetoric.

The campaign's strategy was a model of simplicity. The squatting on and occupation of federal land was conducted in an orderly way.

On the morning of July 4, 1890, hundreds of men marched onto the reserve and with axes and saws began clearing forest and proving up their claims. They were only allowed to file on a maximum of two claims, to prove their intent of settlement and not speculation, as well as to preserve land for others. After building cabins and improving their land, there was a united and concerted demand for title to the land, and pressure applied on the federal government to provide that title. By the end of the year 500 claims had been filed.[12]

The well-organized squatters then flooded their congressman, John L. Wilson, with letters and telegrams demanding that he introduce a bill releasing the desired and squatted-upon federal land. He proved amenable, and with a few timely trips to Washington, D.C. by Port Angeles residents, the land rebels were able to gain title to their plots in early 1894. With the opportunity created by this clever bit of political coercion and land grab by local residents, Aldwell claimed and improved two lots, paid the appraisal fee, and thus gained title. He also bought several lots from squatters who could not afford the appraisal fee. This marked the beginning of Aldwell's career in land speculation, allowing him to accrue land and early wealth while forging the necessary relationships for raising capital and generating support that would prove so critical to the later building of the Elwha Dam.[13]

While land accumulation and speculation laid the foundation for his career and vision for Port Angeles' future, Aldwell later claimed ambivalence about the landscape; it was both a commodity and a source of beauty and inspiration. Regardless, he felt driven to work changes upon the land. "There is something about belonging to a place," he wrote. "You want to control more and more of it, directly or indirectly . . . land was something one could work with, change, develop."[14] The principle of working with, changing, and developing land also governed his attitude about nature—it existed to serve human needs. Like many other boosters and businessmen across the American landscape, he saw and touted the benefits of nature in which a community was being built, while arguing that it had to be improved upon to be perfected and serve human needs completely. The transformation of first nature to second nature, as Cronon argues, required measures such as drainage, river and harbor improvements, railroads, and, of course, dams.

Aldwell would find his lever for transforming first nature to second[15] when he discovered a small claim on the Elwha River. Stating that he discovered the river through a claim he purchased from an acquaintance for $50, his later description of the site reveals or implies an aesthetic appreciation for this location. "The view was magnificent from that hilltop claim . . . and it would have been my claim except that . . . I decided to go on down to [another] cabin."[16] This second claim was situated in a deep canyon, through which the Elwha roared, with vine maples surrounding the cabin and a spring running in front of it. "The scintillating rays of sun were coming through the branches and sparkling on the water," he recalled. "My life had taken me to schools, to cities, to business, but suddenly that spring embodied all of life and beauty I thought I'd ever want."[17] Sublime moments aside, it was here that Aldwell later built the Elwha Dam for the generation of hydroelectric power.[18]

His language of beauty and fulfillment arising from nature anticipates environmental values that were developing at that time among a small cadre of American preservationists. A 1901 article in the *Seattle Post-Intelligencer* described the Elwha River in language familiar to later environmentalists or earlier romantics and transcendentalists: " . . . beautiful, clear as crystal, rushing down from the snow-capped peaks of the majestic Olympics, through gorges, over cataracts, through and among immense boulders, cool, and pure and powerful, containing the energy of thousands upon thousands of horse power . . . The Elwha, sublime in its majestic and awe inspiring scenery, is destined to become a mighty power for good in the hands of ingenious humanity, for the present and future generations."[19]

The rhetoric employed here notes that regardless of beauty and inspiration, the river's highest purpose would be in service to mankind. In 1901 boosters were already identifying the best locations for dams on the Elwha. "There are many places along its course where its energy could be transformed into power for the use of the manufacturer, for lighting, for the tram car, for the street car . . . the two best opportunities for the development of power are the lower of Aldwell's canyon, and the Upper canyon."[20]

This demonstrates that Aldwell was not alone in his desire for hydroelectricity for Port Angeles.[21] Regional boosters had already emphasized the advantages provided the Pacific Northwest by the numerous rivers draining the various mountain ranges on the coast and in the interior. *The Nineteenth Annual Report of the United States Geological Survey* for the years 1897–1898 described the Elwha River:

> *This river rises on the southeastern slope of Mount Olympus, and is the largest stream flowing into the Strait of Juan de Fuca, or Puget Sound, from the Olympic Mountains. Its waters are clear at all ordinary stages, and run over a gravel and bowlder [sic] bottom. It is a tortuous and turbulent stream, winding between high and precipitous mountains, cutting its way through rocky ridges, and forming deep and narrow canyons.*[22]

This essentially accurate description of the river is followed by the repeated myth about large grasslands at the center of the mountain range just waiting to be turned into cattle ranches. The report identifies "Aldwell's Canyon" as a key site and in the following year's report provides even more information about water flow, possible power generation, and expected costs of a dam built on that site.[23]

A 1904 article titled "The Water Power of the Pacific Northwest" analyzed the topography, geology, and hydrology of the region with a keen eye on waterpower possibilities. While the main part of the article discusses how dam construction could facilitate the use of hydromechanical power for milling wheat and spinning wool, the author did note some early and primitive hydroelectric production in Spokane and Oregon City, and then ended the article with a rhetorical flourish probably considered hyperbole by many readers. In fact, in what became the most accurate prediction in the article, the author hinted at how quickly the economy would change in the next four decades in that region. After stating that those who live closest to a resource are least able to understand its value, he wrote, "There are those who will yet discover the Northwest and her resources. When that day comes, the present tide of immigration, great as it is, will increase tenfold; and the Lewis and Clark expedition will only be outdone by an Edison and Marconi expedition re-enforced by a capital sufficient to proclaim this 'Oregon Territory' in its commercial and industrial possibilities greater than any of the acquisitions of the United States."[24]

Leaders of Port Angeles embraced that spirit of capitalism and strove to make their town and region one of great "commercial and industrial possibilities." A booster pamphlet published by the Clallam County Immigration Association, an organization of local merchants and boosters, titled *Port Angeles, the Gate City of the Pacific Coast*, identified hydroelectricity as the key to profitably harvesting nature's bounty. Noting that Port Angeles was well situated for maritime trade on the Strait of Juan de Fuca, and that the local soil was "rich and very productive," the boosters then commented on the role of the Elwha River in their vision for the future. "For the utilization of these varied matchless resources, nature has provided Port Angeles with a magnificent water power, the possibilities of which are almost unlimited."[25] After discussing the potential power available through hydroelectricity, the pamphlet's authors elucidated the various ways in which harnessed power could assist in extracting resources and converting nature's wealth to liquid capital. "And what would be the possibilities of that power? It would turn the wheels of state; it would provide sufficient power for the manufacturers, the electric lighting, the street car service of a large city . . . " While this short list would seem enough work for a river to perform, the list went on, asserting that hydroelectric power could also support an electric railway to lakes (Sutherland, Crescent, and Dungeness) and electric rail lines for logging into the mountains, with plenty left over for other uses. With the boundless optimism of boosters of that era, the piece ended by trumpeting, "Truly, a grand destiny is ours."[26]

The booster literature did not limit the value of hydroelectricity to mere economics. The refrains of utopian rhetoric arose in one article extolling the need for and advantages of hydroelectricity. Boosters believed "innumerable benefits" would accrue from a harnessed Elwha River. Not only would an industrial economy emerge in Port Angeles; the cost of living would be reduced. Waxing ecstatic, the author then argued that with the combination of electrical power and already invented electrical appliances, "The inventions of an inventive age will produce for the betterment of humanity, Bellamy's ideal commonwealth may not be as far in the future as the pessimist might imagine."[27] For the boosters and civic leaders of Port Angeles, hydroelectricity promised to be the tool through which they could not only amass wealth but also improve American society.

The linchpin to this vision was a hydroelectric dam; Aldwell began secretly buying up land needed for the building of the dam and the reservoir. With outside investment and assistance, he purchased the requisite land over a period of 12 years. R. M. Brayne and his son-in-law Duncan Shanks originally invested in the operation. In 1885 Brayne had built and managed one of the first pulp mills, located on Youngs River in Oregon. Aldwell at that time was busy promoting the community through his management of the *Port Angeles Tribune-Times* and securing property for the hoped-for expansion of the Northern Pacific Railroad to Port Angeles and for his own economic benefit. When Brayne stopped by his office in 1894, surely they discussed the critical role of power to the development of the Port Angeles economy. What they certainly did do was organize a partnership to acquire land for the dam and reservoir site with the agreement to be as secretive as possible, using agents to secure the land for them, so word would not get out about their plans and drive up land prices. Brayne and his son-in-law eventually sold their share to George A. Glines, a real estate broker from Winnipeg who had a great deal of money invested in land in the area already. Glines and Aldwell formed a partnership in 1908 and moved forward with their plans to build a dam and hydroelectric power plant. "The instigator and prime mover, Mr. T. T. [*sic*] Aldwell, has put in about eighteen years in securing the sight [*sic*] and adjacent property so that he may not be hindered in any way with water backing up onto the property of others. He owns today about six miles of the river bed on each side of the river."[28]

Even as Aldwell continued with his secret plan to buy up land for the future dam and reservoir, the Port Angeles community maintained its slow, steady growth. The settlers usurped even more Native resources as they expanded and diversified the Port Angeles economy. The opening of a clam-packing plant in 1895 and its quick conversion to canning both salmon and clams tapped a key resource of the Lower Elwha Klallam while extending the wage-labor economy.[29] The construction of an even larger and updated cannery in 1919 on Ediz Hook, where some Lower Elwha Klallam continued to live, increased the dependence of the Port Angeles economy on the salmon resource, and by exacerbating pressure on the salmon, undermined the Natives' economy.[30]

The growth of the settler community of Port Angeles and the surrounding area was subsidized by the wealth of nature and enabled by the displacement of Natives from that landscape. There was the very real physical removal of Indians from large portions of the landscape achieved through the treaty of 1855, and the loss of lands along the Elwha River to homestead whites in the 1860s;[31] beyond that was the figurative removal of the Lower Elwha Klallam Indians and others through economic marginalization. Adding to this, conservationists trying to preserve the salmon further undermined the Native culture and economy. While by 1910 state law required individuals to hold fishing licenses, Klallam and other Indians were not citizens and therefore could not obtain fishing licenses. This may seem ironic but it is more accurately understood as another means of undermining Indian sovereignty and economic self-sufficiency. While this may not have always been intentional, the lack of thought and incidental marginalization of the tribe still deserve criticism. This abuse continued over the years. Boyd lays this out very effectively, pointing out that even after gaining citizenship

Klallam Woman working on a sewing machine on Hollywood Beach, Port Angeles. The juxtaposition of sewing machine with the tent and the canoe, as well as the growing town in the background, suggests the desperate effort by Klallams to modernize and adjust to the dramatic changes imposed on them. Bert Kellogg Collection. Courtesy of North Olympic Library System.

in 1924, Indians in western Washington still faced restrictions on their treaty rights to harvest salmon. She tells of an incident when a Klallam man "was dragged from his bed and down a flight of stairs in the middle of the night and then charged with 'illegal' fishing . . . Klallam children learned to outsmart officers by tying string to their fish and dragging them home through the long grass undetected."[32] As damaging as white settlement, commercial fishing, and enforcement of conservationist policies were to the Lower Elwha Klallam, the construction of a dam on the river would eclipse all of those problems, destroying the salmon almost completely and driving the Indians even closer to their nadir.

PUTTING THE ELWHA TO WORK

In 1910, Aldwell organized the Olympic Power & Development Company. The company included Joshua Green, R. D. Merrill, and Mike Earles on its board of directors. Earles was a prominent local lumberman and businessman. R. D. Merrill was the son of Thomas Merrill, co-owner of the Merrill and Ring logging company of Saginaw, Michigan. Thomas Merrill had built his wealth logging the forests of Maine, Michigan, Minnesota, and Canada. The company owned 23,000 acres of forested land in the Port Angeles area and through his sons, R.D. and Thomas Jr., he was seeking further economic opportunities on the Olympic Peninsula. Aldwell also announced his acquisition of multiple plots of land and intentions to build a dam in 1910. One local paper wrote, "Mr. Aldwell has spent a number of years and no inconsiderable amount of money in organizing his proposition and holding it together until such time as general conditions would justify."[33]

Investment and support were garnered locally, much of it from lumber interests, and the capital stock for the company was set at $1 million. The company had one hurdle to clear before obtaining the franchise for the dam from the Port Angeles City Council. The Port Angeles mayor preferred a plan supported by Seattle investors for a power plant on the Little River. The council overrode the mayor's veto, however, and awarded the franchise to Aldwell's Olympic Power & Development Company. Aldwell promised 50,000 kilowatts in the franchise meeting as opposed to the mere 500 kilowatts that were to be generated by the proposed Little River Dam. Local boosters sought greater investment in their economy and likely concluded that an abundant power source would engender increased investment and, thus, growth. As one Port Angeles newspaper article stated, "Commercial bodies in all cities now recognize this and encourage in every way the development of large water powers, which have a capacity sufficient to supply cheap power to large manufacturing concerns . . . a large constant flow of water is essential to have sufficient power to develop economically."[34] Boosters sought power generation in order to supply power for the anticipated next generation of industrial manufacturing.[35]

Seeking power required that capital also be sought and it was not long before Aldwell began pursuing additional investment for the dam project from outside the region. Businessmen understood the importance of promised power development for recruiting capital into the region. A March 1911 article in the *Seattle Times* on the development of Port Angeles and Clallam County stated in its subtitles, "To Open Resources: Attract Capitalists" and "Money Interests Just Awakening to Vast Resources of District—Elwha River Now Harnessed for Power."[36] The article discussed the importance of the proposed dam for both economic development and for attracting interest from outside the region. "The long-awaited opening of the resources of the country tributary to Port Angeles is now in sight . . . owing to the large undertakings of capitalists who have gone into Clallam County and ascertained for themselves the dormant opportunities for exploitation and development in a country having vast timber, agricultural, mining and other sources of wealth."[37] Knowing the interest of better financed capitalists outside the region and needing capital for his project, Aldwell had to leave his "city of destiny" and head east, because as he wrote, "Power in the West had to be financed in the East."[38] On a trip to Chicago and New York, Aldwell struck gold by convincing the engineering and investment firm of Peabody, Houghteling & Company to invest substantial capital in the dam project.[39]

The investment in the dam by this Chicago firm showed their confidence in the growing Port Angeles economy. Development in the region grew steadily during the years between 1910 and 1914. Logging boomed along the Strait of Juan de Fuca and in the foothills and river valleys of the Olympic Mountains as the easily accessible areas around Puget Sound were increasingly cut over. Logger and businessman Mike Earles contributed mightily to the rise of the Port Angeles economy and community, as well as to the belief that the town could create an industrial economy. He had logged in Wisconsin and like thousands of others came west when the forests of the great northern woods were finished off. In the Northwest he built a regional lumber business with operations in Clallam Bay in the 1890s, as well as in Maple Valley, south of Seattle, and in the Bellingham area. There, he and his partners, Ed Gierin and brother John Earles, built two mills. Their company acquired timber property in Crescent Bay. A logging boom ensued as logs were dropped over the steep bluff on the harbor; a narrow-gauge railway was then built to access timber at higher elevations and further from shore. This benefitted the Port Angeles economy, as jobs were provided locally and workers migrated into the region to work in Earles' and others' logging camps. Conditions were rough, typical of logging camps of the era. Food was bad, crews worked long hours—approximately 11 hours a day, six days a week—in terrible conditions, with a great deal of labor transience resulting.[40]

Earles eventually made Seattle his base of operations and built the first major mill in the Port Angeles area in 1914, with extensive cooperation from Aldwell. This mill received power from the Elwha Dam upon the dam's completion. Earles also financed and managed the building of a railroad from Port Townsend, where boxcars were loaded on barges and shipped to Seattle. Aldwell also cooperated with Earles in this venture. The railroad went into operation in 1915. These developments, along with the building of the dam, greatly increased Port Angeles' ability to harvest, process, and ship lumber.[41]

While these events helped to stimulate steady growth for Port Angeles after 1914, it is important to remember that the extractive economy and the profits of the Olympic Peninsula were largely controlled by capitalists living outside the region. As historian William G. Robbins points out in his study of logging in Coos Bay, Oregon, *Hard Times in Paradise*, and in *Colony and Empire: The Capitalist Transformation of the American West*, migratory capital from outside the region played the critical role in exploiting the resources of the Pacific Northwest and in its economic development. He specifically writes in *Hard Times in Paradise* that "for more than 150 years, the lumber and forest products industry has provided a prime example of migrating capital, rapid liquidation of resources, and boom-and-bust cycles for towns dependent on the forest bounty."[42]

Outside investment certainly controlled the logging economy of the Port Angeles area. A 1908 listing of timberland owners with title to more than 10,000 acres revealed that only one, Mike Earles, lived in the region; he resided in Seattle, and had moved there from the Midwest. The Port Angeles mill built by Earles in 1914 was sold to a California owner in 1915.[43]

RIVERS AND POWER

The spirit of capitalism, so strong and unmitigated in the late 19th and early 20th centuries, played a fundamental role in the construction of the Elwha Dam as well as much development in the American West. Robbins is emphatic when he writes, "It is essential to recognize that for the last thirty years of the 19th century and into the early years of the 20th, the American West was the great natural-resource reservoir and the investment arena for eastern U.S. and western European capital."[44] While boosters spoke of the social benefits of extracting resources and generating electricity, their fundamental interest was in creating capital and accumulating wealth.

In the case of Aldwell and the Elwha Dam, although he was able to generate some local interest and investment, the construction of the Elwha Dam would never have been accomplished without substantial investment by the Chicago firm. It was their capital, much more than their expertise, that resulted in the damming of the Elwha. And unlike the boosters of Port Angeles, the Chicago investors did not conceal their interests behind impressive speeches about improving "the commonwealth" or creating a "glittering metropolis." In a letter to Aldwell, the firm articulated their interests quite clearly after discovering his promise to the city of Port Angeles that it could defer payment for electricity generated by the dam. The Chicago investors unequivocally explained that they would require immediate capital return from the dam from its electricity production, and that in the future Aldwell should make no more such decisions without consulting them first.

Local boosters aggressively pursued investment from outside the region. Port Angeles businessmen sought to entice immigrants and capital to their community. Nature appeared beneficent in the bounty provided for extraction and sale, and local businessmen assured themselves and others that the wealth to be gained from harvesting resources such as lumber, salmon, and minerals would contribute to Port Angeles' growth and success, as well as to the pocketbooks of wise investors. Moreover, clever entrepreneurs were not limited to conventional means of extracting profit from nature. A Tacoma resident proposed a particularly bold idea to the Port Angeles Board of Trade, requesting their investment support. He suggested cutting large pieces of ice from glaciers on the side of Mount Olympus (using heated electric wires), shooting them down a 30-mile wooden flume to Port Angeles, and then shipping the ice from there to San Francisco for use in cold storage houses. The board, maybe recognizing the limits of technology and capital or just stunned by such a preposterous vision, politely declined involvement in this particular scheme.[45]

While businessmen in the Port Angeles area pursued the wealth to be amassed from logging, mining, and fishing, certain limits arose that increasingly restrained their economic activities. The emergence of the Progressive Era conservation movement resulted in resource management initiatives that regulated the laissez-faire economic environment within which American capitalists had long operated. The overexploitation of resources that had resulted in economic booms and busts and incredible environmental damage had also engendered a movement that sought to rationally and efficiently manage resources for the long-term public good. However, in the peripheries of the nation—such as the Pacific Northwest—restrictions on the use of resources were haltingly codified or weakly enforced. The apparent abundance of resources made it difficult for conservationists to convince people of the need to regulate commercial activities and development. For many years entrepreneurs continued to extract from forest, hill, river, and ocean whatever promised suitable profit at whatever price the market would bear, regardless of the environmental and social consequences.

The Port Angeles boosters were not unique in their interest in economic development and using hydroelectricity as an engine of economic growth. Aldwell and the other supporters of the dam were part of a first wave of hydroelectric development in the region. Dams had been built already in the Northeast and California and provided models of energy production to Northwest businessmen eager to tap the unharnessed power of the mountain rivers. The first power plant using hydroelectricity constructed in the United States was built in 1889 at Willamette Falls in Oregon City, Oregon. The company that built that power plant then dammed Oregon's Clackamas River in 1907; the Cazadero Dam and Power Plant further demonstrated the increasing interest in hydroelectricity in the Pacific Northwest. The Puget Sound Power Company was organized in 1902 to build a 25,500-kilowatt dam and plant on Washington's Puyallup River. On the eastern side of the region, the Washington Water Power Company threw up dams on the Spokane River in Post Falls, Idaho, and in Spokane, Washington, to generate power for the local community and for the mining district in Coeur d'Alene, 20 miles north of Post Falls. Four dams were built on the Spokane River by 1910. Back in western Washington, the White River Dam and power plant was built in 1911. The Condit Dam was built on the White Salmon River of Washington in 1913. Dams were constructed on the Missouri River in Montana in 1890, 1910, 1915, and 1918. The Big Sandy River in Oregon was dammed in 1912. Unquestionably, the region's rivers were being brought under control, one by one, to benefit these expansionist efforts and rapidly growing communities.[46]

OF DAMS AND CONQUEST

Informed by historical and personal knowledge of the impact of dams on fisheries in other regions, both Oregon and Washington tried to provide protections to spawning salmon. Oregon's territorial constitution in 1848 required dams and obstructions in salmon rivers to be built with fish passageways. Also, the first legislative session of the newborn state of Washington in 1890 weighed in on the side of salmon. One of Washington's oldest laws required fish passage through dams. Idealistic in tone, in reality these laws commanded little support in resource-extraction-dominated economies and legislatures of these states in the late 19th and early 20th centuries.

Dams for mining operations and irrigation farming, as well as splash dams, all violated these laws.

When Aldwell began moving forward with his great plan, he knew the momentum and interests of his culture strongly favored development and he would not face penalties or criticism for destroying the salmon fishery, even if it meant breaking the law.[47] He appeared untroubled by the damage the dam would undoubtedly wreak on salmon fisheries. This lack of concern did not reflect disdain for nature. In his autobiography, Aldwell spoke frequently of his love for nature, and for fishing in particular. But like most of his contemporaries, he favored quick, profitable development over cautious progress and conservation of resources. To be fair, he probably saw the abundance of salmon in all the rivers and streams of the region and felt that a few rivers could be developed without seriously damaging the salmon resource. However, he also felt that wilderness was a barrier to progress and therefore had to be tamed. In describing his efforts in his autobiography, Aldwell would have us believe he did not tremble at the risks inherent in the building of the dams. Historian Roderick Nash describes the philosophy of the pioneer: "The transformation of a wilderness into civilization was the reward for his sacrifices, the definition of his achievement, and the source of his pride. He applauded his successes in terms suggestive of the high stakes he attached to the conflict."[48] Aldwell interpreted his actions in the same spirit.

In his later years, Aldwell expressed great pride in the Elwha Dam project despite the overall failure of his vision: he was proud of his role in "conquering the wilderness." While many rivers ran thick with salmon, which encouraged a belief in the "unlimited" abundance of fisheries resources, electricity remained in short supply, and the demand for it increased with the steady growth of population and commercial enterprises; therefore, the choice was clear to Aldwell. Instead of worrying about the salmon that would be eradicated by the dam, he saw the potential for profit and the development of an industrial metropolis that hydroelectricity would bring. As historian Richard White writes in *The Organic Machine*, his study of the Columbia River: "Emerson's vision of the machine as a force of nature found its fullest expression as part of the old romance of energy in Western society, a dream of liberation from labor, an end to social conflict and environmental degradation through the harnessing of nature's power to human purposes."[49] The perfecting of the Elwha as an engine of development, prosperity, and social progress was the ultimate goal of Aldwell, his supporters, and their ilk. The Elwha River would be converted into the "organic machine" of the northern Olympic Peninsula. They were certain "a grand destiny" awaited them.

CONSTRUCTION AND CHAOS

Converting the free-flowing river to an engine of economic growth and social improvement required capital, ingenuity, and difficult, dangerous labor. Any human venture will include its share of tragedy and failure and this was as true of the Elwha Dam project as anything else in human history. Equipment failure resulted in two deaths and an injury on March 3, 1912. A great derrick was being used to load gravel into a scow on the lake when the main guy cable snapped, "and as the strain was thrown on the other cables, each parted, the derrick toppling over into others."[50] There was a large number of visitors on that day, viewing the project's progress. One group found itself in the wrong place at the wrong time. "Just before the accident [E. B.] Webster, wife and son, and Engineer Fitts of the Power Co., stepped down to the edge of the canyon, standing alongside [John] Berg and [Walter "Shorty"] Richter, and watching the men working on the scow below." Having walked a short distance up the hill with Mr. Fitts, they heard the derrick breaking free. "One glance back at the toppling timber, its tops a hundred feet overhead, and they started to run. Just then the flying cables were seen and they had not taken more than a step or two when Webster, a few feet to the rear of his wife and Mr. Fitts, was struck by a cable, and Berg and Richter were swept over the edge."[51] Webster survived, albeit with a severe gash and heavy loss of blood. Berg, leaving a family behind in Norway, and Richter, who had been married for two years, died.

Another terrible accident occurred on August 17, 1911. According to the *Port Angeles Tribune-Times*, "Rasmus Nelson, an engineer on one of the derricks at the works of the Olympic Power Company, met death Wednesday forenoon in a fall over an eighty-foot bluff into thirty feet of water as the culmination of a quarrel and a fist fight with Peter Smith, a fellow workman." The men had been arguing and, according to witnesses, Nelson "was the aggressor." While punches were being exchanged between him and Smith, Nelson tripped on a steam pipe, fell over the edge, and apparently hit his head as he plummeted into the gorge. A doctor examining the body stated that a concussion from that blow was the cause of death. Nelson was originally from Rosengarde, Denmark, and Smith was from Poland.[52]

Horrific and fatal accidents were a relatively common occurrence in Pacific Northwest towns where men worked in logging camps and sawmills, on fishing boats and construction projects. These accidents in no way hindered work progress. And as the dam took shape, the Port Angeles community's excitement grew. The *Tribune-Times* crowed that flipping the switch at the power plant would give Port Angeles "one of the best municipally owned lighting plants of any city of small size in the State of Washington."[53] The article also waxed rhapsodic over the quality of the street light system being put in place and asserted that the city would be in a position to provide power for all new needs, hence providing the impetus for more industry to move there.[54] Similarly, an article in late October, near the project's end, raved about the potential benefits of the dam. Noting that the river was finally being converted to hydroelectricity production, the *Tribune-Times* reported, "Yesterday morning the big generators were turned over for the first time, and all the machinery of the plant is reported as working satisfactorily."[55] The article noted that Port Townsend and the Puget Sound Navy Yard in Bremerton were planning to use energy from the Elwha as well. The line to Port Townsend was already completed and workers were hastily attempting to finish the line to Bremerton so Elwha hydroelectricity could be exported there.

Although Aldwell was general manager of the dam project, he argued that his power and autonomy were compromised by the insistence of Peabody, Houghteling & Company on using their own engineers for the design and construction of the dam. Finding himself in the position of having to answer to distant investors must have chagrined the man who saw himself as the agent of civilization and a conqueror of the wilderness. A letter to J. L. Houghteling, Jr. from Aldwell suggests the preemptory tone and attitude of majority investors based in Chicago seeking to extract profits from the hinterlands of the Olympic Peninsula of Washington State: "I have your letter of the 15th regarding the extension of the Port Angeles franchise, before me on my return from Port Townsend, and must say that I am somewhat surprised at its contents. I think it would have been wiser, before you condemned a person so strongly, who is exerting every effort for our mutual welfare, to have made an effort to inform yourself as to the real existing conditions."[56] He stated that his actions were appropriate and served the interests of the company and its investors. Aldwell further explained that delays in building the dam required an extension of the franchise in order to protect the company's business interests, stating that he was unsatisfied with the engineering firm and had followed the Chicago investors' advice to work as closely with the firm as possible. He ended by questioning the technical abilities of the company's hydraulic engineer.[57]

A series of letters between Aldwell and the Chicago firm attests to his legitimate concerns and supports later contentions in his autobiography. Tensions were clearly growing on the building site according to a letter from him to Alexander Smith of Peabody, Houghteling & Company dated May 17, 1912. He wrote, "It is beyond my comprehension why our engineers cannot make some reliable figure. I think we should have had an engineer of our own on the work as they hid from me as long as they could the fact that the foundation, or rather, a portion of it, had gone out. I am not an engineer but so far my predictions have all come true." Aldwell also complained that the supervisor of the firm building the dam was unnecessarily rude, stating that he "is making a personal matter of it and has made some statements concerning me which are almost ludicrous to write about. It is not a personal matter to me at all but I think that it is my duty to keep you informed as well as Mr. Glines as to the progress of the work and whenever I can make an estimate about what I think the cost will be."[58]

In a June 10, 1912, letter, Aldwell addressed the issue of a solid foundation for the dam. Describing his visit to the caisson, he noted that the natural level of the river is 82 feet above sea level and in the canyon the water was approximately 20 feet in depth. Pointing out that this made the natural riverbed about 60 or 62 feet above sea level, Aldwell then complained that after two months of labor and thousands of dollars expended, the firm was still only down to about 70 feet, approximately 10 feet above the natural rock bottom of the canyon.[59] He was legitimately concerned that the engineering firm would not make it to bedrock and anchor the dam effectively. In fact, they had no intention to anchor on bedrock. Their intent was to hang the dam between the canyon walls, which were about 40 feet wide at the bottom at that point. Unfortunately, instead of using chutes to pour wet concrete for the foundation, they sent batches of buckets down. The inconsistent drying of the concrete made the foundation vulnerable.[60]

Aldwell continued in this vein, pointing out problems with the caisson and holes under the foundation of the dam. Numerous leaks sprang from under the bottom of the dam. Sheet steel pilings were driven in front of the dam down into the gravel and rock, across the canyon, in an effort to slow the leakage. Increasingly worried, he escalated his rhetoric as he described the quality of the work on the foundation and the potential for later problems. The angry Port Angeles leader stated that he had gone down to the base of the dam and removed concrete as if picking up gravel and sand, arguing that merely throwing concrete into the river was not a satisfactory substitute for what would have been, in his opinion, the proper action: building a temporary dam, pumping the river dry, and laying down a proper foundation. Aldwell emphasized his fear that there would be a blowout at the base of the dam. In addition to these concerns, the intrepid industrialist grew more and more frustrated by the lack of clear progress in the dam construction, rapidly increasing costs and his inability to obtain an estimate of the cost of completing the dam. The process had clearly escaped Aldwell's control and there was little that he could do about it.[61]

A critical letter from Peabody, Houghteling dismissed Aldwell's worries regarding the building of the dam, revealing that these concerns had been challenged and laid to rest by the contracted firm. Frustrated at the outside interference and the problems beginning to burden his great centerpiece for the future of Port Angeles and the region, Aldwell wrote back that there was a discrepancy between his estimation of the elevation of the natural riverbed and the operating assumption of the contractors building the dam. Aldwell effectively argued that the dam was being built approximately eight feet over the natural bed of the river, the foundation being laid on an unstable bed of cobble and gravel. He was concerned that when the water was released it would blast a hole at the bottom of the dam.[62]

Despite Aldwell's determined efforts, the controversy continued unresolved. He wrote a letter to Chicago demanding the removal of the dam contractors, asserting that they had been covering up mistakes, in addition to the other problems that he had already outlined.[63]

Apparently his power play failed because in a letter responding to J. L. Houghteling, the president of the Chicago company, he struck a conciliatory and explanatory note. "I certainly will be very pleased to see Mr. Summers when He arrives, and go over the matter of the foundation of the dam thoroughly with him, and if his contention is right, which I cannot see how it can be, I will be the first one to admit it and do it cheerfully . . . "[64] Aldwell protested that his only interest was the health of the company, asserting, "Understanding the situation as I believe I do, I could not agree to have water turned on under the existing conditions as I see them . . . "[65]

His complaints having come to naught, the project continued until the arrival of the heavy October rains. The river began rising. Aldwell's concern about the construction of the dam proved prescient, when, on October 31, 1912, a surge of water breached the dam and destroyed the powerhouse.[66]

Aldwell's alarm over the structural integrity of the dam was likely shared by others. An article in the *Port Angeles Tribune-Times* opened its report of the blowout with the following comment, "An accident that for a long time past has been feared by many familiar with the engineering problem involved in the enterprise overtook the plant of the Olympic power company on the Elwha river at about 6:30 p.m. Wednesday evening."[67] The blowout punched a deep hole in the gravel below the dam, allowing the whole reservoir to empty in about two hours. Immediately below the dam, the surge of water reached 30 feet higher than the previous water level and a raft of logs rushed down the river to the strait. Phone calls were quickly placed to warn of the flood; luckily, nobody was known to have been injured or killed in the collapse. Some damage was done to property, including the dam's powerhouse and some of its machinery. The equipment of a logging firm at the mouth of the river and two or three Lower Elwha Klallam fishing boats were lost to the surge of water. Also, a bridge crossing the river was washed out.[68]

The Lower Elwha Klallam Indians remember the blowout well and were saved from drowning by the barking of their dogs, which prompted them to quickly hustle to higher ground and onto the railroad trestle over the river. The flood was high enough to leave dead fish in the branches of trees. Nobody in the tribe was injured but damage was done to their property and the Klallam have always been justifiably nervous living in the shadow of the dam and another potential blowout.[69] The aftereffects were described in the local paper: "Our beautiful lake has disappeared, but we hope soon to see the dam repaired and the lake again make its appearance. The receding water left many logs nicely balanced on the top of stumps and they are quite a curious site [*sic*]." The author of the article also noted how quickly the salmon tried to reenter and use their river again. "Following the breaking of the dam the salmon immediately took advantage of the breach and a number were seen in Little River and Indian Creek. These streams were favorite spawning [g]rounds of the salmon in the past, but since construction work was commenced on the dam, two years ago, they have been entirely shut out as the company made no provision whatever to get by the dam."[70] The *Olympic Leader* reported on November 1, 1912, that the blowout had left "great numbers of salmon and trout strewn over the fields and through the woods, and everyone going down that way got all the fish they could carry home."[71]

THE SECOND TIME IS THE CHARM

Aldwell supervised the rebuilding of the dam using new engineers and increased investment, now to the tune of $3 million provided by Peabody, Houghteling & Company. For the project to have any chance of success, the hole under the dam and the foundation issues had to be addressed. This was a major undertaking and required vast amounts of rock and soil. Before blasting rock from the canyon walls, soil was placed on the exposed rock so that upon blasting and falling into the riverbed, the rock and dirt would mix. In the cavity beneath the dam, 5,000 cubic yards of rock were placed, with even more rock and dirt deposited in the river bottom above and below the dam. Still struggling with leakage under the dam, mats were made with fir branches. These fascines were about three feet thick and were laid down over the rock and soil upstream of the dam. Such bundled branches were commonly used at this time for stabilizing banks or extending jetties (frequently on the Mississippi River). The fir mats were then covered with more rocks and soil. Although seepage still remained fairly high, the dam became tenable at this point, with completion of repairs in December of 1914, and a repair cost of approximately $150,000.[72]

The completion of the Elwha Dam closed off the river to spawning salmon and steelhead. Not only did it prevent spawning chinook, coho, chum, and pink salmon from reaching the upper river and its tributaries, it also blocked the sockeye from passage to Lake Sutherland, which was connected to the Elwha by Indian Creek and located about two miles west of the Elwha River. Damming the river would have other long-term impacts on the Elwha River basin ecosystem, a topic to be explored in greater detail in following chapters. The Lower Elwha Klallam Indians lost access to their most important resource when the dam was constructed, furthering the damage to a culture and economy that had been ongoing since the arrival of disease epidemics and the 1855 Point No Point Treaty.

In his efforts to accrue wealth and build the metropolis, Aldwell actually violated Washington State law. His failure to build fish passageways across the dam violated an 1893 state law that forbade the building of a dam without fishways.[73] In September 1911, two years before completion of the Elwha Dam, Clallam County Game Warden J. W. Pike wrote a letter to State Fish Commissioner J. L. Riseland, sounding the alarm about the dam's impact on spawning salmon. "I have personally searched the Elwha River & Tributarys [*sic*], above the dam, & have been unable to find a single salmon. I have visited the Dam several times lately, was out there yesterday and there appears to be thousands of Salmon at the foot of the

The Elwha Dam under construction. Bert Kellogg Collection. Courtesy of North Olympic Library System.

Dam, where they are jumping continually trying to get up the flume. I have watched them very close, and I'm satisfied now, that they cannot get above the dam."[74] The letter concluded by elucidating the Elwha's virtues as a salmon-producing river, the destruction the dam would wreak on the impending coho salmon run, and the obvious impact it would have on the regional fishing industry.[75] In response, Riseland sent Superintendent of State Fish Hatcheries John Crawford to examine the dam. Crawford acknowledged that there were no fishways at the dam and no means by which the salmon could bypass the dam. Further, he stated that although it was impossible to add effective fish passage at that time to the design of the dam, he was assured by the engineer in charge of construction that a fishway would be built as soon as the dam was in the final stages of construction. This never happened.[76]

Riseland, after meeting with investing members of the Olympic Power Company, representatives of the commercial fishing interests of the peninsula, representatives of the U.S. Bureau of Fisheries, Thomas Aldwell, and the dam engineer, proposed a plan for transporting salmon past the dam. Many experts believed then that a functional fishway could not be built in a dam the height of the Elwha Dam, which, upon completion, exceeded 100 feet. Accordingly, Riseland proposed that the Olympic Power Company build and maintain a fish trap at the base of the dam and, with an elevator, lift the fish above the dam and release them to continue their spawning run. The letter explicitly stated that this action would have to be taken or the Olympic Power Company would be required, in strict accordance with the law, to build a functional fishway. It is informative that the proposed solutions were technical in nature. Given the political economy of the region and era, there was no interest in dam removal.[77]

AN UNEXPECTED SALMON ADVOCATE

Even these limited demands were successfully ignored by Aldwell until the arrival of a pugnacious new fish commissioner. Leslie Darwin was appointed to the State Fish Commissioner's office in 1913 after the election of the progressive Democrat Ernest Lister as governor. Darwin had moved to Bellingham from Texas as a young man and panned for gold on the slopes of Mt. Baker. Later, he remade himself as a journalist, becoming a reporter for the *Seattle Times*, and then managing the Bellingham newspapers, the *Herald* and the *American Reveille*.[78] Under Darwin's leadership the *American Reveille* evinced a strongly progressive tone, calling for a fairer distribution of wealth and greater taxes on rich corporations, and decrying the corruption of corporations and trusts.[79] Upon winning the governor's seat, Ernest Lister sought out a fish commissioner who would enforce fisheries regulations more stringently. Darwin was the first fish commissioner to openly criticize the fishing industry's wasteful practices, representing a significant break from the past, when fish commissioners maintained ties to the fishing industry.[80]

Darwin was representative of an emerging body of scientific managers who assumed the necessary job of regulating industry and managing resources during the Progressive Era. The conservation movement had emerged in response to overexploitation of natural resources and environmental degradation. Historian Clayton R. Koppes explains that the federal government had allowed unfettered economic growth built on widespread environmental devastation through the 1890s, for reasons of a greater prosperity and a wide range of freedoms for Americans, and to facilitate the creative development of American society and its economy: "the government tried to insure the release of human energy in the realm of natural resources by giving individuals wide liberty to secure natural resources and to do with them as they pleased."[81]

Growing public anger at waste and speculation in land and resources, along with increasing awareness of the finite and diminishing resources available to Americans, drove the increasing intervention of federal and state governments in managing resources through principles of conservation. Conservationists of the 1890s and early 20th century acted within the wider Progressive Movement or Era. Historian Richard Hofstadter wrote, "In the Progressive

Era, the life of business, and to some degree, even of government, was beginning to pass from an individualistic form toward one demanding industrial discipline and engendering a managerial and bureaucratic outlook."[82] Most Progressive leaders were members of the professional classes, people of high education and status in American society. Doctors, editors, college professors, small businessmen, and lawyers were active in Progressive campaigns.[83]

The movement gained momentum in a period of economic and political stability. Rather than seeking dramatic change, Progressives sought to adjust the existing order to better adhere to the values that they had been raised with and still valued in the face of a changing society—those of restraint, conservation, support of the community, and participatory democracy. In their eyes, the existing order assigned undue power to those accruing massive capital. Progressives believed that creation of a system of bureaucratic management through government would not only curb the excesses of industrial capitalism, but also would ensure continuation of traditional preindustrial values in American society. The movement is most commonly understood as an effort to curb the worst excesses of capitalism. As Koppes explains it, "Any change in the focus on immediate economic use implied a challenge to a strict market rationale. This did not mean an anti-capitalist stance. Some of the people who were most alarmed about environmental problems were corporation executives who realized that the traditional approach to the environment had to be modified if their firms were to continue to prosper."[84] As members of the Progressive Movement, conservationists sought to regulate and correct the excesses of industrial capitalism in regards to its exploitation of natural resources.[85] Conservationists like Darwin saw themselves as the conservators of democracy, bringing restraint over a new capitalist era that while running amok threatened not only natural resources, but the freedom and opportunities of American citizens as well.[86]

Consistent with his reform-minded contemporaries across the country, Darwin felt that the role of conservationists was to intervene and manage natural resources where industry had both overexploited them and threatened the health of those resources and the enterprises based on them. He explained it well himself, writing, "It has always seemed to me that the responsibility for being the head of the Fisheries Department of this state is a very great one. Millions of dollars are invested in our fisheries; thousands are dependent upon it for employment; the demand has yearly increased, and the efforts to take our fish have multiplied to the extent that some of the salmon runs have shown a great decrease." Darwin then lashed out, revealing his continuing anger at the ongoing destruction of the state's fishery and likely disappointment in his own inability to do much about it. "The people of this state have an interest in perpetuating and maintaining our food and shellfishery, compared with which the right of any individual, no matter how great his investment therein, sinks into insignificance."[87]

Darwin clearly represented the conservationist agenda in protecting and managing resources and also in seeking the greater good for society over the benefits of individual entrepreneurs. Darwin sought not to interrupt or prevent impact to ecosystems from industrial development, but instead strove to manage resources efficiently in order to sustain their productivity and gain the most use from them. In Koppes' formula of conservationists being guided by concerns over efficiency, equity, and aesthetics, Darwin was most concerned with equity. "The equity argument stressed that natural resources belonged to all the people and should be retained in public control in order to prevent their concentration in the hands of a few and to insure that the benefits of resource development were distributed widely and fairly."[88] It is important to not view this approach as complacent or simply complicit in industrial and resource-extractive destruction of the environment. In fact, this position represented a dramatic evolution in environmental thinking in that era and political economy, and rendered the idealistic and aggressive fish commissioner a radical in that culture. He wrote: "Many of those interested in catching and canning fish lose sight of the fact that the state's interest in our fisheries is paramount to the interest of any individual who engages in their taking merely for profit."[89] Darwin was similar to other conservationists of the period, who, according to historian Samuel Hays, attempted to transform "a decentralized, nontechnical, loosely organized society, where waste and inefficiency ran rampant, into a highly organized, technical, and centrally planned and directed social organization which could meet a complex world with efficiency and purpose."[90] While the conservationists appeared to be radicals to businessmen accustomed to a laissez-faire capitalist economy and disinterested government, their perspective and goals were, in fact, moderate, reasonable, and warranted; they merely sought to protect industry and capitalism from self-destruction and conserve natural resources for future use.

As moderate as their perspective seems today, Progressive Era conservationists were fighting powerful economic interests who strongly opposed any form of regulation or management. Darwin grew increasingly angry at the excesses of the owners of commercial fishing operations and equally determined to rein them in. "It seems to me to be a crime against mankind—against those who are here and the generations yet to follow—to let the great salmon runs of the State of Washington be destroyed at the selfish behest of a few individuals, who, in order to enrich themselves, would impoverish the state and destroy a food supply of the people."[91]

The fish commissioner extended his critique, arguing that "every pressure is exerted on behalf of those selfishly interested,"[92] undoubtedly taking a jab at a Washington State legislature dominated by financial interests, as well as at a dominant culture prizing wealth over conservation. Darwin followed this attack by asserting that critics were silenced, vilified, and slandered. Like many conservationists of the time, he believed, and argued in this report, that an informed electorate would rise in anger at such gross waste, corruption, and abuse of power—if only they could learn the truth. "It is my belief that had the people understood the situation, they would have acted long ere this, and would have prevented the practical destruction of some of our greatest salmon runs."[93] Darwin's mission was to "protect and conserve" salmon and other resources, not for nature's sake but for the common good of the people of the state of Washington. He was pursuing a progressive, public-spirited agenda shaped by the area, economy, political structure, and time in which he operated. In the case of the salmon of the Elwha River, Darwin arrived at a seemingly logical and practical solution for the problem presented by the Elwha Dam.[94]

Upon taking office, Darwin soon discovered that the Olympic Power Company had failed to perform the steps ordered by his predecessor. Darwin latched onto the issue of the Elwha Dam immediately and pursued it relentlessly. After a series of letters and telegrams between himself and Aldwell, Darwin proposed the construction of a fish hatchery below the dam. One letter is interesting in that Darwin strongly asserted the state's preeminence over the federal government regarding state fisheries. In response to a conversation held between Aldwell and representatives of the U.S. Bureau of Fisheries, Darwin wrote, "The Federal Government has not the least thing in the world to say concerning any thing [sic] in the State of Washington relative to its food fish." He proceeded to explain his potential delight at the possibility of the federal government building hatcheries for Washington, but ended by reiterating, "But you must appreciate that they have nothing whatever to say whether or not the State shall enforce its laws relative to the construction of fishways."[95]

Having thus asserted the authority of the state over its own fisheries, Darwin then proceeded to offer a solution to the problem. Pointing out that "no officer of the State has any right to waive one of the state's statutory requirements," and that no one was "at liberty to say to you that you will not have to put a fishway over your dam," Darwin proposed a clever, pragmatic, and illegal plan. He suggested that by selecting a hatchery site at the base of the dam and making the dam the obstruction for the purpose of collecting eggs and milt for the hatchery, it would be possible to obviate strict enforcement of the fish passageway law and, therefore, maintain both salmon runs below the dam as well as hydroelectrical generation. To achieve this end, Darwin requested that Aldwell provide a site and funds for the building of a hatchery.[96] This compromise seemingly offered a solution between those seeking to develop the area economically, harvest nature for profit, and transform the Elwha into an industrial river—and those responsible for management of the fisheries.

Demonstrating the dominant ideology of that time and era, Aldwell failed to appreciate the solution proffered to him and continued to resist compliance. He was willing to sacrifice the salmon for hydroelectricity and likely resented the increasing intrusion of the state in the form of a persistent fish commissioner insisting on protecting the state's fisheries. The initial success of his project likely encouraged his intransigence. Besides selling power locally, he temporarily achieved his dream of extending a network of electricity across the peninsula in the fall of 1914, by providing lighting to Port Angeles and Port Townsend, and power for the Bremerton Naval Shipyards and numerous lumber mills and canning plants. Aldwell's vision was that the Elwha River, properly harnessed and employed, would be the engine of economic growth and social progress that he and other Port Angeles boosters had envisioned. Aldwell had no intention of letting a radical fish commissioner get in his way.

As Aldwell resisted compliance, Darwin grew increasingly impatient. After an exchange of several letters, and at the end of his rope due to the dam builder's failure to implement the hatchery plan or respond to his communications, Darwin fired off a short, gruff missive on June 2, 1914. He made it clear that unless he received a response regarding Aldwell's plans within five days, he would issue an official order to build a fishway across the dam. "It is out of the question for us to allow another fish run to beat its brains out against the dam."[97] Aldwell responded in a letter the following day that he was doing everything possible to meet Darwin's requests to provide a hatchery site and $2,500 for construction of the hatchery. Before the end of June they had reached agreement on these terms and initiated the steps toward building a hatchery.[98]

The building of the Elwha hatchery is significant in that it represented Darwin's hopes of using hatcheries not only to ameliorate the impact of dams on salmon-spawning runs but also to increase the number of fish overall. "Every major stream in the State of Washington which salmon ascend and particularly those of Puget

Sound should have hatcheries established thereon . . . in order to care for the growing fishing industry, it would seem hardly possible for the state to have too many."[99]

Darwin believed that salmon fisheries could be managed in such a way that fish stocks could be maintained in the face of heavy commercial fishing and development and also be increased in number. The devastating impacts of overfishing, dams, and logging on salmon runs would be limited by an aggressive campaign of hatchery construction and salmon propagation; nature could be managed, manipulated, and improved upon through the use of science and technology. The construction of hatcheries and raising of hatchery fry constituted the primary mission of the fisheries agencies in the late part of the 19th and early 20th centuries. It may have seemed that hatcheries represented the only solution available to fisheries managers in this early period of little authority and paltry funding, combined with political and public support for all manner of economic development. Darwin was part of a generation of conservationists that embraced and promoted hatchery production throughout the Pacific Northwest. From 1896 to 1915, the total salmon and steelhead fry production for Washington State increased from 4,500,000 to 1,021,174,416. This initiated a period of dependence on hatcheries in Washington history, and also allowed for almost unmitigated use and development of rivers due to the belief that hatcheries would be able to fill the void.[100]

Darwin's eagerness for and reliance on hatcheries was not original to him. In an era when development and growth trumped preservation of nature and game and fish species, those entrusted with the protection of natural resources were compelled to use other tools when they found that blocking development, like dams, was impossible. While regulation of harvests, setting of quotas for salmon, and other management strategies became important, the central beam in the edifice of fisheries management in the Pacific Northwest was fish hatchery production. This did not begin in the Pacific Northwest but rather in the northeastern United States in the mid-1800s, where the Market Revolution had created natural havoc and destroyed the rivers and fisheries of that region and engendered the model of environmental protection and management inherited by Darwin.

"CIVILIZATION DEMANDS
A CALCULABLE AND CERTAIN SUPPLY"

Before 1860, troubled by the decline of fisheries, the governments of Connecticut, Massachusetts, and Vermont began studying hatchery production. In 1864, New Hampshire became the first state to create a fish commission in an effort to reverse the fortunes of the state's fisheries. When, two years later, they attempted their first effort at artificial propagation, New Hampshire fisheries managers had to import salmon eggs from Canada owing to a paucity of eggs in the Northeast. The failure of this experiment and the high prices for Canadian salmon eggs encouraged managers from Maine, Connecticut, and Massachusetts to join together in collecting their eggs from the Penobscot River, and to cooperatively utilize hatchery production to boost salmon numbers in the region. They did so not out of ignorance of the problems posed by habitat loss and overfishing, but because they had so little power over those who destroyed the rivers' fisheries.[101]

In the effort to preserve fisheries in the face of overharvest and habitat destruction, those responsible for the fish turned quickly to science for a solution to the problem—or as historian Joseph Taylor terms it, to "inventing a panacea." Using science to mitigate fisheries destruction promised a solution to managers who held little regulatory power in a society where economic progress was substantively valued over habitat and species preservation. Science offered a solution where there seemingly was none. Henceforth, hatcheries would constitute the primary technological solution to the problems dams posed for fisheries.

Although fish culture in various forms has been practiced for thousands of years (the Chinese raised carp more than 2,500 years ago), modern commercial salmon cultivation arose in France in the middle of the 19th century. Two French fishermen began the practice of artificially propagating salmon after slipping out under a full moon on a November night in 1841 to spy on spawning salmon. Having learned this process, they created an artificial means of salmon reproduction in an effort to stem declining salmon numbers.[102]

The first large, commercial salmon hatchery was constructed on the Rhine River in Huningue under the leadership of French scientist M. Coste. Visitors from around the world studied the strategies employed there, interested in this early model of a "fish factory," as Coste referred to the hatchery.[103] The creation of the American Fish Culturists' Association solidified the emerging fish culture movement and helped to propel fish hatcheries forward as a solution for collapsing fisheries. The creation of the U.S. Fish Commission (USFC) seemed to offer a federal tool for maintaining fisheries. Under Spencer Baird's leadership, the Fish Commission moved to distribute salmon eggs to states throughout the Northeast in order to boost salmon populations in rivers.[104]

The reliance on fish propagation was not merely a stopgap measure resulting from lack of cooperation between federal and state governments and an inability of fisheries managers to enforce laws and regulations meant to preserve fish. It seemingly offered great potential for *increased* harvests of fish. Fisheries professionals evinced excitement and enthusiasm at the possibilities promised by the burgeoning young science. At a meeting in 1876 of the American Fish Culturists' Association, Robert B. Roosevelt, then president of the Association, gave a speech considering the state of fisheries and the move to artificial propagation. "Fish culture has existed only a few years; what will be its condition at its centennial the most enthusiastic can hardly conceive . . . there need be no fear for the future, and in much less than a hundred years the waters of America will teem with food for the poor and hungry, which all may come and take."[105] This speech reveals an early confidence in the potential promise of the science of artificial fish propagation. Along the same optimistic lines, the Maine Commissioners of Fisheries explained how fish culture would improve upon the limits of natural production. "Here fish culture intervenes. Every egg under her careful management is fertilized; nothing is left to chance; ninety-eight eggs out of every hundred are hatched."[106] The implication is that human management and creation of a safe environment would reduce the risks; the eggs would not now be consumed by other fish or washed away in a storm. Thinking like a manager working to remove all inefficiencies and wasteful costs, the natural conclusion was that more eggs protected until hatching was bound to result in more fish. The commissioner then proceeded to illuminate the similarity between this process and careful husbandry. "The helpless young fry, fast anchored to the yolk-sac, are carefully protected until ready and able to shift for themselves, the same as the farmer coops and protects his young turkeys and chickens . . . Civilization demands a calculable and certain supply."[107]

THE HATCHERY SOLUTION

While these comments on the promise of fish culture originate in the 1870s, they provide an early glimpse of the spirit of Progressive Era conservationism, the belief that science and technology could be employed to make nature more efficient and productive even while fisheries were destroyed through overfishing, dam construction, and habitat destruction. Historian Joseph Taylor cogently points out, "Fish culture became the preferred tool of management because it offered to produce an endless supply of fish."[108] A dependence on hatcheries would emerge from a combination of faith in science, lack of regulatory authority, the difficulty of interstate and state-federal cooperation in river management, and the destruction of the environment and concomitant impact on fish populations across political boundaries. However, this was by no means an inevitable development. This have-your-cake-and-eat-it-too solution would continue to hinder meaningful fisheries management and reform far into the future.

Taylor explores this issue carefully in *Making Salmon: An Environmental History of the Northwest Fisheries Crisis.* Explaining that George Perkins Marsh understood early on that it would be very difficult or impossible to limit human impacts on habitat, Taylor then elucidates Spencer Fullerton Baird's failure to convince states to manage fishery harvests based on scientific discoveries about fish populations. This failure compelled Baird to move strongly to the other option, an increasing reliance on the use of technology to maintain fish populations that were rapidly disappearing under the onslaught of industrialization in the late 19th century. As a result, the USFC under Baird's leadership moved toward the promotion of fish culture as a solution to the crisis facing fisheries such as Atlantic salmon in the Northeast. According to Taylor, "Fish culture offered Baird a way to rejuvenate fisheries without treading the political minefield of regulation. And most important of all, a national distribution system allowed Baird to claim that fish culture would benefit all sections of the country. Baird could cultivate broad congressional support by promising fish for everyone."[109] Furthermore, Taylor explains, "To generate support, [Baird] had to straddle the world of politics and science. Fish culture was his bridge; it promised practical results painlessly, and science would improve its methods over time."[110]

In its promotion and pursuit of fish culture, the USFC shipped Pacific salmon eggs east and indeed throughout the world in an effort to establish the salmon in waterways across the planet. Shad, another popular eastern fish, was distributed throughout the Mississippi River basin and introduced into West Coast rivers as well.[111] An inaccurate understanding of Pacific salmon biology and confidence that planting success determined overall success in increasing fish numbers drove the commission in these early days. It didn't help that the budget for fisheries science shrank sharply during Baird's tenure. Taylor uses budget allocations to show the sharp disparity between research and fish culture. For example, in 1872 the USFC had a budget of $8,500, all of which was to be spent on research. But the share of the budget dedicated to research declined as fish culture grew in importance. "In the next seventy years, however, expenditures for science never again exceeded 21 (1875) and usually stayed below 7 percent. Meanwhile the budget for fish culture skyrocketed. From 1873 to 1875 Congress allocated an average of

$25,000 for shad and salmon work. By 1887 that figure had risen to $185,000. Fish culture had become the fiscal engine driving the USFC, employing 105 people and consuming over 73 percent of the budget."[112]

The fundamental ignorance of fish biologists was exacerbated by an inadequate and declining investment in the research budget. The reduction of money for research concomitant with the rapid escalation of funds for fish culture production indicates the agency's early shift toward easy solutions. This switch to fish culture not only reflected a confidence that science could increase natural production but also constituted a response to fisheries managers' lack of regulatory authority. Baird, Livingston, and other hatchery advocates should not be let off the hook, as it were, too easily. In *The Fisherman's Problem*, Arthur F. McEvoy argues that these early promoters of fish culture recognized American culture's destructive tendencies. For example, Baird wrote in 1878: "Wherever the white man plants his foot and the so-called civilization of a country is begun, the inhabitants of the air, the land, and the water begin to disappear."[113] McEvoy points out that the urge to end the exploitation of nature did not run strongly in these men. Driven by the cultural forces of their own day, they believed that "attempts to bring such social forces under control through the deliberate use of law were by their nature vicious."[114] Torn between their ideology of the free market and the need to manage the fisheries efficiently, while also constrained by lack of regulatory power, fish managers at the federal and state levels quickly turned to hatchery production instead of mounting an effective resistance to habitat destruction and the overharvest of fish.

Moreover, the protectors of fish too often were playing catch-up, and took over management once great damage to salmon fisheries had already occurred. After devastating the salmon runs of northern California, the cannery owners turned to the abundant salmon runs of the Pacific Northwest, especially the Columbia River. There, too, the salmon-canning industry sharply reduced the region's salmon populations. McEvoy writes eloquently of this culture of salmon destruction, arguing that members of the salmon industry followed cultural instructions in the same way the salmon followed "a common genetic program." Practices learned and traditions developed in New England drove this salmon economy. "Anglo-Saxon fishers thus had a collective ecological identity no less than the salmon did . . . they inaugurated the industry in California as they fled declining salmon fisheries on the Kennebec [Maine] and other New England rivers."[115] He insists that this destruction is part of a pattern, that nothing different had been visited upon the Central Valley salmon than had been wrought upon the salmon fisheries of New England. This very same process wreaked havoc on the Columbia River fisheries. "In a sense, the industry behaved like a community of swidden, or slash-and-burn, farmers, working one patch of land until its fertility declined and then moving on to another."[116]

William Robbins forcefully argues that migratory capital played the central role in the devastation of natural landscapes in the American West as well as other regions, and he has effectively and convincingly demonstrated this point in *Hard Times in Paradise* and *Colony and Empire*. Accrued capital together with improved transportation systems in the United States were redirected into investment in brand new areas of rich resource reserves. This migratory capital was invested in railroads, mills, canneries, lumber, fish, and in reaping the profits of headlong, wasteful harvests of minerals and other resources. It then moved on to other locations ripe with abundant commodities for harvest and conversion into capital. William Cronon also examined the role of urban capital and credit in transforming western hinterlands, but McEvoy and Robbins more explicitly explore the destruction of the environment in the American West. Both of these historians correctly identify free-market capitalism, migratory capital, and irresponsible exploitation of natural resources as integral to the collapse of the salmon fisheries in the Pacific Northwest. What could protect salmon in such a political economy?

Politicians in the Pacific Northwest responded to the salmon collapse by crafting limited harvest and management legislation in the 1870s and 1880s. However, politicians showed little political will to limit the harvest of salmon from the Columbia River and throughout the region; the laws were weak and went unenforced. The reality is that the political economy of the region and period precluded meaningful salmon regulatory management. Instead, hatcheries would be used to fill the void and replace the lost spawning salmon runs. As fisheries biologist Jim Lichatowich writes of the decision to move toward dependence on salmon hatcheries in the Pacific Northwest, "As might be expected, given a choice between artificial propagation and restricted harvests, the industry seized the hatchery alternative."[117] McEvoy offers a more damning critique of those responsible for the fisheries. "Artificial propagation and exotic transplants offered simple, technical, intuitive solutions to the complex problems of fishery depletion. They appealed to what one economic historian called 'the traditional combination of empiricism and common sense' that had up to the late 19th century proved more than adequate to the tasks, not only of technological innovation but of lawmaking as well." Of even more importance, McEvoy argues, these technological solutions could seemingly provide a solution to damaged ecosystems and depleted fisheries without requiring changes in behavior or increased regulation. "That government and its scientific advisors could replace what civilization's carelessness had destroyed was an article of faith in U.S. fishery policy and one that proved very hard to discredit."[118]

Salmon capitalists resisted regulation tooth and nail. In the face of limited restrictions on the fishery, cannery companies and other members of Oregon's salmon fishing industry signed a petition against the legislation and proposed to pay for and build a hatchery instead.[119] This dependence on hatchery production was supported by a United States Fish Commission that had almost completely abandoned fisheries science research for the singular pursuit of fish production. According to Taylor, by 1890, "fishery management had become synonymous with production, and fish culture was its sacred cow."[120]

The first hatchery built in the Pacific Northwest arose from this decision to employ hatcheries instead of meaningful regulation, a compromise resulting from weakness and based on technology, science, and hubris. Livingston Stone, fresh from his painfully unsuccessful experience with hatchery production on the McCloud River in California, arrived in the Pacific Northwest to assist in the construction of the Clackamas Hatchery in 1877. The Oregon legislature's unwillingness to fund the hatchery at the time compelled the USFC to take control of the facility. The hatchery was soon beset by problems such as flooding, sedimentation from logging in the watershed, interference by mills, and salmon runs blocked by downstream dams. These problems reinforced the fish managers' sense of powerlessness in the face of politicians, timber companies, commercial fishermen, and cannery owners unwilling to suffer restrictions on their activities.

Livingston Stone's fundamental misunderstanding of salmon biology strongly influenced early hatchery production. Ignoring the studies of Canadian fishery managers who saw a link between salmon and home streams, Stone argued that salmon entered streams based on the rivers' particular assets rather than returning to home streams to spawn. While this may indicate a genuine misunderstanding on Stone's part, it also rationalized his preference for using single sources of eggs for far-flung hatcheries, a practice that engendered long-term damage to biologically distinct and diverse salmon runs by populating rivers with genetically similar species that drove out and replaced wild salmon. This belief also lent more credence to the efficacy of hatchery production than if Stone had actually understood the value of a variety of rivers such as the Cowlitz and Willamette, which he laughably considered inadequate salmon rivers.[121] As fish biologists Bill M. Bakke and Joseph Cone write, "One consequence of Stone's misunderstanding of salmon biology was that artificial production of salmon in hatcheries took on a greater importance for salmon production than it otherwise might have."[122] However, it should be noted that he also called for stronger regulations to protect salmon in addition to moving to greater dependence on hatcheries.[123]

Along with demands for strong fishery regulations, fisheries experts began questioning the efficacy of hatchery production. Marshall

McDonald, replacing Baird after his death in 1887 as head of the USFC, announced that there were significant problems inherent in overdependence on hatcheries. He stated that "in this country" there had been too much reliance upon artificial propagation of fisheries, noting the "stupendous scale" of hatchery efforts. Following this he offered an even stronger self-criticism that still resonates today. "We have been disposed to measure results by quantity rather than by quality, to estimate our triumphs by volume rather than potentiality. We have paid too little attention to the necessary conditions to be fulfilled in order to give the largest return for a given expenditure of money."[124]

McDonald then provided a critique of "the hatchery myth," as Lichatowich refers to it, acknowledging that hatcheries could not replace the preservation of habitat and management of the fisheries. Moreover, he pointed out that hatchery production numbers did not indicate overall success in sustaining fish runs in rivers. Others echoed his criticisms. In the same year as McDonald's critique, the president of the American Fisheries Society also turned a critical eye toward hatchery production.[125] However, the criticisms reflected or initiated no change in policy. In fact, under McDonald's leadership the agency increasingly promoted fish culture. And although McDonald had recommended limiting hatchery construction on the Columbia River, the program continued.[126] According to Taylor, "The budget for Fish Culture grew dramatically during McDonald's era. In 1890 funding jumped from $178,000 to $248,000, consuming over 70 percent of the USFC budget. The more salmon declined, the less curious Congress seemed about the cause of decline, and the more basic research dwindled and 'practical appropriations' increased."[127] While concerns emerged about the efficacy of hatchery production, no significant changes were initiated and the commitment to hatchery production even increased. When Darwin escalated the use of hatcheries in Washington, therefore, it was at a time of growing concern over their value. Either he chose to ignore those emerging questions, thought he could do better, or simply had no choice.

Fisheries managers throughout the Northwest increased their dependence on hatcheries as a tool for mitigating the deterioration of salmon and steelhead runs. Conservationists like Washington State Fish Commissioner Leslie Darwin believed that through science and the use of hatcheries, nature could be improved and fish runs increased substantially. While optimistic about the benefits of hatcheries, his optimism masked a dependence on hatcheries due to lack of regulatory power in a state where development and resource extraction trumped conservation. Darwin despised those who overharvested and wasted fish as well as those who blocked and destroyed salmon runs; bowing to their power, however, he accepted a solution—as had fisheries managers in the northeastern U.S. in the late 1800s—that would allow development but only promise to preserve fish populations. Apparently ignorant of failure in the Northeast and exuding a confidence not unusual in westerners, Darwin failed to heed the lessons of the past and initiated a program in Washington State that would do nothing to stem the century-long decline of salmon and steelhead fisheries.

Similarly, Oregon fish managers constructed a series of hatcheries in an effort to increase salmon production even as forests were cut and rivers dammed. Taylor chronicles the series of failures on rivers like the Siuslaw, Clackamas, and McKenzie. Hatcheries in Oregon were troubled by floods, vandalism to collection racks, fishermen harvesting fish needed for egg harvest, and an Oregon legislature unwilling to limit the activities of fishermen in order to support Oregon hatcheries run by the USFC.

Even while fisheries managers in Oregon and Washington rushed willy-nilly into full-scale hatchery production, their neighbors to the north moved in the other direction. After numerous studies demonstrated little production benefit from hatcheries, including a comparative study of natural versus hatchery salmon production in Cultus Lake, British Columbia, in the 1920s and 1930s, the Canadian Fisheries Commission announced the closure of its salmon hatcheries. Although fisheries managers in Oregon and Washington ignored this study, investigations closer to home continued to question the efficacy of hatchery production. A study of Columbia River salmon hatcheries, begun in 1926, demonstrated that "their contribution to the runs was miniscule compared to the results of natural production."[128] In fact, the researcher questioned the popular myth that Columbia River hatcheries were responsible for maintaining fish numbers on the river, writing, "These data prove only that the popular conception, that the maintenance of the pack on the Columbia River is due to hatchery production, is not justified by the available evidence."[129] As early as the 1920s, researchers argued that natural production was superior to hatchery production—a few short years after the ebullience of the Progressive Era. They also questioned the efficacy of hatcheries. This criticism of hatchery dependence continued as the dean of the School of Fisheries at the University of Washington, John Cobb, attacked hatcheries in 1930. According to Lichatowich, "Cobb worried about the region's 'almost idolatrous faith' in artificial propagation, and he regarded the lack of critical evaluation as a serious threat to the Northwest salmon industry."[130]

Following Cobb's death in 1929, W. F. Thompson, the new dean of the School of Fisheries at the University of Washington, shifted the program away from its commercial focus to a greater emphasis on science, particularly in regard to conservation and fisheries biology. This was consistent with the increased focus on research and science in wildlife management in other programs across the country, and it indicates significant doubts about the use of and ongoing reliance on hatcheries. Regardless of these doubts, hatcheries have remained the primary tool for mitigation of salmon losses due to overharvest, dams, logging, development, and other factors. In the face of a culture privileging development and wealth over conservation, fisheries managers continued their overuse of hatcheries despite the past failure of these systems. While dependent on hatcheries because of their own lack of real political authority, they often also believed that the science of fish culture would allow Pacific Northwesterners to continue degrading the environment while maintaining fish runs. The persistent failure of hatcheries in the Northwest in conjunction with accelerated development and destruction of habitat led to an increased but futile reliance on technological solutions to the salmon crisis.[131]

SUBSIDIZING ECONOMIC DEVELOPMENT
WITH SCIENCE

In crafting a technological solution to the Elwha salmon crisis, Darwin was compelled to make statutory changes, because the deal Darwin struck with Aldwell was a continuing violation of the 1893 fish passageway law. Whereas Darwin had willingly used dynamite to remove other small, earthen dams in an effort to restore salmon runs, he was more flexible (or realistic) with a heavily capitalized project leveraging strong political support, such as the Elwha Dam; he struck a deal with a company that had been in violation of the law for five years, years during which the upriver salmon runs were destroyed. While Darwin violated the law, seemingly at least partially in favor of the Olympic Power Company, he was seeking an efficient, timely means to save the salmon runs.[132] Regardless of the letter of the law, Darwin did not command adequate authority as state fish commissioner to remove a dam of such magnitude or force the construction of fish passageways. Darwin pushed hard to get what he could, believing that he had forged a feasible and productive compromise. His fervent belief in the effectiveness of hatchery production undoubtedly made compromise easier to swallow. Darwin's inability to enforce standing salmon laws likely contributed to his belief that hatcheries would provide a solution.

In the first few years of his administration, Darwin accepted seven hatcheries in replacement of wild salmon runs annihilated by the construction of dams. Indeed, the construction of hatcheries became his main goal as fish commissioner, reflecting the trust in scientific management of resources that was typical of the early breed of conservationists and fisheries managers. In this vein, the first two years of his administration, 1913 through 1915, marked a period of busy activity; Darwin labored implacably to enhance propagation throughout the state. He stated that 10 more hatcheries needed to be immediately constructed in addition to those already being built to replace runs destroyed by dams built without fish passageways. From Darwin's perspective this was the only way to ensure continued salmon production.[133]

Collection of eggs during the first year of Darwin's tenure exceeded the greatest previous annual collections by over 50 percent. Five new hatcheries were quickly built, and by 1917 he had built 10 new hatcheries despite an appropriation of only $12,500. Others were either enlarged or reclaimed after abandonment. Darwin was optimistic about the future success of the Elwha hatchery. "The indications are that it will be developed into one of the best hatcheries in the state by reason of the fact that the Elwha River seems to be used by a number of the varieties of salmon."[134] He attempted to increase the gathering of eggs to the greatest degree possible and advocated distributing eggs from productive hatcheries to other hatcheries not gathering sufficient amounts for propagation—a new development in hatchery practices, one that would prove problematic in later years.[135]

By the time of his final report in 1921, the number of hatcheries in the state had been increased from 17 to 31, and the hatching capacity had tripled since 1913. This clearly marked the beginning of dependence on hatcheries in Washington, a development that Darwin believed would make the rivers productive and offset environmental degradation and overharvesting. Rather than bask in his success, Darwin felt frustration and failure as he finished this phase of his career and left office. He wrote, "To him who tries to stand between the greed of those to whose private interest it is to destroy a great natural resource and the state which owns that resource, there is reserved a most unpleasant portion."[136] Despite his efforts, fish runs continued to plummet, especially on the Elwha and Columbia Rivers. Darwin attributed this to overfishing that occurred in 1917 and 1918, harvesting of immature fish, resistance to regulation by fishermen and cannery owners, pollution from industrial and urban development, and, of course, dams.[137]

FAILED DREAMS

On the Elwha River, things went badly for Aldwell, Darwin, and certainly the salmon, not to mention the wider ecosystem and those dependent on it. The Elwha Dam, beset by burdensome costs resulting from the original dam blowout and reconstruction, was sold in 1919 to a subsidiary of Crown Zellerbach to provide electricity for a pulp and paper mill being built by the company in Port Angeles. By 1921, few fish were returning to the dam on the Elwha. And although by 1923, 22,000,000 eggs had been collected below the dam, that year, only two years after Darwin left office, the Elwha Hatchery was abandoned. The electricity expected to power the growth of a metropolis in the end provided energy for one lumber milling operation. Above the Elwha Dam, only memories remained of the flow of sleek red and silver bodies that had once surged through rapids to reach their spawning grounds and build their redds.[138]

In the final analysis, Aldwell and Darwin were unable to fashion a compromise that allowed development of hydropower while maintaining the health of salmon runs. Regardless of failure, this pattern of accommodation and compromise would continue to symbolize the attempted management and eventual destruction of salmon fisheries throughout the rest of the 20th century.

Chapter 3

Fighting a Losing Battle

PRESERVING FISHERIES ON THE ELWHA AND OTHER PACIFIC
NORTHWEST RIVERS IN THE DAM-BUILDING ERA

> *When we used to play around down there by the
> edges of the water and the salmon runs came in, you
> could just see them, glittering. Just schools of them
> going up. Sometimes they would just jump up in the
> air and we would holler and scream, we thought it
> was just the greatest.*
>
> Beatrice Charles, Lower Elwha Klallam Elder

With the collapse of the Elwha River's fisheries and the failure of
the hatchery, the river's meaning had been successfully reduced to
that of a source of industrial power to most residents of the region.
However, the continuing decline of the fishery, the downstream
river habitat, and the coastal ecosystem at the mouth of the river
would sustain an ongoing, although limited, dialogue about the now
secondary meaning of the river: that of a fish producer and still-
critical component of the wider ecological and human community.
Those voices of challenge and protest would ultimately lead the way
to a serious challenge to the industrial Elwha River, an unprecedented
call to tear down dams to restore fish.

With the conversion of the river to a source of industrial power
over its value as a salmon producer, those mandated with the mission
of preserving fish—the Washington State Fish Commission—were
compelled to fight and negotiate on a number of seemingly small
issues in order to preserve any fish at all in the lower few miles of the
river. This moment in the 1920s, continuing into and through the
1970s, marked the nadir for the Elwha River and its great salmon

fishery, as well as for those entrusted with preserving the small remnants of the once majestic run. From that moment, however, a discourse on stream improvement, the importance of salmon, and the responsibility of the state and the dam owners for the salmon would gain momentum and force increased action from the Washington Department of Fisheries. This, in addition to conflicts over dams and salmon that developed in the 1940s and 1950s, laid the foundation for a major challenge to the Elwha River dams in the 1970s and 1980s.

The construction of Glines Canyon Dam. Bert Kellogg Collection. Courtesy of North Olympic Library System.

The successful completion of the Elwha Dam project was followed a decade later by the construction of the Glines Canyon Dam, a second dam that had been anticipated from the late 19th century. Located several miles above the Elwha Dam and now within Olympic National Park boundaries, this dam was state of the art for 1927, when it was completed. An arch gravity design that was 55 feet wide at the base and 273 feet wide at the crest, the dam required anchoring into a large abutment on the east end due to the width of its top and the narrowness of the canyon walls. The plant was automated upon beginning operation, for a time using the largest "single water wheel generator unit" under control of an automated system. This was a technologically advanced dam, a gleaming, impressive monument to local growth and determination to put the river to use. It was designed to be the second of four dams on the river. However, rapid changes transformed the usefulness and meaning of these dams and the river as the Pacific Northwest, with the assistance of the federal government, aggressively harnessed larger rivers for their power. The creation of power pools by larger companies such as the Puget Sound Power and Light Company meant that Elwha hydroelectricity was no longer the sole source of power for Port Angeles, and its energy was increasingly directed exclusively to the mill on Ediz Hook. More important, the construction of large multiple-use dams on the Columbia River, like the Bonneville Dam in 1937 and the Grand Coulee Dam in 1941, eclipsed and made irrelevant smaller dams like Glines Canyon. Their surfeit of produced power, along with the construction of high tension power lines on the Olympic Peninsula in 1949, made the proposed third and fourth Elwha dams superfluous.[1]

From the very beginning of construction of the lower dam, the various dam owners had shown little interest in managing the river and hydroelectric production in a manner that would preserve the remaining salmon in the few miles of the river below the Elwha Dam. Darwin was compelled to constantly pressure Aldwell to pay the bills and fulfill the terms of the contract agreed upon for creation of the Elwha fish hatchery. Soon after the failure of Darwin's hatchery solution, queries about the future of the river and the fish arrived at the Washington State Department of Fisheries. This ongoing refusal to manage the water flow in a way that would not destroy downstream salmon reveals the belief of the dam and mill owners that the river was a source of hydroelectric power and nothing else; to them it was merely an industrial river. Their diminishment of the river through the construction of the two dams was exacerbated by their intransigence and the limited ability of the state to do anything about it. Only a few people in the area insisted that the historic Elwha River be remembered, and to some degree be managed to remain a river of salmon as well.

THE KLALLAM WITHOUT SALMON

The Klallam continued to use the river in their traditional manner as long as possible. Tribal member Beatrice Charles remembers the fish still running strong when she was a young girl, in 1919 and 1920. "When we used to play around down there by the edges of the water and the salmon runs came in, you could just see them, glittering. Just schools of them going up. Sometimes they would just jump up in the air and we would holler and scream, we thought it was just the greatest."[2] She also describes summer evenings by the river, the children wading and swimming while her father read the local paper aloud, translating into Klallam for the elders. Pink salmon were still abundant enough that they kept pots down by the river for boiling gathered salmon.[3]

But these limited opportunities were coming quickly to an end as Washington State passed fishing laws to protect fish populations. This completely enclosed the Klallam from their fish. Because they were not yet citizens, they couldn't harvest the fish without suffering criminal prosecution if caught. They attempted to harvest the fish illegally and continued to do so over the next several decades, but the decline of the lower Elwha began to limit the number of available fish. In addition to the collapse of the fish populations, laws forbidding the harvest of fish, and the loss of hunting, fishing, and gathering land and beaches to whites, the interruption of the downstream flow of sediments led to a decline of the quality of the beach at the mouth of the Elwha, declining clam resources and further diminishing the heart of the Klallam community. Enclosed away from their resource base, their traditional way of life, the Elwha were forced into the wage labor economy to make their way. Lynda Mapes, *Seattle Times* journalist and author of *Breaking Ground: The Lower Elwha Klallam Tribe and the Unearthing of Tse-whit-zen Village*, states the condition of the Elwha in the 1920s quite eloquently: "As for the Lower Elwha Klallam people, they were forced, like the fish, to subsidize the wealth of the newcomers with the sacrifice of their food, their homeland, even their very lives."[4]

FIGHTING FOR THE LAST SALMON

In 1930, Ernest M. Brannon, the superintendent of the Dungeness Hatchery located approximately 20 miles east of the Elwha, evinced a positive tone about the possibilities of protecting the Elwha River's downstream salmon in his letter to the state supervisor of fisheries, arguing that it was a "matter of growing importance" that the conditions of the river (below the dams) be better understood, and steps taken to preserve the downstream salmon and increase their numbers. Pointing out that the whole fishery had almost been wiped out after the construction of the lower dam, Brannon argued that in the intervening years the lower river fishery had managed to restore itself to fairly healthy numbers. He offered evidence from his own work activities to support this point. "This year I fished ten different days catching One hundred eighty one female Chinooks and two hundred fifteen male Chinook Salmon with only a gaff hook. These fish were all very large and in fine shape. Some of the female weighed more that sixty lbs. each and I caught several males that would weigh one hundred lbs. each."[5] Having established the existence of a large and healthy population of chinook on the lower river, Brannon then explained that the females were ripe and full of eggs, poised to spawn. Moreover, he commented on the relative health of the downstream river habitat. "I investigated several riffles and found these fish spawning in large numbers on every one of them. I did 95% of my fishing on one riffle 400 yds below the railroad bridge."[6]

This was when healthy riffles still existed in the lower river. Riffles are shallower stretches of a stream with large and small cobble that create highly aerated water and good spawning beds. The rocks on this stretch of the Elwha that created riffles had rolled downstream from higher in the watershed. The dams having just been built, much of the cobble, and therefore riffles, still remained in the lower Elwha. But this was changing. The dams blocked the recruitment of cobble as rocks piled up behind them in the bottoms of the reservoir. Rocks of various sizes (except for the largest and heaviest) in the riffles observed by Brannon would quickly be washed downstream into the Strait of Juan de Fuca, leaving only a hardened or armored river bottom, unsuitable for spawning salmon. "Gravel and sand once occupied the riverbeds and provided habitats for insects, aquatic species, and spawning salmon. The higher natural sediment loads [before the dams] made the river more dynamic; river channels changed locations and vegetation was scoured from banks and floodplains. Now, well-vegetated islands, low aquatic productivity, and a degraded, channelized river are the norm below the dams."[7]

The riverbed itself, an essential part of the overall health of the riverine ecosystem, was quickly deteriorating even as Brannon believed the fish below the dams could be restored to full health. The river was changing in ways he could neither see nor anticipate, due to a lack of knowledge of the impact of the dam, and because

The picture at the top of the facing page was taken along the shore of the Elwha River several miles above the site of the former Glines Canyon Dam. Note the abundance of small gravel ideal for salmon redds. The lower picture was taken below the Elwha Dam on the Lower Elwha Klallam Reservation before the dam was removed. This is a typical image of large rocks and boulders, with little gravel. The sediment-starved lower river provided poor habitat for salmon reproduction due to the loss of smaller rocks. Courtesy of Jeff Crane.

of research funding by the federal and state fisheries departments that had focused on hatchery production rather than an accurate understanding of salmon biology, river hydrology, and other related issues. Moreover, the dams blocked the flow of organic material from rotting salmon carcasses downstream, reducing the nutrients in and therefore the health of the overall lower Elwha river ecosystem. A dramatic reduction in logs and other woody debris floating downstream (because of the dams) also diminished the lower Elwha. Snags, wood piles, root wads, and other forms of woody debris provide important habitat for smolts and fish, places to hide from predators and find food. The vigor of the river ecosystem was in continuing decline, contrary to Brannon's observations and hopes that improvement was possible in the short term.[8]

Not understanding these changes and observing the healthy, spawning fish below the dam, Brannon expanded his efforts, arguing for the creation of a new hatchery on the river. He pointed out that he had discovered the run late in its spawn and could have easily collected 15 to 20 million eggs if he had only had racks or traps on the Elwha. Clearly, the basis was there for a healthy hatchery fishery and this was an era of heavy dependence on hatcheries. Brannon also discussed the impact of dam operations on the downstream fishery. "There were times the Power Dams would cut the water nearly off but this did not bother the adult fish any because they would lay in the holes while the water was down and not move around any. We found a few salmon that were stranded from the water being shut off and I estimate we picked up fifty young salmon and trout from 4 to 6 inches long that died because of no water."[9] He closed his letter to the state supervisor of fisheries by asking for the construction of a hatchery on the lower Elwha River.

Brannon returned to the river the following year to observe the spawn. In another letter to the state supervisor of fisheries, he described a still healthy salmon run on the lower river. In the hole below the Elwha Dam he saw 14 salmon jump within 30 minutes. Moving downstream from there to the mouth of the river he noted, "There were salmon rolling & jumping in all the deep holes, every one of them were very large ones. There are a number of fishermen fishing with salmon tackle, all of them are having very good luck. I saw three spring salmon caught that would weigh around 40 lbs. Wilson's hardware has had five spring salmon weighing 42 to 48 lbs. each on display this week."[10]

Brannon concluded by noting that there were a number of men who fished at the base of the dam every day. He did not mention whether these included Lower Elwha Klallam fishermen but it is safe to assume it did, although state fishing regulations likely forced them to "poach" at night. While this note makes no specific mention of the need or the strong potential for an Elwha hatchery, the letter was clearly meant to remind the state supervisor of fisheries of that very need.

VOICES OF DISSENT

Longtime resident and river restoration activist Dick Goins remembers that in 1938 low-water releases damaged the downstream fishery. The average flow at the time was 1,500 cubic feet per second (cfs) and on this day in October 1938 the flow dropped to a scanty 10 cfs. "There were people everywhere gathering up these beached chinook. This is at almost the height of spawning time. And the people were gathering them."[11] The deaths of these chinook prior to spawning reduced the amount of eggs in the lower river, diminishing the runs. Explaining that the dam operator reduced flows dramatically on a regular basis, Goins also recalls, "I've seen the edges [of the river] clearly silver carpet [*sic*] with fry, fingerlings, stranded. I have seen them drop it so fast adult chinook were stranded. They did anything they wanted to and it was all bad."[12] Alternatively, sometimes the dam operators released too much water, flushing fish over the banks and stranding them. Lower Elwha Klallam tribal member Adeline Smith remembers, "They'd open the dams and just let the water, you know, come down . . . there would [be] puddles of water all over and the little fish would be in there." Smith and other kids would then use a lard bucket to collect the smolts. "We'd put a little water in there and we'd pick up the fish and keep putting them in there.

Then we'd bring it to the river and dump them in. We were trying to save the little fish because, you know, those puddles would dry up and those little minnows would be dead."[13] According to Bruce Brown, smolts had another unexpected response to being trapped on gravel without water. "The normal response of young salmon to a falling water level is to dive into the gravel substrata, rather than swim unprotected into the current. Juvenile salmon will continue to dig to a depth of several feet as the water recedes, and have even been known to follow underground watercourses into wells and springs."[14] Buried alive, flipping around on dry ground and gasping for air or trapped underground in water, young salmon died in numerous and grotesque ways due to the careless manipulation of water flow for power production. The lack of corporate interest in stewardship and limited regulatory power on the part of the state drove Elwha salmon closer to the edge of extinction more rapidly than would have resulted from the natural deterioration of the lower Elwha habitat.

Some residents of Port Angeles were unwilling to let the Elwha salmon go quietly into the night. At the state level, Director of Fisheries Brennan heard voices of discord from the Elwha River region, receiving mail demanding action on the Elwha River. A letter from E. M. Benn of Port Angeles opened with the suggestion that an informed plurality was interested in the health of the river's salmon fishery. "Calling your attention to a condition which exists on the Elwha River the hydro electric dams [*sic*]. This condition is called to my attention almost every day by people interested in the natural propagation of the salmon."[15] Benn pointed out that an old hatchery had fallen out of operation (Darwin's failed hatchery) and suggested that the power company be compelled to restore and operate this hatchery. He closed by writing, "I believe if some effort was made by the department to force the company to do something here it would be good publicity for the department even if it was impossible to force [the dam owners] to do anything."[16] At the same time Benn suggested action, he also acknowledged the limits of the agency's power to protect fisheries. This marks the beginning of a public–

state discourse over the true meaning of the Elwha River, and the responsibility of the state for the preservation and restoration of its fisheries—a discourse that would gain strength and grow into a full-fledged restoration movement over the next half-century.

The pressure on Brennan accelerated with a letter from Congressman Francis Pearson of the Twenty-fourth District, which includes Port Angeles. In his letter to Brennan, Pearson stated that he had been contacted by many sport fishermen concerned with the fluctuating water flows on the lower Elwha and the impact on salmon. "It seems that on certain days the flood gates of the dam are closed in order to place in reserve more water for a later date. This causes the river below the dam to become very low and leaves all the spawn and thousands of little fish stranded high and dry thus killing an untold number of future salmon."[17]

Recognizing the limits of Brennan's power, Pearson offered assistance:

I am wondering if you have been told of this situation and if you have worked out a feasible solution for the matter. I wish you would notify me as soon as possible so I can have some answer for these men. They expect the spawning to start in earnest in a couple of weeks and have stated that the department es [sic] low on money. They will be willing to volunteer their services to try to move the spawn to some nearby hatchery. They are most certainly very interested down here and I hope that some feasible and reasonable solution can be worked out soon.[18]

This letter indicates significant public concern for the lower Elwha River salmon fishery in the Port Angeles community during the 1930s, as well as a willingness to work on the problem. Brennan responded in great depth and detail in a two-page, single-spaced letter providing the history of the Elwha Dam, Darwin's attempted solution, and the ways in which this effort had hamstrung the fisheries department's efforts to manage the lower river salmon in later years. "This contract, that was entered into and signed by the State of Washington, is so binding that there seems to be little or nothing that can be done further with protecting fish life in the river with the operating companies."[19] In his confidence in the hatchery solution, Darwin had unwittingly given the dam owners carte blanche to use the river in any manner they wanted with no responsibility for the fish. Continuing in the same vein, explaining the near annihilation of the fishery after the construction of the dam, Brennan explained that in fact it was the leakage at the base of the dam that had accidentally preserved the lower river salmon fishery, and that without this leakage, the storage of water by the power company would have left the river completely dry at crucial times and would have extirpated the fish runs.

Having explained the context for the current crisis, Brennan's frustration shone through when he wrote, "The department has made investigations of the subject but has always been handicapped by the existing contract when attempting to formulate any betterment of this situation, particularly in view of the new rights of the industrial diversion."[20] He proceeded to explain in more depth the problems facing the department and efforts to deal with these issues. "It is the desire of this department to make some correction on this situation. While it is improbable that anything can be done in passing the salmon over the Elwha dam, the question of low flow in the Elwha River and the rights of the industrial water diversion should be considered to see if something better than the present situation can be worked out." He further noted the possibility of finding a loophole in the contract that would enable the state to mandate more favorable water releases for the lower Elwha.[21]

Brennan continued in this vein for four more paragraphs, suggesting that creating more local opinion in support of pressuring the companies to act more responsibly would aid the department's efforts, and also advising that any assistance with egg transfer could be coordinated with Brannon at the Dungeness Hatchery.[22] This muted optimism for possible change was starkly contradicted by a letter written to another critic by the next director of fisheries, Fred J. Foster. The language is clear and reflects the reality of the fisheries department as well as the industrial meaning and use of that river as dictated by economic powers in that political economy. "As you know, the State has been powerless concerning the construction of dams on this stream since 1914 . . . This contract is a legal binding action upon the State of Washington which prevents any ordinary actions by this department towards the passing of fish over this dam."[23] Leslie Darwin's clever solution, created from need in a time of political weakness for conservationists and predicated on confidence that the science could work, hamstrung the future fisheries department from doing anything other than running a hatchery on the river, one that might not even function if the company did not release water at the key moments, or released too much. As Foster points out, "no ordinary actions" could be taken; maybe extraordinary actions would be the only solution.

In a 1946 response letter to Charles A. Faussett of Port Angeles, who had inquired about who bore culpability for the salmon crisis on the Elwha, the director of the Washington State Department of Fisheries expressed concern with the state of the river and salmon. Referring to the original contract for the construction of a hatchery in mitigation of the Elwha Dam (Darwin's solution), new director Milo Moore wrote, "You may be assured that this Department is not in accord with the original contract, now [*sic*] do we believe that the dam owners and operators are properly fulfilling their obligation to the migratory fish in the Elwha River."[24] Moore also addressed the problem of downstream migrating smolts negotiating their way past and through the dams, and indicated interest by the department in building a hatchery on the river. While a discourse of critique continued, as did efforts to find solutions to the problems with the downstream fishery, little was actually accomplished.[25]

As the salmon continued their slide, Port Angeles citizens and the state could do little to save them. But they continued to discuss and analyze the possibilities, insisting that this was not only a river for industrial production but also one for salmon. The ongoing insistence that the Elwha River be treated as a salmon river is reflected in letters written in 1951. A letter from the North Olympic Peninsula Chapter of the Poggie Club to the director of the Washington State Department of Fisheries laid out in clear and specific detail the problems on the Elwha and what steps needed to be taken. The author opened with a strong broadside attack against the agency and Crown Zellerbach. "The conditions existing on the Elwha River concerning the salmon and trout fingerlings are about as sorry a mess as can be found. Much has been said in the past about putting hatcheries etc. on this river to try to off-set the conditions brought about [by] the erection of these power dams by Washington Pulp & Paper Company or Crown Zellerbach or whoever built them."[26] He proceeded in the same tone to note that ongoing efforts to plant 100,000 to 200,000 fingerlings in the lower river were meaningless if the dams were operated improperly. "Planting fingerlings in the lower reaches of these streams, below the dams, is not important so long as the man operating these dams is allowed to do as he has in the past."[27] In fact, the author then characterized dam operation resulting in the fluctuating release of water as negligent. Not content only with criticism, the club offered tangible solutions, suggesting a survey "should be made with the idea of promulgating some feasible system whereby a constant flow of water should be maintained, or a slowly decreasing flow of water in an emergency over these dams."[28] The benefits of steady, dependable water flow was pretty obvious from the viewpoint of the author of the letter. "This would then give the thousands of fingerlings, both trout and salmon a chance to move out into deeper water and keep them from being trapped in the shallow pools and furnishing easy food for the gulls and ducks. When the water falls a foot or so in matter of minutes they have no chance."[29] The author did not attack industrialism and dams, but argued for responsible water use so other river values could be preserved and restored.

The letter finished with a meaningless threat of legislation if something wasn't done about the problem of fluctuating water releases and the impact on downstream salmon. All of this discussion focused not on restoration of upstream fisheries but merely on preserving the tiny remnant of the once great run, the fisheries of the lower few miles of the river.[30]

This continuing focus on the lower river salmon—the insistence on a river that was more than merely industrial—increasingly compelled action from the state. The assistant chief of the Fishery Management Division in the Department of Game argued that local voices had made it clear that a gauge to measure water flow needed to be installed downstream of the Elwha Dam in order to monitor "actual daily fluctuations."[31] A staffer of the Stream Improvement Division of the Department of Game also made the same request to the Water Resources Division of the U.S. Geological Survey, showing increased concern over management of the lower Elwha: "You are no doubt familiar with the problem that exists on the Elwha River . . . with regard to the fluctuation of stream flows below the two power dams. People in that area have been pressing us for the past several years to do something about this fluctuation."[32] The letter continued in the same strong tone, closing by insisting that a gauge must be placed in the river and also that he be informed as to whether a gauge would be installed for the coming salmon season, and if not then, when exactly.[33]

It is important to recognize the limited power of state fish agencies and concerned citizens to protect salmon, given the political economy of that era, the overwhelming focus on growth and production, and the conservatism and pressures of conformity in late 1940s and 1950s Cold War America. However, it is even more essential to understand that hot fights over the future of salmon and dams were raging in the Pacific Northwest and the West at exactly this time. The nature of the debate was changing and while nobody was discussing dam removal, the audacity of dam opponents shocked the leaders and shakers of the "go-go era," as Marc Reisner coined it. The days of industry and dam proponents dominating the discussion of a river's best uses were drawing to a close.

PACIFIC NORTHWESTERNERS FIGHTING FOR SALMON

Beginning in the 1930s, large hydroelectric dams transformed the Pacific Northwest landscape and drove the region's emergence as an economic and political powerhouse, while causing serious damage to the greater regional ecosystem. This was true across the American West, in fact. As Marc Reisner argues in *Cadillac Desert: The American West and Its Disappearing Water*,[34] "It is hard to imagine today . . . what the go-go years were like. In 1936, the four largest concrete dams ever built—Hoover, Shasta, Bonneville, and Grand Coulee—were being erected at breakneck speed, all at the same time. In Montana, Fort Peck Dam, the largest structure anywhere except for the Great Wall—which took a third of the Chinese male population a thousand years to build—was going up, too."[35] While these dams served as glimmering monuments to progress, evoking a sense of technological achievement that most Americans took and still take great pride in, the many other dams built following this were less epic in scale, less grandiose in form and beauty. Hundreds of these dams, the construction peaking in the 1950s and 1960s, were built on rivers across the nation.[36]

Monumental projects such as the Grand Coulee Dam not only provided the water for massive reclamation projects driving the growth of an important agricultural economy on the Columbia Plateau, but also provided electricity for the production of aluminum, warplanes, and ships during and after World War II. The construction of these dams and an electricity grid was central to the industrialization of the Pacific Northwest economy. While the spirit of development was strong and these projects were celebrated as icons of humanity's supremacy over nature and the foundation of the new economy, dissent arose over the next major stage of dam construction in the Pacific Northwest. Those marginalized by such projects struggled to challenge the destruction wrought on rivers, fisheries, and human societies. Understanding this broader conflict in the Northwest enables a better understanding of the Elwha restoration effort for two reasons. First, the destruction of salmon due to multiple dam projects (and other causes) across the Pacific Northwest created a context of scarcity, thereby engendering efforts to protect the increasingly valuable and threatened fish. Second, the restoration effort on the Elwha River did not arise from a void but from a wider milieu of concern over environmental decline and salmon loss and a stronger, more sophisticated environmental community.

Concern arose in the late 1930s and early 1940s over the impact of large-scale obstructions like the Columbia River's Bonneville and Rock Island dams on runs of Pacific coast salmon and steelhead. A 1938 report by the Oregon Planning Board "observed that the responsibilities of salmon management were much broader in scope than one state could resolve alone, and it recognized that management fragmented among too many state and federal agencies was ineffective."[37] The board recommended that Washington, Oregon, Idaho, and California cooperate in the creation of a joint Columbia River Fisheries Commission in order to centralize control and management of the imperiled salmon and steelhead fisheries. This suggestion was never implemented. The study was followed by the creation of the Columbia River Fisheries Interim Investigative Committee (CRFIIC) by the Washington State Senate in 1941. Like the earlier Oregon Planning Board, this committee was charged with the task of explaining the problems and possible solutions for declining fisheries on the Columbia River. This CRFIIC study expressed strong concern over the collapsing salmon fisheries and the likelihood of future declines, indicating three major causes for the fishery decline. The first was the overharvest of salmon. As fish biologist and author Jim Lichatowich points out, "The CRFIIC estimated that fishermen harvested 90 percent of the summer-run Chinook salmon. Incredibly, the committee laid the primary blame for overharvest on the Indian fishermen, who provided a convenient scapegoat for the deleterious effects of the industrial economy on the salmon and their habitats."[38] The committee also noted that habitat degradation, including the construction of major dams, was wreaking havoc on salmon runs. And, like the earlier Oregon report, the committee cited the lack of central planning and management as a fundamental reason for the salmon problems. Failure to create a central, interstate fisheries management agency prevented meaningful reform and contributed to the salmon's continuing decline.[39]

The ongoing deterioration of the salmon contributed to protest throughout the region, and in *Saving the Salmon*, historian Lisa Mighetto illuminates continued early dissent against dams in the Pacific Northwest, noting opposition from V. E. Benton of the Washington State Fish Commission against major dams in 1937. According to Mighetto, he demanded a greater commitment by the Corps to financing the research of fish passages on the Columbia. Other dissent came from the American Fisheries Society in 1941 and the Izaak Walton League in the early 1940s. Clearly, prior to World War II significant opposition was emerging to large dams and the damage they would wreak on salmon.[40]

The immediate postwar years in the Pacific Northwest were marked by efforts to restore habitat and preserve salmon and steelhead species. Furthermore, protest quickly arose against efforts to build more dams to produce hydroelectricity. A plan to construct a dam on the Cowlitz River in southwestern Washington, a river that produced prodigious amounts of salmon and steelhead, drew immediate protest from fish advocates. A meeting in late March 1947, hosted by army engineers in Toledo, Washington, drew a large crowd, including "well-represented" game and fishing interests. Members of the Columbia River Fishermen's Union, the Washington State Sports Council, the U.S. Fish and Wildlife Service, and others opposed construction of the dam due to the impact it would have on spawning fish.[41] In May 1947, Director of the Washington Department of Fisheries Milo Moore openly opposed the planned damming of the Cowlitz River, stating that the dam would block 75 percent of the spring chinook and steelhead spawning habitat. He forcefully advocated preservation of the river as an important salmon and steelhead watershed. The opposition of sports fishermen, commercial fishermen, and government fishery biologists represented a growing and increasingly vocal opposition to dam construction that damaged fisheries. However, they failed to stop the dam.[42]

Pacific Northwest Indians spoke out early against the construction of dams and the devastation of the salmon fisheries upon which they depended, and which constituted an important cultural resource.

While they complained about the impact of the privately built Rock Island Dam on salmon fisheries after its completion in 1933, many grew increasingly vocal in protesting the construction of the federal government's Bonneville Dam as it backed up reservoir water over important fishing sites and burial grounds. They registered their complaints with the Corps of Engineers and in more public forums. A Yakama Indian cited his concern in a letter to the *Oregonian* in 1935.[43] Stating first his dislike for Bonneville Dam and arguing that other Indians felt the same way, the letter's author referred to the "shutting" of the Columbia, and having the salmon "pulled from our mouths." The point he made is that the damming of rivers and the killing of fish, on the Columbia as on the Elwha, functions as a reverse form of enclosure. While Indians still live by the river, the loss of salmon weakened them economically, compelling them to seek more wage labor work, and other opportunities elsewhere. The author concluded by writing that "the Bonneville dam will hurt the people worse than the depression."[44] Like the Klallam Indians along the Elwha River, the Columbia Plateau Natives found themselves further marginalized with the construction of fish-killing dams.

The construction of dams on the Columbia, as in other locations, caused the flooding of important fishing sites like Celilo Falls, covered Indian burial grounds, and displaced whole communities. Historian Katrine Barber argues that "Indians fought against the dominant rhetoric of fish values versus power values of both the Army Corps and of Congress. In their effort to estimate the monetary costs of the dam, Army Corps employees neglected the cultural costs of their project, a strategy that had a two-fold effect."[45] Barber argues that this simplified the process for the government because a cost would be simply assessed based on the number of fish caught there. She then adds that by leaving out compensation for the spiritual value of the site "the Army Corps left for debate whether the settlement could have possibly been adequate to the true value of the falls."[46] There were complaints across the nation that the Corps overestimated the economic value of its projects while neglecting other important intangible benefits when providing their cost analyses of proposed dam projects. For instance, in Missouri where the Corps was attempting to build multiple dam projects across the state in the late 1940s and early 1950s, I. T. Bode, director of the Missouri Department of Conservation, wrote the following in a letter to a U.S. senator:

> *Wildlife is not a market commodity in the conventional sense, and it does not lend itself to complete measurement by classical methods of economic appraisal . . . for years now we have participated in cooperative river basin investigations in which the large intangible values of wildlife are recognized in theory, but there is no inclination on the part of project construction agencies to accommodate their plans to these values. When there is a choice to be made the dollar sign reigns supreme—except in the face of an indignant public.*[47]

This reflects the incisive and still relevant critique provided by Aldo Leopold in his essay "The Land Ethic," in which he criticized the economic determinists who insist that the economic value of land and resources is the only important value in land use decisions. Reducing all debates to costs and profits marginalizes all other categories as specious or fanciful. Trapped in the fight over costs and profits, the arguments for the rights of nature, the need for a land ethic, nature as a place of solace or sacred space, as well as recreation or exercise, and finally, the necessity to protect a place of beauty and transcendence hold little sway.[48]

As Barber argues and I. T. Bode asserted, the Corps of Engineers stacked the debate in their favor by reducing all discussion over dam construction to a simple formula of costs versus profits, and the need for economic development as defined by business interests and the Corps. This reductionist approach was instrumental in marginalizing Indians and others who valued nature for reasons other than profit. Moreover, the Corps of Engineers consistently understated the costs of projects while overestimating the ensuing economic benefits.

For Northwest Indians, a conflict over resources became an attack on their way of life, as generations of tradition and culture were damaged by the frenzy of dam building. Indians along the Columbia

River were intimately familiar with the negative impacts of dams long before the debate over dams on the lower Snake River emerged in the 1940s.

SACRIFICING SALMON FOR POWER

The efforts to harness the rivers of the Northwest to aid industrial production, facilitate irrigation, and reduce the impact of flooding developed remarkable momentum in the late 1940s with the revelation of ambitious plans to build a series of dams on major rivers throughout the region. For the most part, this grandiose scheme was received with enthusiasm and approbation. One editorial stated that the plan "is a breath-taking and awe-inspiring concept of how the destructive power in the water can be harnessed and controlled for the permanent benefit of the residents of the area."[49] The editorial then proceeded to common-sensically predict the benefits of the dam program. "The expenditure of three billion dollars, even though spread over a period of a number of years, is obviously not to be taken lightly. But flood control itself is work which can be fully justified as a public cost because of the damage which can be averted and the lives saved: and the power and irrigation features of the program have so conclusively proven themselves to be repayable projects."[50]

Furthermore, the perception of an energy crisis linked to a desire for growth created a call for higher levels of hydropower production—through completion of the McNary Dam on the Columbia River, appropriations for the construction of Ice Harbor Dam on the Lower Snake River, and development of an overall Columbia Basin River Development Plan. The Cold War era demand for power was unequivocal. "The shortage is immediately important to the aluminum plants, which must curtail production at a time when national defense demands are increasing rapidly and the total output is far under domestic requirements."[51] In fact, as historian Keith Petersen explains in *River of Life, Channel of Death*, it would be the demand and perceived need for hydroelectric power to meet defense needs, rather than flood control, irrigation, and navigation (the primary motivations for construction of the dams), that would generate support for building the four dams on the lower Snake River. The specter of the Cold War was a compelling factor here. The role of the Grand Coulee Dam in World War II wartime production and the frenzied rhetoric of the Cold War would make reasonable discussion of the lower Snake River dams almost impossible.

If one needs a reminder of how long the debate over the decline of salmon has played out, a reading of Anthony Netboy's work would suffice to clarify the issue. He provided early, important scholarship on threats to salmon worldwide and particularly in the Pacific Northwest. In *The Columbia River Salmon and Steelhead Trout: Their Fight for Survival,*[52] he effectively details the myriad impacts on salmon populations. His passion for the fish emerges distinctly in his chapter titled "Killer Dams," exploring the impact of dams on salmon and the role played by the Bureau of Reclamation and the Corps of Engineers, both federal agencies. He writes of the Inland Empire Waterways Association as "one of the most formidable lobbyists" supporting construction of dams on the Snake and Columbia Rivers. Netboy describes the complex association of wealth and power in support of dam construction for economic development. " . . . [w]ith headquarters in Walla Walla, supported by every port and would-be port on the river from Astoria to Lewiston, the barge transportation companies, the chambers of commerce, the Bonneville Power Administration, other utilities, the aluminum companies, and others. It was well financed."[53] Noting that the meetings held in Portland were attended by great publicity, Netboy, like Petersen, also identifies Herbert West as the prime mover of the Inland Empire Waterways Association. He notes West's key friendships and alliances within federal agencies and of course, the business community. He "knew how to court allies like Paul Raver, the BPA administrator, and was a close friend of every district engineer, an honored guest when he went to Washington of the chief of the Corps himself, and a master at handling congressional committees. I knew him well. He was rightly proud of the monuments to his lifework—the sleek, magnificent concrete barriers across the rivers built in the 1950s and 1960s."[54]

When boosters of the Walla Walla area and interior Northwest first envisioned an inland port in Lewiston, Idaho, and continued to push that vision, they had no idea of an impending Cold War with Communist-bloc nations and certainly had no interest in using the river to produce hydroelectricity. The desire to build an inland port in Lewiston, approximately 380 miles from the Pacific Ocean, and thereby improve the business environment of that part of the interior Northwest, necessitated a series of dams to create long reservoirs on the lower Snake to make the river navigable for barges year-round. When the U.S. Army Corps of Engineers enthusiastically endorsed this plan following World War II, as the agency was proposing and enacting dam-building efforts nationwide, it seemed inevitable that the dams would be built. However, proponents of dam construction on the lower Snake River were surprised by strong and persistent opposition from fishermen, biologists, and state agencies. Petersen characterizes the protest against the lower Snake River dams as half-hearted and doomed to failure. In so doing, he underestimates the determination of fish advocates to block the dams, and fails to recognize how rare a thing it was to oppose and stop large-scale development plans at this point in American history.

The 1940s and 1950s are generally represented as a period of strong public conformity and consensus on the benefits of growth and capitalism. However, fisheries biologists and agency employees, as well as sports fishermen, commercial fishermen, and Indians initiated strong attempts to block construction of dams on the Lower Snake River. While they finally failed, their efforts stalled the dams for 10 years and lodged complaints and criticisms that reverberate today.[55]

The efforts to block the building of these dams marked the beginning of a shift in public opinion regarding the value of dams; a shift that swelled with the blocking of the proposed Echo Park Dam in 1954 and the emergence of a dynamic and aggressive national environmental movement.

DISREGARDING SCIENCE FOR DEVELOPMENT

Contrary to current belief, biologists understood in the 1940s that dams would negatively affect not only spawning salmon but also downstream-migrating smolts as well. Petersen demonstrates that by 1934 the Bureau of Reclamation had a problem getting juvenile fish downstream past a dam, and this in large part was the reason for building the Grand Coulee Dam without fish passage facilities, thereby cutting off thousands of miles of salmon habitat into the foreseeable future.

Federal dam agency understanding of the problem of smolt transport past dams was expanded with a study by biologist Harlan Holmes, beginning in 1947, that showed that turbines were chewing up the juvenile salmon. The Corps increased their knowledge of the damage rendered by their dams on salmon smolts just a few years later and suppressed the information. According to Petersen, "In 1952, when Holmes estimated that Bonneville Dam killed 15 percent of juveniles passing through, the Corps refused to publish his report."[56]

Even with the growing awareness of smolt mortalities related to dams, the Corps remained opposed to any mitigating steps that would interfere with development and dam construction. This may be ascribed to the predominant focus on growth and development over conservation in the 1930s through the 1950s, but it must also be remembered that there was still a seeming abundance of salmon in the region. This presumption probably legitimized some sacrifice in order to generate greater economic growth. Biologists and agencies responsible for dam construction understood the impact on fisheries before the Corps began construction of the four dams on the lower Snake River, and this compelled them to oppose the Corps's plans. Fishery biologists testified regarding the damage to smolts caused by turbines, expressly declaring to a U.S. Senate Appropriations Committee meeting in 1950 that Bonneville Dam was responsible for 15 to 20 percent losses to downstream migrating smolts. Applying this loss to the planned dams in addition to the already extant Bonneville and McNary Dams, Washington State fish biologists estimated that the dams would destroy approximately one-quarter to over one-third of the smolts making their way to the ocean.[57]

Understanding of the impact of dams on salmon expanded in the 1950s as there was a clear and growing body of scientific material documenting the extent and scope of the damage. Joseph Taylor expresses this point in *Making Salmon*. Studies in the 1950s had shown that dams delayed migration and that northern pikeminnow preyed on smolts in the reservoirs created by dams. Moreover, continued studies in the 1960s demonstrated other migration and spawning problems associated with dams. Certainly, there was no paucity of scientific information on the negative impacts imposed by dams on salmon.[58] Three of the four studies discussed by Taylor preceded the construction of the first of the four lower Snake River dams. Therefore, the assertions of some historians that the Corps of Engineers made serious efforts to deal with the impact on salmon must be questioned; fisheries biologists and the Corps understood that the dams would severely damage salmon and steelhead runs, and built the dams anyway. Development interests and dam construction dominated the thinking of Corps leaders and they weren't going to allow some glitches with fish to impede their vision of a channel river for transportation. Such was the cost of progress.

While the Corps was willing to risk damage to fisheries, fish advocates refused to give in quietly, and organized to fight the building of the dams, focusing on the first project, the Ice Harbor Dam. Although Petersen argues that they held no real hope of winning this battle, it is clear that they attempted to at best stop, and at worst delay, dam construction. Members of the Oregon Fish Commission, the Washington Department of Fisheries, and the Oregon Game Commission organized an extensive and intensive letter-writing campaign to congressional representatives, and provided scientific testimony against the dams. They appealed to sports and commercial fishermen to lobby against the dams, arguing that irreparable harm would be done to the Snake River fisheries. Like the dam boosters' efforts to use Cold War fears, they resorted to

Cold War rhetoric, arguing that a sustainable fishery was invaluable to the strength of the nation in time of war. Furthermore, the agencies accused the Corps of predicting higher revenue through artificially inflated numbers.[59]

It is worth noting that the language of these fisheries experts as well as that of commercial and sports fishermen was strongly conservationist in tone. They did not speak of salmon as icons of the Northwest, or of the aesthetics of free-flowing rivers and huge runs of awe-inspiring, spawning salmon, but rather argued for the importance of protecting an important and valuable economic resource. Like Leslie Darwin on the Elwha and other Progressive Era conservationists, they sought to manage nature efficiently to maintain abundance, and dams threatened their ability to accomplish this. In the face of clear evidence that hatcheries did not offer easy panaceas to the decline of fisheries, they could not respond with the optimism evinced by Darwin 30 years earlier; they had little faith that hatcheries could replace the wild salmon runs that would be destroyed by a series of dams.[60]

Dam supporters saw the legitimacy of fishery concerns and anticipated greater trouble in the future regarding conflicts between dams and fisheries. In November 1948, the Walla Walla district commander for the Corps of Engineers announced the importance of building dams immediately in order to avoid increased conflict in the future. Noting growing opposition to major dams in the Columbia Basin, Colonel William Whipple proved prescient when he stated, "In 40 or 50 years, there will be a real clash between proponents of dam construction and fishing interests."[61] While recognizing that dams would cause problems for downstream migrating salmon and understanding that this conflict and crisis would only grow with time, the response of the Corps was to push its agenda that much harder and get dams in before serious opposition could stop them.

Supporters of the dams prepared for battle with fisheries advocates. As Petersen points out, members of the Inland Empire Waterways Association revealed their ignorance of salmon issues by arguing that dams would make salmon migration easier by providing smooth-water reservoirs instead of the ever-so-difficult rapids. They also employed a strategy that would become the hallmark of dam advocacy in the following six decades. Petersen clearly explains the rhetorical strategy that enabled the supporters of dam construction to divert attention from the impacts of dams on salmon fisheries: "Greedy Indian, commercial, and sports fishers, not dams, were primarily responsible for declining returns."[62] Anyone attending Snake River dam breaching hearings in 2000 would have been stunned to note the marked similarity in testimony between that of dam supporter and booster Herbert West in the 1950s and dam proponents at the end of the 20th century. According to dam supporters, sport fishermen, commercial fishermen, and Indians—not dams—kill salmon.

The urge for power and growth, along with the effective lobbying and deceptions of dam boosters, proved too much for fisheries advocates opposing dams on the lower Snake River. The Pacific Northwest region embraced industrial and economic growth and saw increased hydroelectricity production as the key to achieving that growth. The desire for power and development was so strong that consideration for the health of salmon and steelhead populations was accorded minimal importance. While there had been salmon declines up to this point, the perception might well have been that there was an abundance of salmon versus a scarcity of electricity in a region that had embraced industrial development and growth. Abundance versus scarcity was not an issue for all; some dam proponents found the demise of salmon and steelhead an acceptable consequence of dam construction. One state agency flatly declared: "The overall benefits to the Pacific Northwest from a thoroughgoing development of the Snake and Columbia River are such that the present salmon run must, if necessary, be sacrificed."[63] While fishery advocates were able to delay the building of the dams by 10 years, they understood that they would probably fail in preventing the dams' construction, and in the end the dams went up.

The decline of the salmon fisheries on the Columbia and Snake Rivers resulted from a number of factors, primarily dam construction.

Even as the dams went up and salmon populations plummeted throughout the region, there was growing concern not only on the part of activists but also government agencies about the future of salmon. Lisa Mighetto and Wesley J. Ebel's *Saving the Salmon* is an exhaustive and thorough study of the measures enacted by the U.S. Army Corps of Engineers to mitigate the damage to salmon influenced by the dams built by the Corps. In the preface, the authors write, "From the early planning stages, the Corps recognized that Columbia River dams threatened salmon and steelhead by impeding their migration to and from the ocean. Accordingly, the Corps, with the assistance of fisheries agencies, designed and developed fish passage facilities for all its multipurpose dams on the Columbia and Snake Rivers."[64]

In fact, this is a rather sanguine interpretation of the Corps's role in addressing the deterioration of salmon and steelhead on the Snake and Columbia Rivers. The Corps pushed through the building of the lower Snake River dams over the voice of informed protest, predicting that it had to be done then because 40 years hence the problem would be so severe as to render impossible the construction of major dams.[65] Furthermore, the Corps underestimated the potential impacts of its four lower Snake River dams on fisheries, and exaggerated the future income from business and barge traffic, a point made by the fishery agencies during their opposition to the construction of the dams. Fish advocates accurately pointed out that the Corps was estimating low and that the increased costs would be placed on the shoulders of taxpayers. The degree to which the Corps of Engineers has worked to "save the salmon" has been the result of outside compulsion by means of legislation and prodding by government agencies and citizen groups. Regardless, their reliance on a long string of technological solutions illuminates the tension inherent in the Corps's conflicting mandates, particularly in the Northwest, between promoting flood control and navigation to support business, and preserving threatened and endangered salmon and steelhead runs. The central irony is that the very government agencies who have done so much to bring salmon to the brink of extinction, are now among those responsible for their preservation. The inherent conflict between dams and salmon continues because the Corps is a dam-building agency that consistently places ecological concerns behind its priorities of river development for flood control and navigation. As a result, and not surprisingly, the agency argues consistently for technological solutions while blocking efforts to breach dams. Their own raison d'etre hangs in the balance.

HELPING SMOLTS PAST DAMS AND PREDATORS

Contemporary strategies for resolving the salmon crisis on the Snake River have been heavily technological in nature and breathtakingly expensive (over $3 billion to save Snake and Columbia River salmon by 1997).[66] Their complexity and cost reveal the tension between the widespread desire to save salmon, and the inability to seriously contemplate the removal of major dams. The crisis has engendered clever but ineffective solutions that represent scientific ingenuity, but reveal a lack of political will to substantively address the issue.

The first response to the problem was to create fish passageways—a science that at the time of the Rock Island Dam in the 1920s, the Bonneville Dam in the 1930s, and later the lower Snake River dams in the 1960s and '70s remained somewhat less than perfected. As Mighetto and Ebel point out in *Saving the Salmon*, the plans for fishways over Bonneville Dam remained in a state of constant flux as the dam was constructed and fish passageways designed. "The fishways design 'evolved' and changed sometimes 'day-to-day' during construction of the dam and powerhouse."[67] The authors argue that the Corps made a sincere effort to deal with the upstream passage issue, consulting with fish biologists, Oregon and Washington fish and game commissions, as well as the U.S. Bureau of Fisheries.[68] However, journalist Blaine Harden offers a different interpretation in his book *A River Lost*: "Milo Bell, a hydraulic engineer who worked for the Corps at Bonneville in the 1930s and who invented its fish ladders, told me that the Corps' original design for the dam would not have allowed salmon upstream. Bell, a professor emeritus at the University of Washington, said that without public pressure the Corps would not have spent the money necessary to make fish passage work and salmon runs would have been destroyed. Corps engineers, Bell recalls, made 'a lot of snide comments about salmon.'"[69]

Regardless of the attitudes of the Corps of Engineers toward mitigation of the fish problems they had caused, the agency did invest significant amounts of taxpayer money and research into improving fish passage on mainstem dams. The nexus of this research was the Fisheries Engineering Research Laboratory at Bonneville Dam, constructed in 1955. Here, fisheries scientists and engineers labored to solve the variety of problems associated with fish passage over dams. The variety of species, as well as the diversity of spawning salmon (from the huge spring chinook to smaller coho or sockeye), presented a variety of logistical problems that they sought to solve. One benefit of this location was the ability to conduct experiments and observe the salmon during the actual spawning migration. Researchers investigated such problems as water flow issues, velocity of water in the passageways, the use of light, and the construction of the passageways themselves. The improvement of a vertical slot fish passageway resulted from the efforts to solve the problem of dead shad[70] blocking traditional fish passageways. Vertical slot fish passageways were then installed in several dams, which helped with that particular problem. Furthermore, scientists and engineers used radio tracking and electronic tunnels to better understand the reason for fish delays at dams. Research has improved fish passageways and fish movement upstream, but the salmon runs continue to decline.[71]

Other research has sought to deal with the issues of juvenile salmon migration downstream. This passage has emerged as the most problematic and pressing issue presented by dams, especially the long, slack-water reservoirs that dams create. These reservoirs and the dams themselves radically alter the waterscape of the juvenile salmon's downstream odyssey. Historically, some species of salmon smolts were flushed downstream to the sea in a matter of weeks by snowmelt-swollen rivers. After spending up to two years hiding and growing in their natal stream, smolts are ready for the downstream ride and their physiology begins changing along the trip, preparing them for life as a saltwater fish. Dams and reservoirs have fundamentally altered this journey to the sea. What once took from a few days to two weeks is now transformed into a journey of six weeks or more, marked by several new and enhanced obstacles and dangers, reducing drastically the number of smolts successfully completing their journey to the Pacific.[72]

Slack-water reservoirs created by dams proved problematic in a number of ways. Fish riding the current into the backed-up water are quickly confronted with the need to pick a direction and swim (smolts are biologically programmed to float downstream on spring freshets; now they were forced to swim through placid reservoirs and find their way through hydroelectric turbines. This created a significant obstacle, in contradiction to the smolts' biological makeup and pattern of downstream migration. While finding their way through the reservoirs, they encountered an array of predators, including native fish such as the pikeminnow,[73] which prey heavily on smolts. Bass, an introduced species, and other fish also consume huge amounts of the small salmonids. Evidence indicates that pikeminnow numbers have increased dramatically since construction of Columbia and Snake River system dams. They are particularly heavy on the downstream side of dams, where nitrogen-sickened or bruised and damaged smolts emerge disoriented and weak, making them easy prey. One study estimated the loss of salmon smolts to these fish at between 8 and 61 percent below John Day Dam. The loss of steelhead smolts to the pikeminnow runs at about 12 percent in late spring and early summer.

To address the problem, the Bonneville Power Administration (BPA) has sponsored a bounty program since 1990 and claims to have removed 3.7 million pikeminnow through the payment of bounties, reducing smolt mortality by an estimated 40 percent. Thousands of fishermen pursue the fish for a per fish bounty that ranged from $4 to $6 in 2001 and was raised to a range of $4 to $8 dollars in 2009. The more pikeminnow a fisherman catches, the more he or she is paid. For example, a bounty fisherman currently gets $4 per fish up to the first 100, $5 a fish up to 400, then $8 dollars a fish after that. In 2008, one fisherman made almost $60,000 harvesting the smolt predators, and the top 20 bounty fishermen accumulated a total of just over $430,000.[74]

It is hard to quantify the success of the program, although in the simplest terms, fewer northern pikeminnow should mean more salmon smolts. Interestingly, cultural values imposed on fish play into this equation. Unlike bass or shad, northern pikeminnow are indigenous to the region. However, they are referred to as "junk fish"[75] in contrast to the rapturous language reserved for species such as salmon and steelhead. Further, the costs of the program to taxpayers may outweigh the benefits. In 1991, the Bonneville Power Administration spent $5.5 million to destroy slightly fewer than 200,000 northern pikeminnow, which works out to about $27 per pikeminnow.[76]

Bass and walleye are non-native species that consume prodigious amounts of salmon smolts, too, along with other predators such as seagulls and cormorants. While it is true that some species have always preyed on the juvenile salmon, the problem is now exacerbated by the reservoirs slowing the fish down and leaving them more exposed than they would be in rushing currents.[77] The increased water temperature of reservoirs also results in the death of millions of salmonids. Slack water heats up as summer passes, sometimes exceeding 68 degrees, a fatal temperature for smolts. Higher water temperatures can contribute to sickness and disease as well. Furthermore, the creation of reservoirs reduces the amount of available spawning habitat. The flooding of river and creek mouths and wetlands by the backed-up water reduces the amount of spawning habitat, and the habitat for smolts to hide during the time they spend upriver before heading downstream.[78]

Even the dams themselves kill smolts. Most damaging is the nitrogen sickness acquired by passage through the dams. Mighetto and Ebel argue that the Corps responded immediately to concerns over nitrogen sickness when the issue was understood and publicized in the early 1970s. After organizing a "Nitrogen Task Force" to examine the problem, a technological solution was proposed and installed. According to the authors, the introduction of spillway deflectors has reduced the incidence of nitrogen sickness experienced by smolts, although the number saved is not quantified.[79]

While many of the problems that threaten salmon result from obstacles to downstream migration, there are also problems for salmon traveling upstream to spawn. It is often assumed that dams with fish ladders represent a successful solution to a seemingly impassable problem. It is true that many fish make it successfully up fish ladders. But it is also true that the exertion involved causes problems for salmon. The effort required to cross the dams drains valuable energy reserves that must get the fish upstream to their spawning grounds, since they do not feed on their spawning runs. Turbine discharge makes it difficult for salmon to find the fishways sometimes, although steps have been taken to lessen that impact. Some fish are drawn back into the turbines after passage up ladders. These problems have a cumulative effect. While salmon have always faced numerous challenges in their life cycle, the myriad problems created by dam construction have played the most critical role in the collapse of these fish across the Pacific Northwest. While removing some dams might seem a logical solution, there is strong resistance to this approach, so other efforts must suffice.[80]

FISH BOATS AND FRIENDLY TURBINES

Agencies responsible for the salmon and the damage to them responded to problems created by technology with a mix of technological solutions and stop-gap measures. The trucking and barging of smolts is probably the best example of a stop-gap measure. This program provides a seemingly simple and achievable method to getting the young salmon past the problems encountered in reservoirs and dams. The transport of juvenile smolts by truck and barge began as an experimental program and has become a mainstay of efforts to maintain salmon and steelhead on the Snake River. Initially undertaken by the National Marine Fisheries Service (NMFS) in 1968, the studies continued into the 1970s as Little

Goose and Lower Granite Dams reached completion. This program transports smolts past nitrogen sickness, predators, and long travel through slack-water reservoirs. Barges could seemingly replace the lost functions of the river itself. A Corps of Engineers pamphlet titled "To Save the Salmon" describes the smolt-barging system in an interesting mix of scientific terminology and colloquial language:

> One way to get young salmon downstream through slow-moving reservoirs, avoid problems with dam passage, hungry predators and the perils of gas-supersaturation, is to give them a ride. That's why many juvenile salmon are given a lift [author emphasis] downriver . . . each transport barge and tanker truck is custom made to make the trip as safe and comfortable as possible . . . fresh river water is constantly circulated . . . This not only keeps the water fresh and healthy for the young fish, but also helps them "get to know" or "taste" the river just as if they would if they were still swimming in it.[81]

The casual language of the pamphlet ("Hey little fella, want a ride?") implies a commonsense solution to an intractable problem (of the Corps's own creation); the truth remains more complex. In fact, many fish biologists question the efficacy of the barging program. The biggest concern revolves around the issue of homing instincts.[82] Do juveniles transported downstream in barges retain the ability to find the way home to their natal stream? Various studies offer differing conclusions.[83] Environmental law professor Michael C. Blumm cogently summarizes the debate over salmon and barging, explaining that the barging program had been in operation for over a decade, regardless of its effectiveness, because it precluded interference with various economic interests like soft white wheat farmers, paper companies, irrigated agriculture, navigation, and, of course, the power companies. Like McEvoy's earlier statement regarding the dependence on hatcheries to preclude meaningful protections of fisheries, smolt barging serves the same interest in using technology to avoid disruptions to the economy and special interests. The National Marine Fisheries Service "embraced this program of artificial transport, alleging that a sound salmon restoration program required a systematic comparison of the efficiency of truck and barge transportation versus in-river migration over a four-year period."[84]

Protests from tribes, environmentalists, and the state of Oregon against this program (because it fell far short of the measures required under the Endangered Species Act) met with judicial ratification of the barging in 1997, which allowed continued transport of the smolts in place of stronger measures until 1999. While the survival rate is higher for trucked and barged smolts than it is for those making the trip downstream without aid, salmon spawning numbers have continued to fall, raising questions regarding the effectiveness of this program. Part of this problem arises from failures of transported salmon to return home in predictable and sustainable numbers when spawning.[85]

Dam turbines represent one of the most pressing threats to young salmon and steelhead, and turbine bypass systems represent another technological effort to solve the crisis. The Corps of Engineers has struggled to find solutions to that problem since 1951. According to Mighetto and Ebel, "The fisheries agencies, universities, and the Corps scientists contributed to this effort. Laboratory and field studies included the use of electricity, louvers, water jets, air jets, sounds, lights, and traveling screens."[86] Another effort to reduce smolt mortality in dam turbines was the Corps's creation of "fish-friendly" turbines, so named and touted by the Corps themselves as a partial solution during the debate over breaching of the four lower Snake River dams. Designed with smaller blades and at a cost of $1.25 million apiece, these turbines were estimated to reduce deaths of juvenile salmon by 2 to 3 percent.[87]

Having played a central role in the creation of the Pacific Northwest salmon crisis, the Corps has employed a variety of solutions to deal with collapsing salmon populations. Trucking and barging smolts, improvements to fish passageways, reservoir drawdowns (the reduction of reservoirs to lower levels so the fish will travel through more quickly), turbine bypass systems, and other responses represent a willingness by the Corps to use tax dollars to attempt to mitigate the damage they have caused (or at worst to create the illusion of crafting solutions), rather than consider the breaching of dams to save salmon. This dependence on technology continues and occasionally reaches absurd levels. It reveals a confidence that creative fixes will allow the Corps to avoid the obvious but politically challenging act of removing some of the worst offending dams.

The use of radio telemetry, acoustic tags, and electromyogram sensors to study both adult and smolt migrations is worthwhile because it expands the body of knowledge of what problems the fish encounter and the effects these stresses have on them. Also, this information can help develop future strategies and solutions for salmon preservation. But these efforts still denote a continued reliance on science and technology to solve the problem, or in the estimation of some, to forestall more radical solutions.[88]

Besides attempts to mitigate impacts *on* salmon themselves, there are also efforts to replicate the impact *of* salmon on the ecology of their habitat. An Oregon company has received funding from the BPA to turn salmon scraps into pellets for dispersal in former salmon habitat. The goal is to recreate the historic biological function of salmon carcasses rotting and being consumed after spawning, and thereby contributing nutrients to streams and surrounding terrain. In fact, some hatcheries have instituted a policy of distributing harvested salmon carcasses upstream in an effort to recreate the old ecosystem and the salmon's role in it. The proposal to produce pellets, bag them, and then haul them upstream for distribution is a further mechanization of a natural system. Imagine a spawned-out salmon lying on its side, gasping in shallow breaths for oxygen, its spotted grey-white flesh rotting off in places even as she dies. A black bear steps into the water, takes a big bite from the middle of the salmon and then tosses it a couple of feet up the bank as it wanders upstream to find another fat salmon to eat. As dusk falls, a raccoon slips out of the undergrowth and feeds on the salmon for a little while, breaking it into little pieces that a flock of ravens descend upon the next morning in a raucous festival of feasting, casually spreading salmon parts about them as they hop along the stream bank or fly to the branches of a cedar tree to consume their meal. These little pieces of salmon then rot, enriching oftentimes sterile or relatively infertile mountain soil, or decay in the stream, providing nutrients for a number of aquatic organisms. The idea is to haul in 25-pound bags of pellets and toss them about. This may introduce nutrients to the soil and water. But important stages in the system—the feeding of various mammals, birds, and microorganisms—will be skipped.[89] While these developments constitute ingenious innovation and may provide important information, they at best offer an optimistic alternative, contributing to the myth that the right fix can replace undammed rivers and healthy habitat.

What is striking about such efforts is that they demonstrate a sincere desire to find solutions to the fisheries crisis and restore the environment, even while they implicitly acknowledge the inability of agencies to take more dramatic, meaningful steps. While federal agencies like the Bonneville Power Administration and the Corps of Engineers are defending dams and promoting technological solutions and other measures, many fisheries biologists have led the charge in criticizing the dependence on hatcheries and technology and calling for an increased commitment to habitat restoration.

Ray Hilborn, fisheries professor at University of Washington, sums up the philosophy and failings of the past century of hatchery production on the Columbia River by observing that "fish culturists had little behavioral or ecological understanding. They believed you could just pump juvenile fish into the ocean, and these youngsters would not affect the other fish there."[90] Hilborn then argues that they believed it might be possible to produce salmon without a functioning river ecosystem and history by essentially herding the smolts to the "sea and use the 'vacant' ocean pasture."[91] He concludes by pointing out that probably more smolts are released into the ocean currently than were produced naturally before the arrival of Europeans, but the *return* of adult salmon is only a "tiny fraction" of the earlier numbers.[92]

Fisheries biologist Jim Lichatowich's study, *Salmon Without Rivers*, provides a powerful and convincing critique of the hatchery system or "myth" as he terms it. Toward the end of his book he provides an ideological explanation for the continuing dependence on hatcheries. He refers to the arguments of physicist Freeman Dyson that a commitment to technological answers that arises from ideology prevents an acknowledgment that technology is failing and requires even more money and research dedicated to technological solutions. Because of this, the proponents of techno-optimism can admit failure only when it is manifest to all. By then the damage is overwhelming or even irreversible. Lichatowich argues with great passion that "hatcheries have been ideologically driven . . . promoted not because they were scientifically justified but because they supported the prevailing development ideology." Not only would hatcheries provide fish resources for the canneries, they allowed for the complete control of rivers and destruction of salmon habitat. "To acknowledge that artificial propagation has failed would call into question not only the hatcheries but also the ideology from which they were derived. It has been far easier to construct and maintain a 'conspiracy of optimism.'"[93]

Historian Paul Hirt coined this phrase "conspiracy of optimism" in his study of the Forest Service after World War II. Lichatowich demonstrates the parallels between the management of salmon fisheries and the management of the national forests. "Columbia River salmon managers became trapped in what historian Paul Hirt has called the 'conspiracy of optimism.' The goals of stewardship and conservation were displaced by techno-optimism—the belief that it was possible to maximize salmon production through technology, even in a watershed simplified and degraded by a series of continuous impoundments."[94] He argues that even as the hatchery solution failed to work, managers continued to employ technology over other meaningful solutions. Lichatowich again refers to Hirt's conspiracy of optimism, arguing that "when programs based on techno-fixes fail, the technology is never blamed for the failure; rather, the fault is said to lie with the politicians who did not provide sufficient funds to buy enough of it. On the Columbia, the result of this kind of thinking has been a spiral of escalating costs with few tangible results."[95]

Other fish biologists have both critiqued the dependence on hatcheries and called for an increased emphasis on restoration of habitat and returning rivers to states of more natural river flow. Fish biologist Gary Meffe provides a thorough explanation for the failure of hatcheries. He explains some reasons why hatcheries contribute to the problems with salmon in the Pacific Northwest. Noting the massive expenditures for and limited success of hatcheries, he writes, "Severely limited state and federal monies spent on hatcheries could be redirected to local and ecosystem-level habitat restoration, or to prevention of further decline through land purchases. The latter would also benefit other species and maintain ecosystem services in the region."[96] Habitat restoration helps many species while hatcheries, in theory, help only fish. The author also argues that hatcheries are not sustainable in the long term, pointing out that they are "a biologically unsound approach to management that can result in negative genetic changes in natural populations."[97] He asserts that even when management practices change to deal with concerns regarding fish genetics, there is still general negligence in maintaining the proper population sizes, and around transfers of stocks between different river watersheds and areas within the watershed, "disregarding potential local adaptations . . . has resulted in the genetic and ecological interaction of native and hatchery stocks, with repeated degradation or loss of native populations."[98]

Meffe then argues that hatchery production results in larger harvests of salmon. While hatchery production goes up, wild stocks continue to decline. "Successful hatchery production seems to provide a psychological license to increase harvest rates, which reduces wild stocks, thus defeating the initial purpose of hatcheries."[99] His final point is an important one. "By financially supporting hatchery production as a standard mitigation practice, the hydropower companies and other development projects that are largely responsible for environmental degradation can 'buy out' of their moral responsibilities for salmonid losses and habitat destruction by demonstrating their concern for and dedication to the declining resource."[100] Whereas in the early days of development in the Pacific Northwest it was believed that hatcheries were palliatives to overharvesting and habitat destruction, it has become abundantly clear that hatcheries contribute to the problem of wild salmon deterioration. The continuing dependence on technology, as pointed out time and again throughout this chapter, allows government agencies and power companies to avoid making the hard choices, always asserting that the technology will lead us out of the current quandary.[101]

Those entrusted with the fate of salmon and steelhead, who have dedicated their lives to this work, have offered some practical suggestions for preserving and possibly restoring salmon populations. With reference to the Columbia River, one article notes "river basin management is dominated by technological operations supporting the region's economy (e.g. hydropower production, irrigation systems, flood control, commercial barging). Operation of the river via the hydropower system is driven largely by economic considerations of water usage in the basin; the associated management decisions constrain conservation and restoration efforts for anadromous and resident salmonid fishes."[102] The article articulates the need to restore natural processes to the greatly modified and industrialized Columbia River. While the article does not call for dam removal, there is enough emphasis on habitat restoration and the need for natural river conditions that increased scrutiny of dams is implied, regarding their economic and social benefit versus their destruction of the river and salmon. Finally, the article boldly calls for a reconceiving of the Columbia as a river once again.

There have been additional calls by fish biologists and activists to create salmon parks or refuges in order to assure large pieces of protected salmon and steelhead habitat. While a great deal of criticism of hatcheries within the fish biology field persists, many still believe in the efficacy of hatcheries, or argue that the tool is simply misused rather than fundamentally flawed.

FROM FAILURE TO RESTORATION

From where did all of this techno-dependency arise, with regard to addressing the fisheries problems created by dams? The answer is complex. Fisheries agencies have shifted their position several times over the last century and a half. For example, while they have tried hatcheries, they have also often made demands for protection of habitat and increasingly for restoration of habitat for fish. Jim Lichatowich effectively argues that the dependence on hatcheries on the Snake and Columbia Rivers arose from a belief in the efficacy of hatcheries. But this interpretation partially rests on the traditional omission of the fisheries agencies' protests against the construction of the lower Snake River dams. Upon losing that battle and arguing that river production of salmon was superior to hatchery salmon, fisheries managers were forced to increase their dependence on hatcheries in order to fulfill their mission.

The failure to deal effectively with the salmon crisis indicates a failure at the cultural and government level. Federal agencies like the U.S. Army Corps of Engineers and the Bureau of Reclamation, having built the dams that are destroying the salmon, continue to insist that science and technology are the keys to recovery, even as they strive to protect their key assets, the dams. These technological fixes have failed, but still the agencies turn to science and technology to further the illusion of meaningful effort, while avoiding the risks of making sacrifices to preserve salmon. But our government reflects our culture, and for many years there has been an assumption that we could harvest cheap power and preserve salmon, too.

The continuing failures of fisheries management compel consideration of another, more commonsense, approach: restoring rivers. The fight to restore the Elwha River and its salmon was a natural next step in the efforts to protect and restore fisheries. On the Elwha, local activists attacked the central issue and problem, the dams. In so doing they ushered in a new era in American environmentalism and fisheries management.

Real anger was manifested at times by citizens in the Port Angeles area. A 1949 letter to the editor was penned in high sarcastic dudgeon.

Writing in vague terms while adopting a pretense of confusion, the author expressed bewilderment at how one man suffers a long prison sentence for a minor theft, while another steals a million dollars and goes to Europe. He finally got to his point: "Two men dynamite a stream for fish and kill a few. They get 30 days in jail, [a] $50 fine and plenty of adverse publicity. Another man kills millions of fish every year and not a word is said or published. Is that justice weighed on the same scale?"[103] Arguing that a farmer who wants to irrigate has to take steps to not damage wildlife or fish (which was only partially true at that time), he got back to the issue of the lower Elwha River. "But another can lower or raise a whole river in less than fifteen minutes and he does not need any permit. For example, on Sept. 28, 1949, one of the branches of the lower Elwha River was about a foot deep and was alive with spawning salmon. On Sept. 29 the river was lowered so much that this stream was absolutely dry. What happened to the millions of fertile eggs that were spawned the day before? Is that justice? Is it just that one man can control a river which belongs to all of us, kill millions of fish each year and not even one word is whispered about? And if you or I ever even gaffed one salmon we would be convicted. I am still confused."[104]

As throughout the Northwest, the pressure was slowly increasing to do something tangible about the salmon problem on the Elwha. One 1956 letter writer to Washington State Department of Fisheries Technical Director Milo Bell (the former Corps of Engineers consulting engineer) got right to the point with both evidence and angry rhetoric. "I'm sending you 66 small salmon fry which I picked up dead," the author wrote, noting that he found them on a beach of the Elwha River. The next passage demonstrates the dam owner's complete disregard of the downstream fisheries. "I arrived at the river about 10:30 A.M. and the water was low. Then about 11:30 they raised the water up about 14 inches—and then about 1:30 P.M. the water was dropped about 12 inches and these fish were picked up at approx. 2:00 P.M. They had been stranded on the rocks of [the] beach because of lack of water. I wonder who is responsible for this destruction of small fish?"[105]

Another letter writer also sent salmon to Milo Bell. As the author lived only a few streets away from the previous scribe, it is reasonable to assume they were in cahoots. But this second letter also included a threat of sorts. "I am sending a sample of some dead fish that were picked up yesterday Sept. 3, 1956 on the Elwha River. The water was dropped Sept. 2, 1956. You will be supplied with the necessary proof when desired. There were lots of dead fish, Mr. Bell. You will receive these fish from time to time."[106]

Bell responded to the letter writers, noting their concern over water releases and stranded salmon. He also asked them to keep track of such events and to estimate fish losses, but to no longer send salmon via the mail.[107]

Who was responsible indeed? Most obviously the owners of the dam, for creating such extreme water fluctuations. But to some degree the fisheries department bore responsibility as well, for failing to resolve a known and thoroughly understood problem in the intervening decades between 1914 and 1956.

The increasing strength of the challenges to the industrial Elwha is indicated by a 1971 study of the river's fisheries and the possibilities for improving it, conducted by the Washingon Department of Fisheries but funded by Crown Zellerbach. The authors surveyed the river for its salmon-producing potential, examined the impacts of the dams on the salmon migrating upstream and smolts transported downstream through turbines, and estimated the costs of the dams in terms of lost revenue from the commercial salmon harvest. It is no surprise that the researchers deemed the river upstream of the dams as excellent habitat for salmon spawning and smolt survival. The words "excellent" and "ideal" are seen time and again in the descriptions of gravel for spawning, riffles, healthy habitat, pools for resting, and transportation corridors up the river. The authors emphasized the pristine nature of the river and watershed within the park boundaries, as later restoration activists would do. "Special emphasis must be expressed regarding the excellent salmon spawning and rearing habitat of the Elwha watershed that is within the pristine area of the Olympic National Park. Although salmon have not spawned in the upper watershed for years, the gravel is not compacted as would be expected in a logged watershed."[108]

After evaluating the potential for the river to become a major fish producer once again, the report estimated the value that could be regained by restoring merely the spring chinook, only one of the five salmon runs historically active on the river, at approximately $370,000 a year. The cost of making necessary repairs to dams and installing fish passage facilities and electrical barriers was estimated at approximately $550,000, with yearly costs of around $32,000. If these numbers are taken as approximate values, the restoration of the spring chinook alone would have offset mitigation costs in two years. They did not estimate what restoration of other chinook, sockeye, coho, pink, and chum salmon runs would generate economically, nor did they examine the impact of a restored salmon fishery on the Elwha River watershed ecosystem. They also did not estimate how restoration would impact the health of the local human populations, particularly the Lower Elwha Klallam, for whom the salmon were essential, both economically and culturally.[109]

Arguing that restoring fish to the river could be done economically and with an immediate financial benefit was one thing. Creating the means to do so was quite another. Typically, the report advocated for technological solutions to the natural problems created by the dams. The two predominant issues were grounded in two concrete barriers, the Elwha and Glines Canyon Dams. Therefore, upstream migration of spawning salmon past dams without fish passage facilities had to be resolved, as did the migration of salmon smolts downstream through turbines and over one very long drop, approximately 60 feet in the case of the Glines Canyon Dam. In order to deal with upstream passage of spawning salmon, the authors recommended using an electrical barrier dam, trapping the fish, then trucking them upstream to continue their voyage into the "pristine" upstream salmon-spawning habitat. Downstream migrating smolts presented a more complex set of challenges. The costs of screening turbines was deemed "prohibitive," so the best solution was a combination of fish passage traps in the spillways of each dam, with an effort to "smooth the spillway surface to minimize juvenile mortality during periods of spill."[110] The authors never hinted at, suggested, or mentioned dam removal—making the dramatic pace of change heralded by the call for river and fisheries restoration in the 1970s and 1980s even more remarkable.

The construction of the Elwha rearing channel by the state in 1975 was an effort to keep the lower Elwha chinook sustainable by providing them a spawning site. As part of a settlement with the Washington Department of Fisheries, Crown Zellerbach provided the funding for the channel. In a continuing effort to keep the lower river producing fish, the Lower Elwha Klallam initiated use of a hatchery in 1978. This stemmed from the famous Boldt decision of 1974, assuring Indians half of the salmon harvest, as guaranteed by treaties they signed in the 1800s. The hatchery was built to provide more fish to serve the tribe's needs. The pace of events however, suggests another point. The construction of the hatchery, and the challenging of the Federal Energy Regulatory Commission (FERC) relicensing of the dams at around the same time, supports a point made by Robert Elofson, manager of Elwha River Restoration for the tribe and a tribal member himself. He argues that the Boldt decision is not only important with regard to restoring the Indians' access to a crucial resource, but also because the requirements for managing the fishery called for increased tribal governance. Elofson suggests that the skills, knowledge, and logistical issues related to building a hatchery, and managing and building a salmon population required the development of expertise and managerial skills that strengthened the ability of the tribe to govern itself. If that is the case, it might help explain the increasing assertiveness of the tribe regarding the dams that had caused them so much trouble.[111]

The Lower Elwha Klallam were fed up. In 1976 they launched the first blow in the struggle that would lead to legislation mandating the removal of the dams to restore the river and its fisheries. Crown Zellerbach was required to seek relicensing of its Elwha project from the FERC every 50 years. The tribe filed and gained status as petitioners in the case, and moved to block relicensing of the dams for multiple reasons. This escalation in the efforts to restore the salmon of the Elwha, in opposition to the industrial users of the river and the government, took the discourse to another level. It led directly to a new step in American environmentalism: demands that the dams be removed, and that the river and its fisheries be completely restored.

Chapter 4

Meaning Runs Through It

RECONVERTING THE ELWHA
FROM INDUSTRIAL RIVER TO SALMON RIVER

*If the wild salmon can no longer survive here,
one might ask, where can they?*
Bruce Brown[1]

"Torpedo the Dams, Full Speed Ahead," declared the flyer announcing a party to celebrate the impending demolition of the two dams on the Elwha River, located on the Olympic Peninsula of Washington State, about six miles west of Port Angeles. River restoration advocates had won a startling victory in 1992 by convincing Congress to pass legislation to restore the Elwha River, including removal of both the Elwha and Glines Canyon Dams if necessary. This was the first time federal legislation had been passed for the removal of dams to restore a river and its fisheries. However, while the activists had won groundbreaking legislation and complete victory seemed imminent, the battle would drag on longer than activists could anticipate, despite ushering in a new environmental era of dam removal and river restoration.

The story behind the Elwha River activists' success is one of cooperation and creativity resulting in a broad coalition of unlikely allies. The fact that these dams were still standing nearly 20 years later reveals the continuing tension between economic development and salmon restoration in the Pacific Northwest.

While numerous environmental debates dominated the headlines in the Pacific Northwest in the 1980s and 1990s, one of the most important and heated was that over the extinction of salmon and steelhead populations and the likely future decline of runs throughout the region. The movement to restore the Elwha River and its salmon represented a remarkable environmental and political effort, which seemingly reached fruition with the passage of the Elwha Restoration Act in 1992. An examination of the Elwha restoration effort demonstrates shifts in environmental values in America and the Pacific Northwest. Of more interest is how the Elwha River was reevaluated in the modern era for nonindustrial uses, and the remarkable strategy of consensus employed to craft and pass a bill calling for restoration of the river and its fisheries.

Bruce Brown's *Mountain in the Clouds*,[2] a book exploring the history and collapse of salmon fisheries on the Olympic Peninsula, with a strong focus on the Elwha River and the episode between Darwin and Aldwell and their attempted solution, helped build support for the idea of river and fisheries restoration in the region. After his book was published, Brown even suggested in a keynote address that dam removal should be considered as an option. The idea of river restoration through dam removal began to gain traction quickly. A letter from the National Parks Conservation Association to Olympic National Park Superintendent Robert F. Chandler in March 1985 suggested the park service purchase the two dams so that they could be removed at a later date. The letter also criticized the construction of the Elwha Dam and the hatchery solution as a key factor in the destruction of Northwest salmon fisheries.[3]

It was clear that the status quo on the Elwha River could not be sustained much longer. A proposal by the administration of Olympic National Park in March 1985 for reintroduction of anadromous fish called for strong measures and private money to initiate a serious effort to restore salmon above the dams in two phases. In the opening paragraph of the report, the loss of both salmon and access to excellent habitat was emphasized, as it would be time and time again in future activist media efforts. Also, the report made the point that there was more at stake than just salmon, or the lack thereof. Because the river was one very important thread in a complex mountain watershed ecosystem, the loss of salmon above the dams created significant impacts throughout that watershed. Spawned out and decomposing salmon contributed nutrients to the river and its tributary streams and also fertilized the soil surrounding the waterways. The lack of those fish made the river, streams, and soil less fertile and less productive. This was clearly an expanding and much more ecological way of thinking about the impact of the dams on the environment, beyond just salmon survival. Moreover, the loss of salmon had negative impacts on the numerous species that depended on the fish, such as raccoons, otters, bears, ravens, and others.[4]

The Olympic National Park administration then fired the proverbial shot across the bow, foreshadowing or paving the way for arguments for dam removal, by stating that mitigation would be necessary to lower mortality rates of *downstream* migrating smolts as part of a plan to reintroduce salmon *above* the dams. The long years of ignored protest over the health of the river's fisheries were quickly drawing to a close. The report emphasized the importance of the mitigation measures and the consequences of failure. "Certain procedural changes in operation of the dams may reduce this mortality [of downstream migrating smolts]; however, if these do not reduce it to acceptable levels, additional measures will be necessary."[5]

The report then laid out the steps necessary for mitigating the Elwha fisheries. Some of these steps included: modification of the spillway on the west bank of the Elwha Dam by removing rock outcroppings and resurfacing, elimination of use of the east bank spillway during the period of downstream smolt migration, and a reduction of water flow through the west spillway during the same period. The park also insisted that both dams modify turbine operations and water release at critical times in order to reduce mortality of juvenile salmon. This was intended to protect young fish migrating downstream from above the dams, through their turbines, and then down to the Strait of Juan de Fuca. Clearly, an important shift was underway and gaining momentum. Apparently, the days of status quo acceptance of a deteriorated river and poor management of downstream water flow by the dam owners were over. The report also addressed the issue of upstream fish passage by demanding construction at the Elwha Dam of a weir for adult salmon, a short ladder, fish trap, cableway, and hopper. In addition, a fish truck loading area, truck ramps for fish release in both reservoirs, the purchase and maintenance of two trucks for the above reason, and annual funds of $30,000 to operate the facilities would also be required. The park also set a strict timetable for implementation of these improvements, emphasizing that these were "minimum measures" that would have to be expanded as necessary.[6]

REIMAGINING THE RIVER

As interest in upstream fisheries restoration, and even dam removal, gained momentum, Rick Rutz of Olympic Park Associates analyzed the possibilities of dam removal. According to political scientist Virginia Egan, "Rick Rutz began to research the feasibility of the dam removal option. Several activists in this period relate how Rutz first developed the language for an intervention and 'shopped it around' to various Seattle offices of key environmental organizations."[7] This apparently worked, because on May 15, 1986, four conservation groups—Seattle Audubon Society, Friends of the Earth, Olympic Park Associates, and the Sierra Club—also joined the groups seeking to block relicensing of the dams. Another factor in the involvement of these environmental groups was the recent passage of the Electric Consumers Protection Act (ECPA) in 1986. Mandating that environmental issues be given weight during the review of a request for dam relicensing, the legislation effectively strengthened the hand of environmentalist groups, brought more interest groups into the escalating Elwha restoration movement, and increased the likelihood that dam removal could happen. According to Egan, the environmental groups were interested in testing the ECPA, and the Elwha case seemed a perfect candidate.[8]

While there was some talk of dam removal, few Elwha advocates saw that as a real possibility. The FERC (Federal Energy Regulatory Commission) had never refused a license (thus damning a dam to removal) for environmental reasons and had proven strongly resistant to considering environmental issues in the relicensing process in general. Therefore, the focus was on using the relicensing process to force a real consideration of the salmon issue and push for extensive mitigation of the dam's impact on the fish. Although the environmental groups were granted intervenor status in relicensing, they demanded dam removal from the beginning. In the mid- to late 1980s, theirs was a minority and marginal position.

The Joint Fish & Wildlife Agencies (JFWA) and the Elwha Relicensing Steering Committee (ERSC) were organized by salmon advocates to facilitate negotiation and gain as much as possible from the FERC and dam owners Crown Zellerbach and James River Corporation. Ironically, and consistent with its history of powerlessness since 1914, the Washington Department of Fisheries, because of Darwin's earlier agreement, could not oppose relicensing the dam. They were, however, allowed to sit in on the meetings. The JFWA coordinated research on restoration, mitigation, and the feasibility and logistics of dam removal, and reviewed material and findings in order to present a consistent message and united front in the release of public information. This group also provided a forum for resolving disagreements and conflicts among the member groups.[9]

The ERSC was dedicated to the distribution and exchange of information and ideas for advocates of Elwha restoration. Meeting for the first time on October 1, 1985, the group also sought the active participation of both Crown Zellerbach and the Lower Elwha Klallam. The group continued to expand with invitations to and increasing participation by Conservation Intervenors, including those demanding dam removal. Notes Virginia Egan, "Toward the end of the FERC relicensing proceedings, as they were beginning to conclude that mitigation measures would be cost-effective for the company, representatives of JRC [James River Corporation] and Daishowa America[10] also attended."[11] (Daishowa had become owner of the Port Angeles pulp mill by this time.)

This process of coordination, cooperation, and open communication would prove critical in the efforts to restore the

Elwha. The crafting of a consensus solution reflected the mastery of those three strategies and culminated in the remarkable legislation of 1992.

Before evaluating the success of the consensus effort, it is necessary to understand the unique qualities of the Elwha. While there are many dammed rivers in the Pacific Northwest and the nation, few have generated the vociferous support expressed for Elwha restoration. The beauty of the river, its location within a national park, and the dramatic loss of a bountiful salmon fishery were all factors contributing to support of the dams' removal. Moreover, unlike the Columbia River or Snake River dams, the Elwha River dams were reasonable targets for removal and river restoration. The watersheds of many other rivers like the Snake and the Columbia have been seriously degraded under the pressure of agriculture, logging, and other resource extraction activities along with urban and suburban development. By contrast, the Elwha River's watershed is little changed since the pre-dam era. Approximately 84 percent of the watershed exists within the Olympic National Park and most of it is old-growth forest, providing abundant and healthy salmon-spawning habitat. Furthermore, the dams were of little economic significance, providing partial power for only one Port Angeles pulp mill. Strong arguments can be made for the restoration of many rivers, but the ecological health of the Elwha River watershed as well as the economic insignificance of the two dams provided a realistic scenario for dam removal and river restoration.

OF SALMON PAST AND FUTURE

The Lower Elwha Klallam tribe has lived for centuries on the banks of the Elwha River and sought to regain access to a healthy and productive river. The demise of the river occurred within two generations; fisheries manager and tribal member Rachel Kowalski recalls her grandmother speaking of the river teeming with fish. And as Kowalski states: "It's not just a matter of dollars and cents for us . . . the loss is ever present."[12] Their involvement was important for several reasons. The tribe had already challenged the relicensing of the dams on the Elwha. They were also economically and culturally dependent on the river and stood to benefit from a decision to restore the salmon runs. Additionally, the Indians of the Northwest were guaranteed the right to access and harvest fish in the treaties of the mid-19th century, as clarified by the Boldt decision of 1974, which required that salmon harvests be split evenly between Indian and non-Indian commercial fishermen. Underlying the discussion of restoring the salmon to the Elwha was the knowledge that the Lower Elwha Klallam had lost their traditional access to the salmon fisheries and that legal action was a possible outcome of this violation of treaty rights.[13]

The possibility of litigation provided the Lower Elwha Klallam and other river restoration activists with strong leverage in their endeavors to restore the river, and this potential outcome fueled efforts to remove the dams through other means. Like many Northwest Indian tribes, the Klallam suffer from high unemployment rates along with other economic problems, and see a restored Elwha River as a means to strengthen their local economy and reinforce important cultural traditions centered around the river and its fish. "The tribe has long struggled to advance its concerns regarding the subject," wrote the tribal council to Washington Governor Booth Gardner in 1989. "At issue is a devastating loss of income resulting from the destruction of the river fishery . . . The disruption of natural river flow has resulted in a loss of a valuable beach area and associated uses including shellfish harvesting."[14] Restoring what had been the very heart of the community for untold years would of course be both powerful and poignant. But pragmatic arguments were the key to getting the dams removed. A Klallam study indicated that a restored Elwha River could bring as much as $150 million to the tribe over a period of fifty years.[15]

Writers and activists pursuing river restoration celebrated the inherent aesthetic and productive characteristics of the Elwha. They generally portrayed the river as pristine, bountiful, and magnificent. A *Seattle Times* editorial advocating removal of the dams declared "that the dams decimated the Elwha's rare five-species salmon runs, including legendary giant kings that exceeded 100 pounds."[16] The emphasis throughout pro-restoration editorials, brochures, and letters was on the size and abundance of the salmon runs as well as the weight of individual chinook salmon. Indeed, the size and weight of chinooks became a focus of restoration rhetoric. "Flowing out of the heart of pristine Olympic National Park, the Elwha River once sustained all five species of Pacific salmon.[17] Giant chinook salmon weighing more than 100 pounds once spawned in the Elwha . . . two hydroelectric dams were constructed on the river, destroying its once prolific anadromous fish runs."[18] An article on the Elwha River restoration in a Friends of the Earth bulletin reinforced this narrative of abundance lost, referring to the Washington State Department of Fisheries estimates of 8,000 chinook a year and a quarter million pinks every other year, noting, "So many pink salmon used to jam into the Elwha that they once lifted a canoe right out of the water— or so the story goes."[19]

Spawning male pink salmon in the Elwha River. Courtesy of National Park Service. Olympic National Park Web site, http:// www.nps.gov/olym/naturescience/fish.htm.

This anecdotal reference to canoes being lifted out of the water resembles other archetypal stories of people crossing rivers on the backs of spawning salmon and spooked horses having to be backed across streams and rivers packed with salmon. These popular stories colorfully recall the abundance of the salmon runs and the awe they inspired in early observers; use of these anecdotes also reflects powerful nostalgic longings. Accordingly, Don Hannula of the *Seattle Times* described the historical Elwha chinook in reverent tones: "They came in spring—the biggest breed of salmon this state has known—and began their steep, grueling journey up 65 miles of river rushing from the majestic Olympic Mountains. These were the fabled giant Kings of the Elwha—salmon that tipped the scales at more than 100 pounds."[20] This prose served as the introduction to an editorial supporting Elwha restoration, and imbued the reader with a grandiose, romantic interpretation of the value of the Elwha River and its salmon. While it is tempting to believe that humans have always viewed nature in such a way, the perspective stems in fact from cultural changes over the last century and a half. The language used here to describe nature and ascribe to it particular aesthetic values can be traced to the American preservationist tradition and earlier to the romantics. The early preservationist period in American history radically changed and continues to influence the way many Americans view, talk about, understand, and, finally, use nature. It is difficult to understand the values and emotions driving the Elwha restoration movement without examining the culture of environmental preservationism, at least in a limited way.

The shadow of Sierra sage John Muir stretches long over this preservationist impulse. Muir argued that nature contained value besides that of human economic interests, and special places deserve to be set aside not only for reasons of biological health but for aesthetic and particularly spiritual reasons as well. Seeking to protect his beloved Yosemite Valley, Muir wrote:

It seems strange that visitors to Yosemite should be so little influenced by its novel grandeur, as if their eyes were bandaged and their ears stopped. Most of those I saw yesterday were looking down as if wholly unconscious of anything going on about them, while the sublime rocks were trembling with the tones of the mighty chanting congregation of waters gathered from all the mountains round about, making music that might draw angels out of heaven. Yet respectable-looking, even wise-looking people were fixing bits of worms on bent pieces of wire to catch trout. Sport they called it. Should church-goers try to pass the time fishing in baptismal fonts while dull sermons were being preached, the so-called sport might not be so bad; but to play in the Yosemite temple, seeking pleasure in the pain of fishes struggling for their lives, while God himself is preaching his sublimest water and stone sermons![21]

Clearly for Muir, as with the many preservationists who have followed him, including the environmentalists pursuing restoration of the Elwha River, nature holds an intrinsic worth, a value beyond its practical and economic usefulness to humans. While transcendentalists such as Ralph Waldo Emerson and Henry David Thoreau spoke of nature in the same language of wilderness romanticism and primitivism, it was largely through the efforts and writings of Muir that this interpretation of nature gained a wider acceptance in American culture gradually over the early 20th century.[22] Indeed, perceiving spiritual values in nature has gained greater acceptance among Americans. A 1995 sociological study of Americans' attitudes toward nature showed that Americans of different religious faiths shared an awe, reverence, and respect for nature, even finding that agnostics used the metaphor of "God's Creation" to support their environmental values.[23]

For many Americans, spiritual values are implicit in nature, particularly in places that trigger feelings of the sublime like Yosemite and the Grand Canyon. The spiritual aspect of nature represents a central impulse for preserving some natural places. Furthermore, the preservationist impulse once found in only a small segment of the American population now constitutes an integral element of contemporary environmentalism. To limit our understanding of the effort to restore the Elwha River and its fisheries to the legal motions and negotiations is supremely reductive. Any analysis that refuses to examine the whole complex weave of ideas, values, and emotions tied to nature—and particularly nature at its most magnificent, beautiful, and even monumental—is overly materialistic and, in the end, useless.

The language employed by those seeking restoration of the Elwha and its fisheries echoes the rhetoric established by Muir and other early preservationists. Letters written to Washington State Governor Booth Gardner supporting the removal of the dams in 1989 and 1990 also described the Elwha River in terms similar to those used in editorials and environmental brochures. One writer declared: "We need to restore the wonderful salmon runs that existed before these dams were built and to begin to repair the damage they have caused to this magnificent area of the Olympic National Park."[24] Another letter stated, "What is gained is a natural free-flowing Giant with return of its tremendous anadromous fish production."[25] The phrase "a legendary run of huge salmon,"[26] repeated often with slight variations, best clarifies the perceived monumental character of an undammed Elwha as expressed by environmentalists.

MONUMENTAL FISH

Preservationist attitudes are important in understanding the effort to restore the Elwha River, but other elements were in play as well. The description of the Elwha River and its salmon echoes a theme historian Alfred Runte refers to as "monumentalism." Runte argues in *National Parks: The American Experience*[27] that the urge to create parks and monuments arose in part from a strong sense of American cultural inadequacy resulting from the violent separation from Europe and its cultural legacies entailed by the American Revolution. By emphasizing the wonders of nature such as Niagara Falls, and later places like Yellowstone and the Yosemite Valley, Americans could replace the lost cultural monuments of Europe with natural monuments already available on their own magnificent continent.

Indeed, for many preservationists, the wonders of nature constituted a higher value than that of European art and architecture. John Muir wrote, in reference to the Merced Valley, "The whole landscape showed design, like man's noblest sculptures. How wonderful the power of its beauty!"[28] Americans at the turn of the 19th century viewed nature as a romantic landscape that filled a cultural niche missing for citizens of a young nation. Monumental landscapes, waterfalls, mountains, and geysers served as a replacement for the lost and longed-for European heritage of ancient cathedrals, castles, and ruins. Furthermore, these monumental places also suggested the golden future awaiting the young republic. Besides all of these reasons for setting aside and protecting monumental nature, the turmoil of the late 19th century, when the creation of national parks and monuments began, contributed to the effort to iconize certain majestic places such as Yellowstone and Yosemite. The idea was that these places also served to unify Americans as one people. This was a powerful impulse in the wake of Reconstruction's failure, the Populist movement, and the labor-capital conflicts of the 1880s and 1890s.

Monumentalism engendered a tendency to set aside lands not based on their resource values or ecological significance but, rather, for their beauty as reflected in a monumental way: towering granite cliffs, cascading waterfalls, awe-inspiring glaciers. Historian Roderick Nash articulates a similar idea when he talks about the role of wilderness in defining America in *Wilderness and the American Mind*, arguing, "In the early nineteenth century American nationalists began to understand that it was in the *wildness* of its nature that their country was unmatched."[29] As Nash explains it, Americans felt that while other countries might enjoy and celebrate a limited, tame form of nature, only Americans could brag of owning and conquering a "wild continent." The idea of wild nature being central to American identity went beyond physical challenges and abundance. According to Nash, "If as many suspected, wilderness was the medium through which God spoke most clearly, then America had a distinct moral advantage over Europe, where centuries of civilization had deposited a layer of artificiality over His works. The same logic worked to convince Americans that because of the aesthetic and inspirational qualities of wilderness they were destined for artistic and literary excellence."[30]

While arguments supporting restoration of the Elwha River stressed the significance of the ecosystem and the chance to restore a potentially complete and healthy biotic community—an increasing rarity in these days of ecosystem fragmentation—their language reflected the American tradition of monumentalism as well. It might even be that the efforts to restore nature, in this case the salmon runs of the Elwha, are driven by a nostalgia for an imagined better American past. Restoring monumental nature may be a fundamentally conservative act (in both senses of the word) insofar as it restores nature of a certain kind—in this case, an abundant fishery. Arguably, monumentalism is the cornerstone of American exceptionalism and a powerful impulse indeed. Regardless, leaders of the restoration movement realized that arguments for restoration of the river had to appeal to more than aesthetic nationalism and ecological preservation if they hoped to achieve a consensus of support for dam removal in a rural community. They needed to make sense ecologically, economically, and, finally and most problematically, politically.

BUILDING SUPPORT FOR DAM REMOVAL

While river restoration activists believed there were many good reasons for removal of the dams and restoration of the river, the political and cultural context of America and the Pacific Northwest in the 1980s necessitated a pragmatic approach, an approach that focused on building popular support for dam removal by pointing out the numerous benefits of river restoration, primarily with a focus on the potential economic benefits. The "wise use" movement of the 1980s articulated an anti-government and anti-environmental position in the West. The Reagan administration had not only abandoned and condemned the moderate environmental stewardship of earlier Republican administrations but had also moved to undermine environmental laws and agencies responsible for the environment. In the Pacific Northwest, and particularly the heavily affected Olympic Peninsula, many residents were in an uproar over the spotted owl and restrictions on harvesting of old growth timber to protect owl habitat, resulting in severe economic impacts for many logging-dependent communities. At the same time, there was a broader recognition in the region of a worsening crisis of salmon and steelhead extinction and decline, with dams perceived as the primary culprits.

In a milieu of resistance to environmentalism and concern over loss of jobs to owls and salmon, the environmental groups escalated their opposition to the relicensing process and moved toward a legislative solution. In March 1988, Olympic Park Associates, the Seattle Audubon Society, Friends of the Earth, and the Sierra Club filed a petition for the FERC to declare that it did not have jurisdiction over the Glines Canyon Dam relicensing. They also demanded that the FERC immediately "phase the proceedings." The environmental groups argued in this petition that the Federal Power Act of 1920 along with further legislation in 1935 banned dams in national parks and prevented the FERC from providing licenses for such projects. James River Corporation had argued that because part of the project (the Elwha Dam, power lines, and other related equipment) was on non-park land, the FERC had the authority to issue a license even though the Glines Canyon Dam resided within the park boundaries. The environmental groups' response to this was caustic. "Even if true, the relevance of this is difficult to discern. The statute makes no such convoluted distinction and such a construction should not be forced upon the statute without especially good reasons. Here, there are good reasons why James River's reading should not prevail."[31] The environmental groups referred to precedents in earlier cases where the FERC had declared its inability to license on national park lands.

The whole licensing process allowed the intervenors to develop more scientific material and understanding of the impact of the dams and the potential for restoration. It also enabled the groups to sort out competing and conflicting interests and organize the most effective way to move forward. Moreover, during this process it became clear to James River and Daishowa America that the costs of mitigation would be prohibitive, so they began supporting dam removal. How to best achieve this goal and overcome an intransigent FERC became the overriding question, with lawsuits seeming the best answer.[32]

In late 1990, the intervenors shifted to a new strategy. While pursuing a legal strategy before the Ninth Circuit Court would likely bring success, it wasn't certain that the court would find in favor of removal of both dams, or not split jurisdiction of the FERC over the dams between the Elwha Dam and the Glines Canyon Dam. Advocates were concerned that they could get only a partial victory. Both James River and Daishowa were concerned enough that they lobbied hard for legislation mandating dam removal. This would obviate the need for FERC cooperation while swiftly cutting the Elwha knot. Unfortunately, the Commission refused to join the removal advocates in supporting legislation, even though its own Environmental Impact Statement (EIS) research was indicating that dam removal would be necessary.[33]

Congressman John Dingell, Chairman of the Subcommittee on Oversight and Investigations to the Committee of Energy and Commerce, was a critical player in building support for this legislation and making sure it saw the light of day; without his support, the bill would never have left committee. In a 1989 letter to Democratic Congressman Al Swift of Washington's Second Congressional District, Dingell indicated that he had met with several people from the Northwest on the Elwha issue, including representatives of the Lower Elwha Tribal Council. While agreeing that the Elwha fisheries had been poorly managed for too long, he also stated that it would be impossible for him to support legislation for restoration without "a great deal more information and understanding of the impacts and consequences."[34] He had therefore asked the General Accounting Office (GAO) to study the issue and legal ramifications. "I have also written to the Secretary of the Interior and the Federal

Energy Regulatory Commission (FERC). Enclosed are copies of both letters. You may want to release them."[35] Dingell clearly sought to bring public attention to this legislation, possibly indicating that he supported further exploration of this issue if not actively endorsing the legislation.

In the letter to the comptroller general of the GAO, Charles A. Bowsher, dated the same day as the above-mentioned letter to Congressman Swift, Dingell employed activist language for restoration. In his letter, Dingell refers to the dams providing power for only one mill and being owned by one company, a key point cited often and early by restoration advocates. He also incorporates the language of "Nature Lost" so central to activists' efforts and discourse. Dingell made the common reference to all five species of Pacific salmon, and the fame of the run in terms of quantity and quality of fish. He also argued that restoration would improve the ecosystem of the Olympic National Park and Washington State anadromous fisheries.[36]

It would have been difficult for an environmental group brochure or letter from an activist to state the case much more clearly or cogently than this. In so doing, Dingell reinforced the central arguments of restoration advocates. However, and maybe more interestingly, they had clearly crafted an effective rhetoric of pragmatism and opportunity that was evocative, easily repeated and explained, and poignant. Activists employed clear, precise, and powerful rhetoric with significant impact early in their efforts.

In pursuit of the necessary information, Dingell instructed Bowsher to perform a number of tasks within 90 to 120 days. Among these tasks were the need to address legal issues regarding dam removal, a history of the dams and the river fisheries, the impact of the dams on the Lower Elwha Klallam, the impact on employment, and the deignation of who would be responsible for restoration of the fishery. He also directed the GAO to determine the jurisdictional status of the FERC regarding the Elwha dams and also whether the commission could force dam owners to mitigate for damage to fisheries.[37]

Dingell's letter to Secretary of the Interior Manuel Lujan, Jr. and FERC Chairman Martha Hesse displayed a discernible edge. Notifying them of his role in the proceeding legislation, Dingell wrote that he was concerned about the safety of the dams and their impact on the fishery. Stated worries as to who would pay for restoration were followed by a strong indictment of FERC behavior. "Foot-dragging, finger pointing, and unreasonable delay seem to prevail in this matter, while efforts toward sound and reasonable solutions seem to be eluding everyone."[38]

After bringing up the issue of jurisdiction, questioning the National Park Service's contention that the FERC lacked jurisdiction over the dams, and inquiring into the issues involved in ordering the removal of a dam, he also requested that the commission provide a detailed and comprehensive history of the dams' licensing, environmental, and safety issues. Toward the end of the letter, Dingell's rhetoric grew sharper again, like a prosecuting attorney hitting a defendant with a series of tough questions. "What actions has FERC taken under the law to restore and mitigate fishery losses from these dams? Why has FERC never apparently re-opened the licenses to deal with the fish and wildlife issues? What are FERC's plans concerning fish and wildlife under the Federal Power Act?" Dingell was clearly pushing the Commission to take the ECPA seriously, reminding the commission that it was now required by federal law to also consider environmental issues when reviewing the relicensing of a dam. He continued in his attacking vein, specifically questioning the actions of the dam owners in earlier years. "What are the responsibilities of the licensee, including prior licensees or owners, for dam safety and fishery losses? In this regard, please identify the original licensees and explain how the present owners succeeded to them under the law. Also, are the dams operated for the 'sole purpose of providing electric power to Dauhowa [*sic*] of America's pulp and paper mill?' Is that consistent with the requirements of the Act?"[39] Not only was Dingell trying to amass information, he was asking what had been done or not done to allow the situation to reach such a point.

The potential burdens of a long relicensing process, intertwined with a series of judicial rulings likely to require extensive mitigation measures, compelled Daishowa America to show more interest in a legislative solution to the Elwha salmon crisis. The concerns of the company were numerous; first among them was the desire to keep electricity costs low. One of the central reasons for buying the Port Angeles mill in the first place was the availability of cheap power (significantly lower than market costs) produced by the two dams on the Elwha, providing 40 percent of the mill's power needs. In addition to protecting its low power costs, the company also wanted compensation for investments in the dams since 1986, to avoid having to pay for mitigation requirements (estimated at $64 million at that time), and protection from any liability associated with future damage to Elwha River watershed habitat and salmon. The company had numerous incentives to take a seat at the legislative table.[40]

Daishowa was in a strong position to protect its interests and achieve the above-mentioned goals through legislation because of its prominent position in the locally depressed Port Angeles and timber economies. Nobody wanted to cost the local economy the 400 jobs at the Port Angeles plant, or to suffer the political blowback of a plant shutdown. So, all efforts were made to create legislation that would protect Daishowa and the local jobs.[41]

JOBS AND SALMON

While it is obvious that political opposition created by anticipated job losses could have stopped the restoration effort dead in its tracks, Virginia Egan makes the critical point that the earlier vociferous and ugly conflict over logging restrictions to protect spotted owl habitat informed the concern of restoration activists for protecting local mill jobs.[42] It is hard to overstate the impact of the spotted owl controversy in the Pacific Northwest. Loggers and their supporters construed the habitat and logging restrictions as the impositions of an oppressive federal government dictated to by activists more concerned with birds than the health of logging communities. Clearly, if jobs were threatened by efforts to restore rather than preserve salmon, the rhetoric and conflict would likely spin out of control. More generous actions could stave off a discourse of "environment/fish versus jobs/ livelihood" or even the coarser rhetoric of outsider environmentalists and urbanites pushing their agenda onto hardworking rural folk. That was the kind of rhetoric that had been common in the spotted owl debate and is often responsible for stasis in environmental issues.

Supporters of river restoration recognized the need to depict the restoration of the Elwha River and its salmon as a rational and economically desirable decision. While the evidence clearly supported this position, it was necessary to devise a support strategy built on reducing economic dislocations arising from dam removal. The linchpin in this effort was the "creative solution" offered by environmental activists and supported by Congressman Al Swift. One of the most vexing problems facing restoration advocates was the issue of the lumber mill powered partially by electricity from the Elwha dams, and the potential loss of jobs. While blocking relicensing seemed a promising and straightforward strategy, it also would amount to a federal "taking" and could result in a series of lawsuits delaying the removal of the dams. Elwha restoration activists sought to forge a legislative solution based on consensus instead of employing lawsuits and depending on the FERC relicensing process. Broad community support might lead to a quicker and more popular solution to the problem presented by the dams.[43]

The "creative solution" became the key to this process. This was an initiative by the restoration advocates and Congressman Swift's office, which sought to find replacement sources for the power that would be lost with the dams' removal, thereby preventing the closing of the Daishowa mill and the corresponding loss of jobs. The replacement of power at no additional cost to Daishowa left the company with no justifiable opposition to the removal of the two aging dams. Jim Baker, then the assistant Northwest representative for Friends of the Earth, argued it was important to achieve a win-win solution that would benefit all the parties concerned with the Elwha River, its salmon, and hydroelectric production. The fact that the Bonneville Power Administration (BPA) could provide replacement power at the mill and the increasing pressure brought on and by the FERC to evaluate the environmental impacts of the dams improved the chances for favorable negotiation toward a solution that would lead to the removal of the dams, with protection and benefit for the parties involved.[44]

The determination of restoration advocates to pursue consensus through the "creative solution" was reinforced by the fact that the above position was articulated after the General Accounting Office had released a legal opinion consistent with advocates' positions that the FERC could not relicense the Glines Canyon Dam, and had the authority to order removal of both dams.[45]

Those who had always depended on the river played an ongoing and persistent role; the Lower Elwha Klallam were essential to the overall success of the restoration efforts. They steadfastly insisted on dam removal at all costs. As part of their overall political strategy, the tribe agreed among themselves to give up other goals where necessary while sticking fast to dam removal. For instance, they had hoped to gain access to traditional lands on Ediz Hook for the creation of a cultural center as well as for seasonal homes, as had been their practice earlier in the century before they were displaced. However, Port Angeles, as part of its negotiations in this process, insisted on renewing its lease on the Hook, asserting that the city had plans to develop the land. The Elwha Klallam also gave up on the hope for a massive infusion of federal money for housing, as Senator Slade Gorton slashed that request from $20 million to $4 million.[46]

Along with the local Native population, Congressman Al Swift played a crucial role in the effort, particularly in building consensus for dam removal. Swift kept the support of the local community uppermost in his mind as he worked for restoration of the river. From beginning to end, he realized and fought for Port Angeles issues such as water purity, jobs, and the economy. Staff notes of a meeting in December 1991 between Al Swift and Port Angeles Mayor Jeff Palmerance stress the economic benefits that would accrue from the Elwha Restoration Act. They emphasized the importance of preserving economic security while removing the dams.[47] These notes also pointed out that water purity would be assured and restoration would lead to increases in salmon and steelhead, improving the local tourism economy. What started with a river and fish was turning into a complex plan benefiting multiple sections of Port Angeles and Elwha River regional society.[48]

When the Department of the Interior confidently announced that the FERC would not relicense and the Interior would take ownership of the Glines Canyon Dam and possibly the Elwha Dam, it was clear to members of Swift's staff that this could lead to serious economic consequences for the local community, and they chose not to follow this course.[49] Cooperation between restoration advocates and Congressman Swift provided the necessary nudge toward consensus. The owners of the Daishowa mill hesitated to allow BPA energy audits of the mill's energy efficiency and use, a necessary step in the creative solution. Environmentalists were quick to let Swift know of the mill owners' obstructionist behavior.

> *You have frequently stated to us, to the companies, to the other intervenors, and to the public that litigation over the Elwha River dams should be avoided. We agree. In the hopes of providing a basis for convening negotiations among all the principal parties, we have taken this initiative of communicating to you and to BPA our findings on energy conservation at the Daishowa mill. We respectfully urge your office to take whatever steps are feasible to persuade the principals to convene negotiations at the earliest possible date—certainly before FERC actions or other events force any party to resort to litigation over the dams.*[50]

Broad support for this effort, the real threat of legitimate legal action, FERC intervention, and pressure applied by Congressman Al Swift all convinced the mill owners to cooperate with efforts to build consensus for dam removal through application of the creative solution.

FROM RESTORING SALMON TO PUBLIC WORKS

Activists focused on achieving consensus on dam removal. Besides the creative solution, they stressed the fishery production capabilities of the river, and how that could result in dollars not only for commercial fishermen, including Indians, but also, for the local economy through increased sport fishing and tourism. They, like the Lower Elwha Klallam, relied increasingly upon economic arguments for dam removal; supporters of restoration stressed the economic contributions from dam removal and sediment removal jobs to the local Port Angeles economy.

In a struggling economy depressed by cutbacks in logging, the promise of money and jobs was an effective way to cultivate local support. "At least half of the removal cost would be pumped into the Olympic Peninsula economy in the form of wages to workers doing river restoration," stated a 1994 Department of the Interior report supporting restoration.[51] In releasing this report, Assistant Interior Secretary George Frampton Jr. pointed out the benefits of Elwha restoration for "preserving and creating jobs."[52] Specifically, the restoration would provide "$90.4 million in gross income to workers in Clallam County . . . National Park Service spokesman Joan Anzelmo said she had been involved in discussions at which the total number of jobs over the 20-year life of the project was estimated at about 1,500, with a maximum of 400 to 500 jobs at any one time."[53] Letters to the editor identified the economic benefits that could be gained from a restored Elwha River: "Restored salmon runs will generate millions of dollars of new revenue every year for sport, commercial and tribal fishing. Businesses on the Olympic Peninsula will experience large increases of tourism dollars from visitors who come to see firsthand the restoration in progress. And dam removal will also restore an attractive, free-flowing river segment, providing increased opportunities for the growing whitewater boating industry."[54]

A *Seattle Times* editorial combined the aesthetic and wilderness ideal with an economic argument, encapsulating all the values now inherent in the anticipated Elwha River, a river flowing with multiple meanings. "Restoration of salmon runs would provide an economic boost by increasing tourism for the Olympic Peninsula. A free-flowing, 70-mile [actually, closer to 42] stretch winding through

Olympic National Park would make the Elwha one of the country's great wilderness rivers."[55] The Elwha River was clearly again being asked to do a lot. The same editorial also clarified another aspect of the pragmatic strategy. In response to worries that removing Elwha dams would stimulate a widespread call for further dam removal on the Snake and Columbia Rivers, the editorial stated, "Restoration of the Elwha would set no precedent for the Columbia River and its tributaries. Hydroelectric dams on the Columbia are an essential part of the economy. The Elwha Dams pump out a piddling amount of cheap power at a heavy environmental price."[56] The editorial asserted an important point that became ubiquitous in the Elwha River restoration efforts: that the Elwha would set no precedent for dam removal on the Snake and Columbia Rivers. As the editorialist pointed out, the electricity pumped by the dams on the Columbia and Snake Rivers, not to mention reclamation projects supporting agriculture and inland navigation, implied much more significant economic costs should dams on those rivers be removed. Additionally, the Elwha River watershed is a fairly small ecosystem and, as already mentioned, remains relatively intact, healthy, and protected in a way that the Columbia and Snake rivers are not.[57]

In addition to all the other arguments for the exceptional nature of the Elwha River dams and the benefits of their removal, Olympic National Park Superintendent David Morris stated succinctly and pragmatically what made the Elwha River restoration project more promising than other projects: the fact that the "removal of the Elwha Dams would provide 'the biggest bang for our bucks.'"[58] While other issues such as environmental health and ecosystem restoration played a key role in generating restoration support, the linchpin of success was supporters' ability to prove the project would make sense economically. The issue of potential job loss was dealt with in one fell swoop—not only would jobs not be lost, they would be created by this restoration effort.

Since the 1980s' debates over the spotted owl in the Pacific Northwest, a general dichotomy had emerged in the media and public rhetoric asserting that an urban, liberal environmental movement, with values based on recreation and aesthetics, was impinging on rural, resource-extraction-based economies against the will of local blue-collar residents.[59] Just as the Lower Elwha Klallam Indians portrayed the benefits of a restored Elwha River in largely economic terms, many Port Angeles letters relied on utilitarian and resource-related arguments in favoring restoration. This is not to argue that Port Angeles residents ignored or were unaware of the aesthetic values inherent in a restored Elwha. Rather, restoration advocates in the Port Angeles area were probably more aware of economic issues and local attitudes, and they constructed their arguments for restoration with these issues in mind. They sought to build consensus around a theme of economic improvement. While this can be chalked up to strategy, it is also worth noting that as members of the community, they had to think more carefully of the impacts on friends and neighbors. Many Port Angeles residents offered strong and detailed arguments elucidating the economic benefits of dam removal. "Plans to renovate and to expand the mill need not be shelved due to dam removal. Modernization and conservation can turn the mill into a showcase of production and energy efficiency. Predictions of mill-closure related job loss can be offset by the labor requirements of the dam removal and canyon rehabilitation projects."[60]

Those supporting the restoration of the Elwha and its salmon represented a broad and varied constituency, but they shared some common beliefs and goals. Primarily, they believed that intact ecosystems are an integral part of a healthy nature; removing the Elwha River dams reflected an effort to restore a river ecosystem to wholeness. Secondly, they acknowledged that science and technology had failed to artificially propagate salmon runs and remake nature into a productive factory of biological commodities. Management of resources is essential, but must be predicated on the protection and conservation of healthy habitat. Moreover, it is necessary to restore and protect nature in such a way that ecosystems can operate successfully on their own and be sustainable. The removal of the Elwha dams and restoration of the river and its fisheries would be the culmination of a remarkable strategy and implementation of a new environmental management model. However, passage of the legislation was one step. Implementation would provide another set of difficult challenges.

RESISTANCE AND LOCAL GOVERNANCE

Despite the direction the 1992 Elwha Restoration Act seemed to be taking toward dam removal efforts, unforeseen events marked the start of a long and drawn-out journey before any real action occurred. The political support evidenced in the legislation's passage crumbled quickly after Republican victories in the 1994 congressional elections. According to the *Tacoma News Tribune*, "With budget-cutting Republicans taking over Congress, a $200 million plan to restore salmon runs by tearing down two Olympic Peninsula dams is probably dead, two members of Washington's delegation say."[61] Democratic Congressman Norm Dicks reversed his already tentative support of dam removal, and Republican Senator Slade Gorton, remarking to Dicks "Welcome to the party," embraced the Republican moment and continued his opposition to the removal of the dams.[62] Gorton, who originally voted for the Elwha Restoration Act, reversed his tentative support for dam removal prior to the 1994 congressional elections. The position of Senator Gorton was key to the future of the Elwha River because of his seniority in the Washington congressional delegation and his position on the U.S. Senate Appropriations Committee, controlling government spending.[63]

Even as Gorton stalled and proposed funding for fisheries enhancement rather than appropriating funds for the dam purchases and removal, local resistance to dam removal emerged. Following the release of the second environmental impact statement (EIS) in the summer of 1995, some local residents questioned the exclusive focus on dam removal and agitated for reopening discussion of other options such as mitigation measures short of tearing out the dams. While there had been numerous opportunities to comment and debate on the proposals presented from 1989 to 1994, these opponents, probably encouraged by the conservative turn in the nation and

Congress at the time, as well as the rhetoric of Senator Slade Gorton, threw themselves into public meetings for the implementation of the EIS draft in the summer of 1995, and both sides debated the future of the river, dams, and salmon.[64]

The group leading the opposition, Rescue Elwha Area Lakes (REAL), spearheaded by area resident Marv Chastain, was shocked and angered that something as radical as dam removal was actually being considered—and close to implementation in their own neighborhood. According to Chastain, "I thought that the idea of destroying two lakes and dams that produced power was too ridiculous to contemplate. But as time went by, I began to realize it *was* being contemplated and it probably was going to happen."[65] The group began organizing around early 1994. At a January 25, 1994, gathering held at Aggie's Restaurant in Port Angeles, approximately 120 people attended an informational meeting aimed at stopping dam removal. Organized by United We Stand America and Chastain, the attendees first watched a movie produced by REAL, laying out their criticisms of the restoration plan. In one of the more familiar arguments, the film declared that the lakes hosted an abundant and diverse wildlife population (including trumpeter swans) and should be preserved as ecosystems for their value. The film also stated the Secretary of the Interior had said on multiple occasions that he was eager to press the plunger and blow up the dams, that removing the dams would necessitate the purchase of power from other, more expensive sources, and that silt from the restoration would destroy what salmon did remain in the lower river.[66]

In addition to the impact of downstream silt, the film raised the oft-stated concern of dam removal opponents that unsightly and smelly mudflats would be exposed, reducing property values and creating an unappealing aesthetic. This particular concern has been proven false in numerous cases where raised, such as dam removals in Maine and Wisconsin, but they could not know that in 1994, before dam removals began happening on a regular basis. Concerns over the diminishment of water quality and damage to local wells were articulated in the film, as was Marv Chastain's consistent refrain that there is plenty of spawning gravel in the lower river, a patently false claim. Finally, the film advocated fish ladders and expressed concern over what the real costs of this project would be.[67]

The post-film discussion was animated and ranged from reasonable concerns to the paranoid. For example, sensible points were made and questions asked regarding the impact of sediments downstream, the costs of restoration, and whether 100-pound salmon would actually return to the Elwha. Paranoia kicked in with assertions that the government really wanted to shut down the local mills, that the Olympic National Park was using this to expand, and that "a very powerful group of people in this country merely want to trash the Olympic Peninsula."[68] The references to park expansion and land grabs reflect ongoing tensions over the recent restrictions of logging public lands to protect the spotted owl, as well as even older local debates over park boundaries and resource access and use dating back to the late 19th century.[69]

REAL was able to gain the interest or support of approximately 300 people and donations amounting to around $3,000, which then was used to hire a consultant to analyze the government reports produced during the research, planning, and implementation process. In the end, they responded in the traditional way—recommending preserving the status quo with techno-optimistic solutions such as screens, fish ladders, trap and haul programs, and such. No matter that the research for the restoration had ruled these options out as ineffective, nor that these "solutions" were failing on rivers throughout the Pacific Northwest; the focus was on keeping the dams right where they were.

In what some might see as a postmodern move, REAL argued that the second nature of the Elwha River dams and reservoirs should be protected from a return to first nature (or third nature?) because of the natural values embodied in the harnessed Elwha River. Moving away from the shock of the idea that dams might actually be removed, taking away precious electrical power, REAL argued that new wetlands and reservoirs had been created by the dams and species dependent on these, such as lake and rainbow trout and migrating waterfowl, would be damaged by dam removal. The rest of the group's arguments against the proposed dam removal were based on several issues: questions over whether restoration would actually work; a belief that the downstream habitat was a good one for chinook salmon—although fisheries biologists had substantively explained why it was bad habitat (not enough cobble, too warm, flow problems, etc.); and a belief that the city might need the power produced by the dams in case of an emergency—although the power generated by the dams was barely enough to run the Port Angeles hospital. The "in-case-of-emergency" argument echoed those of the Inland Empire Waterways Association that the lower Snake River dams should be built in case the Cold War turned into a hot war.[70]

With this vocal, conservative, minority opposition, Slade Gorton seemingly had his proof that locals opposed dam removal. More than happy to construe the Elwha dam removals as the urban, liberal elite imposing their will on poor, benighted, underrepresented, less-urbane types (an argument that plays well in rural Washington State) who "work for a living," Gorton tapped into or manipulated some of the ongoing local animosities against federal power and Pugetopolis recreationalists. This also helped fuel ongoing anger from the earlier spotted owl controversy that created so much division on the Olympic Peninsula. Clearly the local community, the average Port Angeles folk, would never really support something as radical and unjustified as the removal of two perfectly good dams. Demanding a community-based plan for the Elwha (thereby trying to pit the locals against the outsider environmentalists) that he assumed would substantiate his assertions, Gorton unwittingly opened the door to the next stage of the Elwha restoration process. The Elwha Citizens Advisory Committee would demonstrate that the restoration plan had greater support than Gorton assumed and would likewise defy simplistic categorizations of environmental efforts as urban-based policies imposed against the will of rural residents.[71]

PORT ANGELES WEIGHS IN

Despite these political setbacks, advocates of restoration pushed forward with their plans. Those seeking restoration, including environmentalists, the Lower Elwha Klallam, and federal agencies such as the National Park Service and U.S. Fish and Wildlife Service, continued their efforts to restore the river, creating a plan for restoration in 1994 and an implementation plan published in April 1996. Both plans strongly urged complete removal of both dams, removal of accumulated sediments, replanting of indigenous plants in the old reservoir beds, and moderately aggressive salmon restocking programs. However, most of the funds to accomplish this would have to be appropriated by Congress, and Senator Slade Gorton blocked every attempt to earmark funds for this effort.

The Clinton administration lent its support in 1996, probably for legitimate environmental reasons as well as to improve relations with environmentalists angered by his signing of the salvage logging rider. Gorton sustained his opposition to the Elwha Restoration plan, saying that President Clinton was "proposing that we sacrifice Hanford jobs in the Tri-cities but spend millions of dollars to tear down dams on the Peninsula."[72] This seeming non sequitur reflected Gorton's efforts to perpetuate the idea of job losses associated with environmental policies and projects, and to always align the Elwha River restoration with the Columbia and Snake rivers. Job loss was not an issue in the case of the Elwha River plan. Certainly Hanford had nothing to do with the Elwha.

Democratic Senator Patty Murray strongly favored river restoration and was joined by Republican Representative Rick White, who suggested taking money from Columbia River salmon programs to use for Elwha restoration. In 1996, support for dam removal became more pronounced, with Interior Secretary Bruce Babbitt stepping up his efforts to have the dams removed and Olympic National Park Superintendent David Morris calling for their removal as well.[73] Bruce Babbitt made a trip to the Elwha River in 1997, seeking to reinvigorate the issue but also enunciating a more cautious approach than in 1994, mindful of the need to win Senator Gorton to the cause again. Cautious due to the firestorm he had earlier ignited with ranchers, farmers, and industrial interests in the West with calls for dam removals, Babbitt repeatedly stated that the destruction of the Elwha dams would provide no precedent for other dam removals.[74] The considerable power and influence of Gorton in resolving the Elwha restoration battle was demonstrated by his effectively blocking funding for several years, as well as by the words of Babbitt in 1997: "The bottom line is that Senator Gorton is a guy who would be likely to have the final say on this issue."[75]

While evaluating the actions of politicians is central to understanding the progress of activists in restoring the Elwha River, it is equally important to consider an interesting development in the Port Angeles community. The Elwha Citizens Advisory Committee, a group assembled in Port Angeles to offer formal advice on the Elwha issue, announced its support of river restoration, although it called for a 13-year restoration timeline rather than rapid dam demolition and restoration. The decision of this committee to support river restoration through dam removal represents the success of the consensus effort pursued by restoration activists, and demonstrates the degree to which Slade Gorton's political maneuvering violated the popular will. At this point, Gorton and other opponents' tired but still-effective accusations of urban environmentalists attacking rural communities for questionable goals proved untrue, for this committee was not some gathering of wild-eyed Port Angeles "tree-huggers." Rather, it represented the more traditional and conservative elements of the community. One member, Jerry Newlin, was president of NTI Engineering and Surveying Company as well as president of the Clallam County Economic Development Council. Bart Phillips was executive director of the Clallam County Economic Development Council and spokesperson for the group. Clearly, the economic interests of Port Angeles were well represented on this committee.[76]

Although originally opposed to dam removal, the committee ultimately arrived at a consensus advising dam removal over an extended time period. Through a process of education and inviting people concerned about the Elwha issue to speak up via debates and public meetings, the group decided dam removal made the most sense for the Port Angeles community. The support of the advisory committee demonstrated not only the effectiveness of the consensus strategy but also the pragmatism of the dam removal and river restoration plans. Furthermore, the creation of legislation for river restoration and the support for this project illustrates a remarkable process of democracy and compromise in action.

ECOLOGICAL DEMOCRACY IN ACTION

The committee's report, "The Elwha River and Our Community's Future," was released on April 30, 1996, and must have shocked Slade Gorton while offering general relief to restoration advocates. Gorton's probable assumption, based on his career rhetoric that rural Washingtonians would automatically oppose environmentalism generally and dam removal specifically, was shattered by the report's endorsement of dam removal and fisheries restoration. But this was not a simple endorsement for immediate removal of both dams as proposed and imagined by the National Park Service. This was a more complex proposal that the committee members believed was more realistic than the Park Service plan, a position that has since been validated.

Noting the importance of the salmon culturally, economically, and ecologically for the broader Elwha River ecosystem, the authors supported restoration but believed that financing would prove problematic. Hence they proposed an extended, sequential, and somewhat complex model of restoration and dam removal that protected the numerous interests of the community, would be successful over the long term, and most important, was also more economically pragmatic. Arguing that the "case for dam removal is compelling," the committee also made the now notably prescient case that financing the removals would be problematic. "The climate in Congress clearly does not favor such an extreme and expensive idea. For Congress, there may be some willingness in the future to consider removal subject to adequate funding. This would be more plausible if the Elwha Restoration Fund is successful . . . "[77]

Because they believed federal funding was highly unlikely, the committee members proposed an Elwha Restoration Fund financed by park dollars, revenue from power generated by the dams once they were owned by the park, federal appropriations, and state money. Financing the restoration in such a way would allow for steady, slow progress but would also build momentum and show the commitment of the community to restoration. This was not the clean, immediate solution favored by restoration activists but it did reflect the opinion of the community and also demonstrated both caution and optimism regarding the realities and benefits of Elwha restoration.

Political scientist William R. Lowry explains the complexity and nuance of the committee's proposal in *Dam Politics*. He argues that the proposal was "appealing" because the committee wanted to reduce the initial cost to the federal government and minimize the effect on the Port Angeles economy. It also recognized that immediate removal of both dams would likely damage the Elwha River's native salmon stock. While noting that hatcheries could be employed to supplement the fish population and reduce losses, the proposal also argued for active dredging of sediments to hasten the process and reduce in-river turbidity.[78]

Regardless of this flowering of ecological democracy in Port Angeles, the heated nature of environmental debate, the fear of the ramifications of successful river restoration by opponents, and the determined opposition of one senator all undermined the committee's 1996 restoration plan for the Elwha River and blocked the democratic will of the Port Angeles community.

WILL THE DAMS COME TUMBLING DOWN?

For a time, the senator seemed to be swayed by the tide of popular support for the restoration, switching positions again in 1998, perhaps temporarily convinced by the endorsement of the Elwha Citizens Advisory Committee for dam removal. In early 1998, President

Clinton announced that $86 million would be appropriated in the 1999 budget for removal of the lower dam and partial restoration. Furthermore, President Clinton stated that he would seek $13 million the following year to remove the Glines Canyon Dam. Meanwhile, Senator Gorton attempted to use support of Elwha restoration as a way to prevent dam removals on other rivers, stating that his support for removal of the Elwha River Dam would be contingent on two major stipulations. One was that 12 years pass before the removal of the Glines Canyon Dam, in order to ascertain the effectiveness of removal and restoration on the lower river—a seemingly reasonable request. However, postponing removal of the upper dam would only perpetuate continuing problems regarding lack of gravel recruitment and suitable spawning habitat for salmon—something that any fisheries biologist or anyone minimally educated on river ecosystems understands. Without concurrent removal of the Glines Canyon Dam, the restoration effort would be of limited effectiveness. His second stipulation was that the Elwha River dams could not be removed without a guarantee that Columbia and Snake River dams would not be removed, revealing his larger concern. While Gorton finally seemed to consider the local community's mandate, his tentative and qualified support for Elwha Dam removal was merely part of a larger strategy of blocking other, larger environmental programs, and preventing the precedent of dam removal for salmon.

Debate over breaching dams on the lower Snake River in the late 1990s convinced Gorton to switch positions on the Elwha yet a third time. Environmentalists, predicting the demise of inland steelhead and salmon stocks, demanded the breaching of four lower Snake River dams, and agriculturalists, industrialists, politicians, and others quickly organized an effort to block them. The debate over the dams on the lower Snake was integral to Elwha restoration because Gorton was able to employ his position on the Appropriations Committee. Funding leverage for the Elwha River restoration would require surrender on the current debate over Snake River dams and prevent any such demands for removal of Columbia River dams in the future.

This strategy reveals the tendency of conservative politicians and industry to see environmentalists as one bloc or movement, rather than recognizing the local character and legitimacy of specific efforts, such as the one on the Elwha. This type of thinking necessitates a victory-at-all-costs mindset, with the presumption in this case that any defeat would lead to the demolition of many more dams. It typifies the strong conservative response to many dam removal efforts.

Formalizing his strategy, Gorton did indeed introduce legislation in the spring of 1998 requiring that funding of Elwha restoration be contingent on a pledge that no dams would be removed from the Snake or Columbia Rivers in the future. He used the removal of the Elwha River dams—regardless of the decision of the local community and the actions of Congress—as leverage to ensure the continued survival of dams on the Columbia and Snake Rivers. This legislation ultimately failed, but inflamed the debate over dams on the lower Snake River and delayed funding for the Elwha River dam removals and for necessary research and planning for several years. What Senator Gorton accomplished was to create a level of inaction that has prevented Elwha restoration for almost two decades following the passage of the Elwha Restoration Act.[79]

Several arguments were made for restoring the Elwha and its salmon runs. However, the primary approach enabling an effective coalition of support for restoration was the argument that removing the dams made sense economically as well as ecologically. The political maneuvering by Gorton that blocked removal of the dams and restoration of the river had little to do with the process that resulted in the passage of the 1992 legislation. Continued delay in river restoration has been the unfortunate by-product of the debate over breaching other, larger dams and an unwillingness to take bold steps to restore salmon runs. But the dams have been removed and the river and fisheries restoration has begun. This reflects a quiet nationwide effort to remove hundreds of ecologically damaging and economically useless or marginal dams to restore aquatic ecosystems.

The efforts to remove the Elwha dams reflected the increasing strength, complexity, and creativity of the American environmental movement in the late 20th century. Similarly, these undertakings also denote at least a temporary high-water mark as environmentalists took on seemingly sacrosanct targets—dams—as powerful symbols and tools of industry and development. The campaign to remove the Elwha dams incorporated environmental and economic arguments, a creative solution, and determination to build consensus in support of restoration. The overall goal of the dam removal effort was the reconstruction of a functional and productive ecosystem, reflecting a broader trend nationally and an increasing sophistication of American environmentalism. While the dam removal program is important insofar as it demonstrates the strength and sophistication of the environmental movement, both regionally and nationally, what is of particular importance is the goal of ecological restoration. In the late stages of industrial capitalism, Americans are positioned to evaluate the economic benefits of dams versus their environmental impacts, specifically analyzing particular dams on rivers and watersheds across the nation. The result, as intended with the Elwha effort, attempts redress, removing dams that provide little economic benefit yet perpetuate intensive ecological damage. Possibly the most important lesson of the Elwha River restoration campaign is that 150 years after the beginning of industrial capitalism in America, it is possible to address environmental deterioration in an intelligent and cooperative manner. "Torpedo the dams, Full speed ahead" may have been a cry of victory that failed to anticipate resistance to change. But it captured the spirit of a movement seeking to find the proper balance between economic development and environmental health.

Conclusion

Find the River

RESTORATION AND THE NEW ELWHA RIVER

The river glideth at his own sweet will
from "Composed upon Westminster Bridge,
September 3, 1802"
William Wordsworth

This book landed on bookshelves mere months after the dams were removed. Even as the Elwha's story found readers, and the author checked the book's rank on Amazon, the first salmon began nosing their way past the old dam sites into an expansive river ecosystem of salmon possibilities.[1] We are left wondering: what is the importance of the Elwha River and its restoration?

First, from a historical perspective, following the story of this river and its short period of development and industrial use allows for an examination of attitudes regarding nature in American society in general, and the Pacific Northwest specifically. By studying the history of the river, it becomes clear that American ideas about nature have changed radically over time, reflecting dramatic and sometimes unthinking economic growth, the emergence of important and popular ideas about ecology, the role of a healthy nature in human society, and the necessity to restore ecosystems where at least practical and necessary. The second part of the question's answer springs from the issue of restoration.

My job would be easy if I could say that the efforts to restore the Elwha River and its fisheries led to the dams being promptly razed and the fish runs at least partially restored, allowing me to argue that this very action had initiated the beginning of an active era of dam removal and habitat restoration across the nation. Of course, reality and history are often too complicated for an elegant narrative getting us from there to here.

In the current era of environmental crisis, with an increasing emphasis on ecological restoration, the Elwha River restoration effort played a key role in opening a discourse on dam removal in the United States. Hundreds of dams around the country have been removed, including major projects such as the Quaker Neck Dam on the Neuse River in North Carolina, and dams on Bear Creek in Oregon, Mad River in California, and various sites in Wisconsin, with consistently successful fishery restoration. The fish return every time, and in healthy to astounding numbers, proving the legitimacy of dam removal as a restoration strategy.

When the discussion of dam removal on the Elwha began in the mid-1980s, removal was perceived as a radical and unprecedented move. Moreover, it seemingly required a unique and powerful set of circumstances, as presented in the Elwha case, to even contemplate the removal of functioning dams. Yet, by the late 1990s, as a furious debate raged over the future of dams on the lower Snake River, activists were pushing hard to remove numerous other dams around the nation. By tilting their lances at these watermills and providing a model of challenge and strategy for taking on dam companies and the FERC, the Elwha restoration activists helped usher in a new era of dam removal and river and fisheries restoration. The revolutionary change in discourse—demanding dam removal for fish restoration on the Elwha River with accompanying legislation—proved the success of such activism and helped launch efforts nationwide to remove dams to restore fisheries.

A remarkable momentum has developed in the years since the early 1990s. There has been a large-scale and highly successful effort to remove small dams throughout the country and even some large dams in various regions. According to the environmental organization American Rivers, at least 465 dams have been removed with approximately 100 more slated for removal or under serious consideration. This is not a large percentage in a nation with about

The Elwha Dam in 2011. Courtesy of Jeff Crane

75,000 dams, but it does represent a fundamental shift in thinking and ecological priorities.[2]

Better understanding the role of the Elwha fight in the current era, and its role in American environmentalism, as well as grasping a fundamental shift in environmental activism and American attitudes about development and nature, necessitates a look east toward a river running the opposite direction of the Elwha.

HOW A RIVER IN MAINE CONNECTS TO THE ELWHA

Today kayakers and canoeists travel the flow of the Kennebec River in Maine, past the old mill site on the southern bank in Augusta. Below them shad, striped bass, herring, and alewives all migrate upstream to the next dam in the river. Five-foot-long short-nose sturgeon break the surface of the water, then plummet back. Fishermen revel in the great runs surging up to Waterville and beyond.

It hasn't always been like this. What brought this river back to life was in great part due to the removal of Edwards Dam—an action made possible by a change in federal laws regulating pollution and the uses of nature, a group of committed activists who could envision a restored Kennebec, and a remarkable process of negotiation and compromise at the local and state levels to put it all together. The fishery restoration project on the Kennebec is a stunning success—to this date, environmentalists' strongest evidence of the efficacy of dam removal for fisheries restoration. Two years following the removal of Edwards Dam, over 1,000 juvenile American shad were collected upstream of the dam site, and many of these appear to have originated from wild stocks migrating upstream.[3]

Both the FERC decision not to relicense Edwards Dam and the actual removal of the dam generated increased cries for dam removal and general euphoria on the part of river restoration activists. Upon the removal of Edwards Dam, Peter Rafle, then director of communications for Trout Unlimited, declared, "We are going through a process of re-evaluating how we value rivers. Obviously, in the developmental stage of this country rivers were primarily a means of transportation and a source of power for industrial development. They still serve those purposes, but I think less so, and we are learning anew to appreciate the other things rivers can offer."[4] Margaret Bowman, director of American Rivers, stated, "It [removal of Edwards Dam] is a very important symbol; it symbolizes how reasonable and practical dam removal can be for river restoration."[5]

The active removal of the pieces of infrastructure that power the industrial economy (many of them from the beginning days of that very economy, like Edwards Dam, built in 1837) is a powerful and symbolic act. Such acts of ecological restoration show the development of the American environmental movement and suggest a process by which philosophy and environmental action are joined in recognizing that an ethical consideration of the rights of nature as well as the desires of humans sometimes necessitates dismantling that which Americans had so proudly built many years before.

THE FIGHT TO RESTORE THE KENNEBEC

In the middle of the 20th century, the Kennebec River was simply too polluted to consider restoring a healthy fishery in the river. The Clean Water Act of 1972 helped bring the river slowly back to life, as did the ending of log drives on the Kennebec in the mid-1970s. These two developments, the result of decades of environmental efforts, brought some semblance of ecological health back to the Kennebec. As the river slowly recovered, residents of the valley began imagining a free-flowing river with Edwards Dam removed. Efforts to make the river "swimmable and fishable" between 1972 and 1990 cost the state of Maine over $100 million for water treatment facilities; by 1990 the river was believed to be 95 percent cleaner than it had been in 1972.[6] While the river still suffered from some pollution problems, it increasingly resembled a healthy river ecosystem, leaving an old dam in Augusta as the final challenge to restoring the river and its fish populations.

The cleanup of the river water was a critical first step in the restoration of the river itself. Advocates and government representatives took the second critical step by boldly proposing the removal of Edwards Dam to complete the restoration of the lower portion of the river and its fish. The Edwards Dam battle was similar to that of the Elwha in many ways. Environmental groups worked together on a focused strategy and recruited the assistance of fisheries experts in state and federal government. Furthermore, they sought to craft a solution that gained the support of the wider community. While the residents of the Kennebec River Valley were more divided over this dam removal than were residents of the Olympic Peninsula, a clever and pragmatic solution in the Kennebec Valley helped build the necessary support. As with the Elwha, activists found ways to offset the economic losses from removing Edwards Dam. Unlike the Elwha case, however, negotiations broke down in Maine. Activists and the state of Maine finally chose opposing the relicensing of Edwards Dam by the FERC over crafting a legislative solution. Their strategy, while seemingly less democratic, would in fact in the end be more effective than the consensus strategy adopted for the Elwha River effort.[7]

Fisheries biologists had already been working for years to bring healthy fish populations back to the Kennebec River. In fact, when a flood breached Edwards Dam in 1974, Thomas Squiers, a fish biologist in the Maine Department of Marine Resources, approached the governor and asked him to block efforts to repair the dam so fish could gain access to upstream habitat. Too far ahead of the cultural shift regarding dams and fisheries, his request fell on deaf ears.[8]

In 1985 fish biologists again embarked on a plan for fish restoration on the Kennebec. "The Strategic Plan for the Restoration of Shad and Alewives to the Kennebec River above Augusta" sought to increase alewife production to 6 million a year above Augusta and also to "achieve an annual production of 725,000 American shad above Augusta."[9] In order to better facilitate this plan, the Maine Department of Marine Resources crafted cooperative agreements with dam owners on the Kennebec River. All the dam owners signed agreements except Edwards Manufacturing Company, the owner of Edwards Dam. The agreements called for owners to provide funding for a fish trap, truck, and release program for the alewives and shad to help them get around the dams. By providing funding for this program, the Kennebec Hydro Developers Group (KHDG) would be allowed to delay the implementation of fish passage facilities at their dams.[10] The refusal of Edwards Manufacturing Company to join this project presented a problem for fisheries restoration efforts because Edwards Dam was the most damaging in the Kennebec River ecosystem. This refusal to cooperate probably reflected Edwards Manufacturing Company's assumption that the government would continue to support economic interests over ecological concerns, as it had for the previous century and a half.

However, efforts to restore fisheries gained enough momentum to compel the owners of the dam to begin construction of a $200,000 fish passage facility in the 1980s. At that point, supporters of fish restoration were not talking about dam removal, but were specifically pointing out the possible economic value of a healthy Kennebec River fishery. In supporting the fish passage facility, Representative Donald V. Carter argued that a healthy sport fishing industry could help the local economy, and that Maine needed to use its clean air and open spaces to improve life for its residents. While the proposed fish collection, sorting, and passage facility reflected growing interest in fisheries restoration on the Kennebec, it also represented the continuation of the old, traditional reliance on technological fixes before the era of dam removal began.[11]

When, in 1989, a coalition of sportsmen's groups and environmentalists declared their intention to pursue removal of Edwards Dam, many perceived this goal as quixotic, although activists believed that removal of the dam would be the most effective way to restore the fisheries.[12] Very few others spoke of dam removal in 1989, although the Elwha River activists were aggressively pursuing a similar goal far to the west in Washington State. The idea of removing hydroelectricity-producing dams for fish restoration was thought to be simply preposterous. The head of the Natural Resources Council and the publisher of *Maine Sportsman* both agreed that dam removal would be the best solution for the river ecosystem, yet also asserted that gaining control of the dam through the FERC process and then removing it would be "a long shot."[13] But the river restoration advocates moved forward on their plan. At the center of the restoration effort, the Maine Natural Resources Council and the Kennebec Chapter of Trout Unlimited formed the Kennebec Coalition and made a long-term financial commitment to the campaign. Support from the Atlantic Salmon Federation and from American Rivers was also key to the early development of the coalition and its campaign.[14] The Kennebec Coalition hoped to block relicensing of the dam when the license came up for renewal in 1993. They moved quickly to put together the legal muscle necessary to file objections with the FERC, to conduct extensive research to accurately depict the ecological and economic impacts of the dam on the river and the community, and to conduct a public education campaign to build grass-roots support.[15]

While advocates of dam removal made their intentions clear, Edwards Manufacturing Company, the owners of the dam, notified the FERC that they intended to spend $30 million to increase the dam's generating capacity from 3,500 kilowatts to 18,000 kilowatts. They also stated that they intended to install a "state-of-the-art fish passageway."[16]

Fish passage technologies had been tried in the past with little success. For example, a fish pump installed in the dam in 1988 had proved of little value, and in late 1989 the Department of Marine Fisheries publicly criticized the Edwards Manufacturing Company for allowing the destruction of thousands of downstream migrating alewives in the dam's turbines.[17] Blaine Harden, a reporter for the *Washington Post* and author of *A River Lost*, described the dam and its impact on the river and Augusta in passionate prose: "The dam cheats both fish and electricity consumers while funneling the bulk of its benefits into the pocket of a company that employs just four people. It does not control floods. It irrigates no fields. Its turbines produce one-tenth of 1 percent of Maine's power needs, which is sold at three times the going rate for electricity in the state. And the dam halts upstream passage for nine species of migrating fish. Even Mark Isaacson, a vice president for the company that owns Edwards, conceded . . . that 'it is hard to make a public-policy argument in favor of this dam.'"[18] A dam of little value degraded a river to provide an insignificant amount of expensive electricity and profit for one small company. A decision that may have made economic sense in the Market Revolution at the heart of the 19th century now clearly made no sense in the late 20th century post-industrial economy of Augusta.

In 1990, Maine Governor John McKernan supported the removal of Edwards Dam even while the Edwards Manufacturing Company participated in concurrent negotiations with the City of Augusta and the Maine state government in an effort to preserve its dam. *Kennebec Journal* reporter Ken Brack characterized the Edwards Manufacturing Company as a "wily adversary" whom many believed was playing the state government against the City of Augusta in an effort to preserve the dam. Governor McKernan raised the stakes by threatening to use eminent domain to condemn and remove the dam. Passage of a bill giving the Atlantic Sea Run Commission authority to remove the dam would give the state negotiating power with the dam owner. Ron Kreisman, who was counsel for the Maine Natural Resources Council and a key player in the efforts to remove the dam, criticized the Edwards Manufacturing Company's tactics when he said, "We have always felt they want to drag out the licensing process as long as possible and are not serious about a new project." The willingness of the Edwards Manufacturing Company to use numerous ploys in the face of restoration efforts necessitated an increasingly interventionist and aggressive approach by river restorationists and the state.[19]

Meanwhile the City of Augusta was working out a deal to become a co-licensee with Edwards. In turn, for helping the Edwards Manufacturing Company obtain its new hydroelectric license, the City of Augusta would gain a portion of the electricity sales, which could have amounted to between $40,000 and $80,000 a year for the city coffers. Furthermore, as part of the plan, Augusta would have the option of buying the dam in 1998. Central to this agreement were the proposals by the company to improve the dam, greatly increase hydroelectric generation, and install improved fish passage facilities. Clearly, the Edwards Manufacturing Company believed that accepting the city as a partner was the key to preserving the dam and their profits. They were also willing to move from their long-term intransigence on fishery issues and improve fish passage in the interest of keeping the dam in place.[20]

During these negotiations, fisheries biologist Thomas Squiers accurately predicted that removal of the dam would increase aeration of the river and would improve the river for striped bass populations.[21] The national environmental group American Rivers announced their support for McKernan's plan in March, 1990. They supported the state's use of eminent domain to condemn and acquire the dam and predicted that intervention in the FERC relicensing process would only extend the process unnecessarily, an accurate prediction of the effort that would eventually stretch out over another nine years.[22] Dam removal advocates turned to the FERC arena after Edwards petitioned to relicense the dam in 1990 and Governor McKernan broke off negotiations with the company, asking the commission to deny the relicensing petition. The governor believed that Edwards was no longer negotiating in good faith over the future of the dam and river.[23] From that point on, the effort to restore the river and remove Edwards Dam focused on the relicensing process.

In their public education campaigns, the Kennebec Coalition and Maine state government strategically chose to emphasize the positive goal of river restoration rather than the negative goal of dam removal. Research provided an important foundation for this process, as the coalition had to demonstrate the historical fish numbers and varieties on the river to make a compelling case regarding the ecological impacts of the dam and the possibilities of restoration. While they worked to produce high-quality, well-researched reports for the FERC, Kennebec Coalition activists also produced sizable crowds at public hearings on the relicensing. "We turned out large numbers of people, primarily from the Kennebec Chapter of Trout Unlimited coordinating them, enabling them to speak articulately . . . we . . . worked very hard to coach a lot of the people, asking them to be respectful, to be patient, to talk from their heart."[24]

The release of the FERC's draft Environmental Impact Statement (EIS) in 1991, calling for the construction of fish passage facilities, a solution that had failed so often in the past, energized the coalition to step up its efforts. The Kennebec Coalition responded by hiring consultants and working more closely with federal agencies to craft stronger technical arguments supporting removal of the dam. The coalition also used consultants to counter arguments raised by defenders of the dam, including assertions that dam removal would be costly, cause riverbank erosion, and increase downstream flooding.[25]

Like the Elwha River restoration advocates, the Kennebec Coalition stressed the particular qualities of the dam and the river that justified dam removal. Like the Elwha and Glines Canyon Dams, Edwards Dam was relatively insignificant as a power producer, providing only 3.5 megawatts of power. The dam was old and relatively unstable, having been breached as recently as 1974 and many other times in its history. Furthermore, the dam blocked critical upstream habitat and miles of rivers and creeks that could contribute to fisheries production, as did the Elwha and Glines Canyon Dams.

Therefore fisheries advocates were able to make both economic and environmental arguments for removal of Edwards Dam. Like Elwha advocates, they argued that the economic benefits of a restored fishery would outweigh the benefits of a dam that produced little power but created insurmountable ecological problems. It was clear as well that the economic benefits of a restored fishery would be more widely distributed than the profits from the dam, which went only to the owners of the Edwards Manufacturing Company.

Edwards opposed dam removal for obvious reasons; they wanted to continue reaping the profits rendered from the high electric rates garnered through a contract signed during the 1970s oil embargo. Reasonably enough, they also feared being forced to pay for the removal of the dam. In an economy where businessmen and women rarely pay for the externalities of their business, the owners of the dam were unwilling to consider the prospect that they bore responsibility for damage to the environment or could be forced to pay for the destruction wrought by the dam on the river and its fisheries.

As co-owners, the Augusta city government supported the company's desire to keep the dam, deriving profits and tax revenue from its operation. And there were other property concerns that prompted the city government to support Edwards. According to interim City Manager Dave Jowdry, "Are there riparian rights for landowners in the 17 miles above the dam? Many of these people—residents of Augusta, Sidney, Vassalboro, Winslow, and Waterville—purchased riverfront property and may have the expectation that there will be water in the river. That may not be part of FERC's deliberation, but we should be sensitive to the concern."[26] Faced with a landmark proposal to remove a dam, the city government chose to support a continuing business interest and practice caution.

As events progressed, the owners of Edwards Dam eagerly cast themselves as victims of organized environmentalists bent on the widespread removal of dams nationwide. As Mark Isaacson of Edwards Manufacturing Company opined, "They are very interested in establishing a precedent for dam removal . . . the dams they really want to remove are not on the Kennebec but in the Pacific Northwest and they thought we'd be a good place to begin. We're a small, private company with four employees."[27] While this statement portrayed the dam owners as victims, a status the original dam builders would have hesitated to claim with their visions of glory and wealth, Isaacson was accurate in his estimation of an emerging national dam removal effort with the Elwha dams in the Pacific Northwest preceding the Kennebec efforts. However, his assertions of a vast environmental conspiracy were broadly overstated. The Kennebec restoration effort was an organic movement conceptualized, organized, and completed by members of the local community who sought to improve the river and their own quality of life.

Perhaps the Edwards Manufacturing Company earned its status as an antagonist to the maturing environmental movement since the company had earlier demonstrated little interest in restoring the Kennebec's fisheries. Now that more dramatic solutions were on the table, Edwards Manufacturing was willing to cast itself in the role of victim.

CRAFTING A SOLUTION AND A REVOLUTIONARY FERC DECISION

Gubernatorial candidate Angus King included support for removal of Edwards Dam in his 1994 campaign, and sustained that support after his election. According to Evan Richert, Maine's state director of planning and point man for the state's efforts to remove the dam, the state worked in close communication with the Kennebec Coalition. "We talked a lot with them and the federal agencies, so we knew what they were doing and ended up focusing on the economic arguments . . . "[28] The state made it clear that it generally supported hydropower, in fact advocated hydropower, but sought to intelligently evaluate each dam and its economic benefits and ecological impacts on a case-by-case basis. Edwards Dam no longer made economic sense, while it had never made ecological sense. As Richert cogently points out, "The cost–benefit just wasn't there to keep the dam. It was going to be different in other situations and we look at them differently in different situations."[29]

According to Richert, the state produced reports for the FERC filing process even as the Kennebec Coalition filed their own extensive sets of documents. When the Edwards Manufacturing Company decided to throw in the towel, they approached the state rather than negotiate with the Kennebec Coalition.[30] The state negotiated with Edwards and the City of Augusta. While Augusta was forced to go along because of Edwards' decision to give up fighting the FERC decision, the city was reluctant to give up the economic perks of its relationship with Edwards without a fight. The timely arrival of Bill Bridgeo as Augusta's new city manager contributed positively to the transition and the city government's acceptance of the future demise of Edwards Dam. His vision for a dynamic downtown development plan partially funded by state money contributed to the willingness of Augusta city government to support the removal of the dam.

Negotiation was only one aspect of the Maine state government's strategy for dam removal. Officials worked actively to promote the dam removal, address concerns, and educate the public in general. There were many concerns: fear of industrial contaminants in soil backed up behind the dam, potential downstream flooding, a reduction in riverside home values, and the elimination of river access for communities that had built piers and docks for the lake. While some of these were reasonable fears, concerns were increased because opponents of dam removal crafted dire predictions of such negative consequences. Thus, these concerns needed to be addressed to create public support for dam removal.

The decision by the FERC to not relicense the dam came as a shock to many. FERC chairman James J. Hoecker explained the decision saying, "Today's order requiring the removal of the Edwards Dam reflects a balanced view of environmental as well as social and economic considerations."[31] Peter J. Howe of the *Boston Globe* announced the FERC decision by writing, "For the first time in U.S. history, federal power regulators refused to extend the operating license for a hydroelectric dam yesterday, ordering that a structure that stretches 900 feet across Maine's Kennebec River be ripped out so that sturgeon, bass, salmon, and smelt can reach their spawning grounds."[32] The battle over the dam's future culminated with a 2–1 vote by the Commission to not extend the license again and to order the dam's razing.[33] Media accounts of the order focused on a shift in resource policy, many overstating the case while comparing rivers of electric power production versus productive rivers of fish.[34]

Fish restoration advocates reacted to the FERC announcement with exultation. Evan Richert said, "This is a big win for the environment and the economy. It is also a terrific example of how federal officials listened to the evidence and struck the right balance in their decision."[35] Stephen Brooke added that "the facts brought FERC to the same place where all the rest of us have been for a long time . . . [the] time has come to remove the Edwards Dam so that abundant fish populations can again return to this magnificent river."[36] The dam owners were somewhat more glum in their response. Isaacson criticized the decision as bad policy and questioned the FERC's authority to deny the license and require removal of the dam.[37] Businessmen and members of the hydropower industry worried that this step might set a precedent for the removal of more dams in the interests of ecological restoration.[38] Certainly a successful river restoration effort through dam removal would provide sustenance to an environmental movement increasingly interested in targeting dams nationwide to reestablish rivers and fisheries.

DANGEROUS DAM PRECEDENT

While the national newspapers and magazines focused on the FERC decision and the unprecedented nature of the order as well as the possible nationwide ramifications, the removal of the dam was far from a *fait accompli*. The Edwards Manufacturing Company, with support from the hydropower industry, mounted a legal challenge to the FERC decision. In their appeal, they requested that the Commission vacate the decision and announced that they would challenge the decision in federal circuit court and possibly demand federal compensation for the taking of their property.[39] The Edwards

Dam owners and City of Augusta filed a re-hearing request in an effort to have the FERC decision overturned.[40] Joining them in this request were "the National Hydropower Association, the City of Tacoma, Washington (which receives a portion of its power from a dammed river in the Olympic Mountains), and the Edison Electric Institute, a national organization representing more than 75 percent of the national electricity generators and an almost equal percentage of the nation's consumers."[41] The other parties to the appeal feared the precedent that decommissioning Edwards Dam might set, and the increased concern regarding environmental issues expressed by the FERC in relicensing procedures since 1986. Further, these groups as well as the owners of Edwards Dam were concerned that the owners of dams failing the relicensing process would be saddled with the cost of removing their own dams.[42]

Additional challenges came from other quarters. Four conservative Republican members of the Senate Energy and Natural Resources Committee challenged the FERC decision. Senator Larry Craig of Idaho (undoubtedly concerned over ramifications of the decision for dams on the lower Snake River and a consistent opponent of environmental causes), Senator Frank Murkowski of Alaska, Oklahoma Senator Don Nickles, and Representative Jon Kyl from Arizona informed the Commission that they were disappointed at its failure to provide a requested stay of implementation of the FERC decision for the dam owners.[43] Ironically, if the Kennebec River Coalition had sought a legislative solution, these legislators would have been well positioned to block dam removal, just as former Senator Slade Gorton blocked removal of the Elwha River dams. However, due to the decision to challenge the dam through the FERC relicensing process, these opponents could only voice their concerns while the process moved forward.

A great deal of distance remained between dam owners, the City of Augusta, and those seeking restoration of the Kennebec River and its fisheries. The final removal of Edwards Dam was more than the simple enactment of orders from the federal government. The crafting of a solution that allowed for benefits all around precluded what might have become a nasty court battle over the future of a dam, a river, and fish.[44]

The Kennebec Coalition and state government patched together a solution in an effort to avoid a lengthy series of court cases. Director of State Planning Evan Richert announced the state's interest in helping create a solution as soon as the FERC decision was announced. "We want to work with the owners and find ways for them to meet their obligations. The governor has a genuine concern that we don't pile costs on the dam owners. We intend to treat them fairly and with respect in trying to reach an expeditious solution. If that's not possible, we'll defend the decision in court."[45] Dave Cheever, a *Kennebec Journal* reporter during the negotiations, noted that it was this plan that finally resolved the issue and cleared the way for dam removal. His interpretation is, however, a little less rosy than that of others. He asserts that the city council and Edwards Manufacturing were given little choice in the matter insofar that this deal was going to happen regardless of their consent.[46]

The solution crafted was a complex one, but it, like the consensus crafted on the Elwha River, offered something for everyone and expedited the process of removing the dam and restoring the fisheries. In an unprecedented move, Governor Angus King appeared before the city council and gave a presentation on the plan for dam removal. The formal agreement between the city, the state, and the dam owners was signed on May 8, 1998. This solution protected the city and the dam owners from legal liability during the dam removal process, made the state responsible for acquisition of the dam with money provided by Bath Iron Works, and required Edwards Manufacturing to pay approximately $250,000 to the city for the last royalty payment to the city, taxes for the year, and a portion of the sale of materials salvaged and sold from the site. The agreement also provided some opportunities for downtown economic revitalization with funds from the state available for development and planning.[47]

The linchpin for this complex financial arrangement arose from a deal struck with Bath Iron Works, a shipyard located in Bath, Maine, alongside the lower Kennebec River. Bath has produced ships for hundreds of years, and Bath Iron Works still builds ships and provides jobs in the region. Bath Iron Works needed to improve its facilities along the river and as a result brought needed money into the dam removal effort. The Iron Works' desire to expand and flatten their shipbuilding yards threatened 13 acres of wetlands that were prime habitat for sturgeon and other species. Facing the need to provide mitigation for this habitat destruction, the company offered to contribute money to the Edwards Dam removal efforts. The $2.5 million provided by Bath Iron Works was key to the final resolution of negotiations and the removal of Edwards Dam.[48]

ENVIRONMENTAL BENEFITS OF DAM REMOVAL

Since the removal of Edwards Dam, most of the fish have returned to the Kennebec, and the river now more closely resembles an organic and dynamic ecosystem rather than an industrial waste ditch. The water quality has improved dramatically with increased water flows and a corresponding higher oxygenation of the water. Insect counts have doubled and tripled with a wider variety of aquatic insect species in the collections, a reliable indicator of higher water quality. The striped bass fishery has improved dramatically on the river, and the fish, along with shad and alewives, quickly moved upstream to the dam in Waterville. Studies of the river above Augusta demonstrated additional spawning in the newly accessible areas as well as general increases in numbers of several other fish species. Two million alewives traveled upstream immediately. Newspaper articles and personal stories have celebrated the resurgence of fish upriver above Augusta, over 160 years since the building of the dam. In fact, it is common to see five-foot-long sturgeon breaching the river's surface from downtown Augusta. This is certainly a success story and offers an alternative to the declensionist narratives that more typically describe the stories of human destruction of nature. The restored river and fisheries provide a powerful precedent for those supporting dam removals in other parts of the country.[49]

AND THE DAMS COME TUMBLING DOWN

The story of the successful restoration of the Kennebec River, although exceptional at the time, is now indicative of a wider movement, as environmentalists and government agencies nationwide seek to reevaluate dams and river use in a context that includes not only economic issues but also measures the value of ecosystems. In fact, small dams are being removed and fish populations restored in many locations throughout the country. The success of this experiment and others like it will determine the future of still more dams and rivers across the country.

On the Kennebec River itself, the success of the Edwards Dam project led activists and biologists to cast their eyes toward the Fort Halifax Dam just 17 miles upstream on the Sebasticook River, a tributary to the Kennebec. After a tough fight, the owners of that dam agreed to remove it, and in the summer of 2008, 9 years after the Edwards Dam fell, this one went as well. Now, the fish travel upstream to yet another dam. The falling dams on the Kennebec and its tributaries are emblematic of the national process, heightened and strengthened by the Edwards Dam fight. Each time a dam is removed with environmental benefits and, it is hoped, economic benefits as well, the momentum piles up behind another dam somewhere in the nation. What will the future Kennebec River watershed look like? Will the resurgence of fish lead to a resurgence of the economy or will those issues remain more ambiguous?

In fact, the Augusta downtown economy has not recovered in the way that restoration advocates and the city manager anticipated it would. Home values along the river have increased, however, and there has been some increase in revenue from tourism, fishing, boating, and other recreational activities. While it is reductionist and short-sighted to be cornered into making economic arguments for removing dams, other unanticipated economic benefits do arise. For example, the town of Benton, along the Sebasticook River, north of the former Fort Halifax Dam site, saw its first alewife run in approximately 160 years, a run that may be the largest in the

United States. Citizens of the town, under the supervision of a newly appointed alewife warden, harvested 350,000 alewives for an influx of $15,000 to town coffers.

Dam removals have nearly all resulted in rapid and notable ecological restoration. For example, the Quaker Neck Dam was removed from the Neuse River in North Carolina in 1997–98, and two other dams upstream were removed, including one blown up by the Marine Corps. At one time, the Neuse River had produced more striped bass and American shad than any other river in North Carolina, a state that has always been a top producer of these popular commercial and game species. The construction of the Quaker Neck Dam in 1952 inflicted severe damage on this fishery. The catch of 700,000 pounds of American shad prior to the construction of this dam stands in strong contrast to the mere 25,000 pounds caught in 1996. Efforts to improve estuary ecosystems led to the plan to restore the river. Specifically, the Albemarle and Pamlico sounds of North Carolina were impoverished by the Quaker Neck and other dams on the Neuse River. Dam removal would allow for the spawning of anadromous species, which included not only striped bass and American shad but also sturgeon, herring, and alewives, enriching both the rivers and the estuary.[50]

The solution was relatively simple, as in the case of the Elwha and Kennebec rivers—remove a dam. Then, remove more. In many cases, dam removal, enabling natural processes to function again, leads to quick and impressive improvements in the river ecosystem. The result has been a resurgence of the striped bass and American shad runs on the Neuse as they work their way into several hundred miles of stream habitat blocked by the dams. Beyond that, and unexpectedly, there has been an increase in amount and size of the popular flat-head catfish, as they aggressively feed on the spawning fish now available after removal of the dams. Elizabeth Grossman, the author of *Watershed*, explains how the removal of one minor dam can radically open up and transform an entire river ecosystem, writing "with the obstacle of Quaker Neck removed, 75 more miles of the mainstem and 925 more miles of streams that feed into the

Neuse are now available to fish." Federal agencies, the dam owners, and local groups worked cooperatively to remove the dams and restore fisheries in a way that created little conflict and that has resulted in an improved fishery. The science was clear that the dam removal would unequivocally improve the river and fisheries, and the owners of the Quaker Neck Dam were willing to cooperate, making this a relatively straightforward process. Now, the Milburnie Dam in Raleigh is the primary obstacle to spawning fish on the Neuse River and there is increasing pressure for its removal. An owner of a store that rents canoes and sells bait on the Neuse River said, "I like it with the [Quaker Neck] dam gone. There's more bigger fish, a lot more variety, and people aren't afraid to eat 'em."[51]

The Waterworks Dam on the Baraboo River in Wisconsin was also removed in the late 1990s. The removal of this dam created dramatic improvements in water quality along with improved fisheries.[52] In fact, Wisconsin environmentalists have made great strides removing dams for environmental reasons, primarily restoration of native fisheries. According to Grossman, over 60 dams have been removed over the last 40 years on such rivers as the "Milwaukee and Manitowoc Rivers in eastern Wisconsin, the Kickapoo and Yahara Rivers and Turtle Creek in the south, the Flambeau River in northern Wisconsin and the Willow River, a tributary of the St. Croix in western Wisconsin."[53]

The success of river restoration efforts has enabled leading groups like American Rivers and Trout Unlimited to hail these efforts, as the fisheries consistently return quickly after the removal of dams. While it seems obvious that fish will return to previously blocked rivers (and the evidence so far supports this assumption), opponents of dam removal consistently deny the potential success of future projects even as the list of successful removals and restorations continues to grow. As an article in *Bioscience* points out, migratory species have returned and increased their numbers after dam removals on Bear Creek in Oregon, Mad River in California, and Clearwater River in Idaho. Furthermore, dam removal has allowed nonmigratory species like smallmouth bass to extend their range and displace introduced species like carp in streams in the northern Midwest.[54] On the West Bend River in Wisconsin, dam removal resurrected the river and created a thriving bass fishery. The old reservoir, predicted by opponents to become an eyesore and mud pit (similar to predictions made by the opponents of Edwards Dam removal), has actually been transformed into a park. The removal of three dams from Butte Creek in northern California allowed a salmon fishery of less than one hundred spawners to rebound to a run of approximately 20,000.[55]

In Maine, inspired no doubt by the success on the Kennebec River and other restoration efforts, activists, government representatives, and business and community leaders put together a remarkable and arguably unprecedented effort to restore the Penobscot River. As with the Kennebec River, dams built on the Penobscot during the late 19th and early 20th centuries had destroyed once-famous and profligate runs of Atlantic salmon, striped bass, shad, herring, and other species, reducing the quality of the overall river ecosystem. Also like the Kennebec River, two dams are to be removed entirely and another one partially modified for upstream fish passage, in order to restore the fisheries of this once great river. This restoration, funded with a combination of federal and private funds, will open up approximately 1,000 miles of river and tributary spawning habitat.[56]

The effort to restore the Penobscot bears some similarities to the process on the Elwha River. A coalition of environmental groups, the Penobscot Indians, government agencies, and the owners of the dams forged a compromise that will benefit everyone involved. An editorial from the *Kennebec Journal* praised the proposed restoration:

It is, it seems, often much easier for humans to destroy than it is to create. For generations, the Penobscot River fed both the Indian tribe that took its name from the river and the landscape of forest and ocean that surrounded it. That connection was severed with the advent of industry and hydropower. To many, the riches that resulted were worth it. But to the river and those who loved it, it was not. So now, a growing and determined group has set out to bring life back to the Penobscot. John Muir once said of his beloved western forests that 'God has cared for these trees, saved them from drought, disease, avalanches and a thousand tempests and floods. But he cannot save them from fools.' You could call those who destroyed the Penobscot 'fools' but it would be fools as well who would now decree that all industry on the river must stop to make up for that damage. Instead, with wisdom, these river restorers have found a way to balance both nature's needs and the demands of our economy.

We—and the river—are in their debt.[57]

This editorial, penned in a community that has already seen the benefit of dam removal, articulates a position rarely heard in the mainstream in this region, or even the nation, a short 20 years earlier. Adopting a nuanced position addressing the shifting uses of the river, based on the requirements of the human community, the editorial writer makes the point that restoration of nature is a fundamental human activity. This echoes the argument made by famed entomologist and environmentalist E. O. Wilson that the 21st century has to be the century of restoration. Furthermore, this editorial argues, as have activists on the Elwha River, Klamath River, and others, that a better balance should be struck between nature and industry; that the excesses of industrial growth can be addressed and corrected to create a more sustainable natural economy. In so doing, activists are showing the way to constructing a land ethic while restoring nature.

A project that compares in scope and ambition with the Penobscot River restoration is the Northwest's proposed Klamath River restoration. The first dam was built in 1918 and eventually four dams on the river helped destroy one of the largest salmon runs on the Pacific Coast. This long, winding river enters the Pacific on the coast of northern California and then extends into the desert of eastern Oregon. Historically, Klamath, Yurok, Karuk, and Hoopa Indians depended on the fish of this river for subsistence. But, as was the case everywhere, they were forced onto small reservations (some of the tribes were actually eliminated and lost federal recognition) and the land opened up for settlement, logging, and agriculture—particularly problematic for the uses of the Klamath River today, in the desert of southeastern Oregon. Four dams, multiple constituencies, and declining salmon runs (with two species listed as endangered) led to an explosive situation in the summer of 2001, when drought threatened farmers dependent on irrigation from the Klamath River in southeastern Oregon. Since that time, after a massive salmon die-off in 2002 because of the draining of water for farming, and amid protests, face-offs, and threats of violence, the various stakeholders in the basin—many of them economically, politically, and ideologically opposed to each other—hammered out a compromise agreement to restore the salmon fishery. There is a great deal of healthy habitat in this watershed, so the potential for recovery of salmon populations is strong.

The Klamath River is not the only watershed in Oregon undergoing restoration. A dam dating from the same era as the Elwha Dam, the Marmot Dam on the Sandy River was removed in 2007 in an effort to restore the river and its salmon and steelhead fisheries. Owned by Portland General Electric (PGE), the dam was built in 1913 and like the Elwha, blocked salmon and steelhead from migrating upstream. While the company is upgrading its other hydropower generating facilities for improved production and compliance with fish protection requirements, the executives decided that upgrading this dam would have been too expensive and removal was a better option. The accompanying dam on the Little Sandy River has been removed, as well as a wooden flume running from that dam to the former Marmot Dam reservoir. PGE also donated 1,500 acres of land from the project to the Western Rivers Conservancy.[58]

On the Rogue River in Oregon, another dam fell to make way for salmon. In the summer of 2009 work commenced to remove the Savage Rapids Dam near Grants Pass. Built in 1921 for irrigation purposes alone, the removal of the 39-foot-high and 500-foot-wide dam represents one of the larger projects up to this point. Poor fish-passage facilities and the general plight of salmon on the Rogue River prompted the national environmental group Water Watch to block a water rights permit request by the Grants Pass Irrigation District (the owners of the dam) in 1991. Years of debate and lawsuits and the listing of the Rogue River coho salmon as an endangered species culminated in a negotiated agreement to remove the dam, which will open up another 500 miles of spawning habitat to salmon and steelhead. Fisheries biologists believe that this action will add over 100,000 salmon a year to the river's population.[59]

On the other side of the continent, one of the great industrial states has aggressively stepped up its removal of aging and obsolete dams. Pennsylvanians have removed over 100 dams, with many more slated for removal. Some date back to the 17th and early 18th centuries and provided power for sawmills, grain mills, and textile mills, representing an important component in the early industrial economy. Abandoned for many decades, their impact on fisheries was largely irrelevant for a long time because the rivers and streams were so filled with industrial and sewage pollutants that they were biological deserts. As on the Kennebec River, the Clean Water Act led to cleaner water and a resurgence of riparian biota, prompting the question of what would happen if the dams were removed? Activists and fisheries biologists envisioned a further restoration of the river and stream ecosystems, with the return of fish like the American shad. Now, creeks and rivers like the Pennypack, Darby, Brandywine, and the Schuykill more closely resemble their historical selves as shad are surging upstream into healthier, accessible habitats. The hope is that eel and striped bass will soon follow.[60]

THE LAND ETHIC AND DAM REMOVAL

To situate dams properly in their cultural and economic context, it is important to understand the social and economic displacements as well as the environmental damage created by dams. American environmentalists, fisheries experts, and communities are evaluating dams in a more complete way, weighing the costs, and removing the dams that create more damage than good. Removing dams is *not* eliminating productivity or eradicating human use of the river.

Nor is it harming the capitalist economic system or laying unfair burdens on rural communities. Nor is it really restoring a river to its "natural" preindustrial state. Rather, it is a matter of choosing to work intelligently with natural systems to allow them to function under fewer overt restraints and controls—in the process, providing a new but also a reconstructed ecosystem replete with an entirely different set of functions, values, uses, costs, and economic benefits. And it is judging the changed system to be desirable, more beneficial, sustainable, and finally, in the sense that Aldo Leopold meant when he wrote of the need for a land ethic, a system that is more ethical in that the value of nature and other organisms is recognized alongside human needs. The restoration of rivers and fisheries through dam removal is an effort to enact Leopold's land ethic.

Some might argue that the Elwha River restoration effort indicates the weakness of environmentalism in America. The fact that it has taken approximately 20 years to get to dam removal after passage of the Elwha Restoration Act prompts that very question. Add to that 20 years the many decades of effort prior to the passage of the legislation, and the question gains even more weight. It is essential to remember that removing large dams for environmental restoration represented a major step in environmental action, a large shift in thinking about the proper uses of nature, and to many represented an attack on industry in America. Resistance and discomfort were to be expected. Consider also that the Elwha dams, unlike the low-head dams that have been removed in the intervening years since 1992, are high-head. Their removal moves the river restoration movement forward significantly because of their size and the potential for high profile, successful fisheries restoration. More to the point, the oppositional role of Senator Slade Gorton, particularly once he folded the Elwha River restoration effort into the ugly fight over the lower Snake River dams, can hardly be overstated. He held almost all the cards, and was willing to ignore not only the legislation but also the advice of the local community via the Port Angeles Advisory Committee, to prevent such an important and precedent-setting move as these dam removals represent. It is important to note that the opposition has been overcome. And while it has taken longer than many had anticipated (except the Port Angeles Advisory Committee), the very lag period that is regretted by many Elwha advocates makes the Elwha River restoration even more powerful and important. The "bottom is out of the tub," as President Lincoln once ruefully commented.

Over the last 20 years, hundreds of dams have come down with generally positive results. More fish have returned, the water is better aerated and there is very little of the decline in property value and the ugly, muddy banks that were predictions of dam removal opponents in other places like Maine and Wisconsin. Fisheries biologists, activists, politicians, and all stripes of Americans are learning of dam removals and seeing the benefits of those efforts.

Now that the dams are removed, advocates and opponents will watch with interest to see how quickly the Elwha River returns to a productive salmon fishery. When the trickles and then stronger runs of salmon and steelhead arrive, the Elwha will provide yet another example of how dam removal in some cases is a reasonable and successful strategy for restoring ecosystems and economies.

A PROPER UNDERSTANDING OF
DAM REMOVAL AND RIVER RESTORATION

Richard White's *The Organic Machine* was one of a raft of books on the Columbia River that were published in a short period in the mid- and late 1990s. This study provides a history and analysis of the Columbia River and its place in American society. White argues that the current Columbia River is one that is made and remade by numerous human activities: commercial and sport fishing, irrigation, pulp mills, hatcheries, aluminum production, dams, hydroelectricity, and so forth. All are necessary endeavors that have created a new kind of river, an Emersonian "organic machine" that is both natural and produces labor for our use and benefit. While noting the problems with treating a major river as a machine, a mere collection of parts, his broader point is that this is the river we must live with now; that it can never be the "natural" river it was before, returned to a

Pool and riffles on the Elwha. Courtesy of Jeff Crane

perceived simpler time of salmon abundance and river health. That may well be—this river commands a complex and large constituency that for the most part sees it as more important for its industrial purposes than for its fish production.

In "Salmon," the final chapter of *The Organic Machine*, White seems to take special pleasure in denouncing some environmentalists. "To call for a return to nature is posturing. It is a religious ritual in which the recantation of our sins and a pledge to sin no more promises to restore purity. Some people believe sins go away. History does not go away."[61] The arrogance of this statement, in its massive disregard for the complexity and intelligence of the environmental community, is reminiscent of some of my students who brush off environmentalists as "tree-huggers." White posits the most extreme position regarding restoration of the Columbia River and its fish, then denigrates it further by referring to these calls as "posturing," comparing these views to religious excess. This was 1995. The calls for dam removals had begun early on with the Elwha legislation in 1992 and then with increasing demands for removal of dams on the lower Snake River. Any desire to remove Columbia River dams at that point were limited either by an acceptance of reality or by the acknowledged difficulty of removing the lower Snake River dams first. As White worked on this book, he must have felt that he was catching this misguided movement in its early stages—and setting it straight.

In point of fact, if you are willing to set aside the Columbia River for a moment and consider the growing and remarkably successful river restoration movement, White has been proven quite shortsighted. The Elwha River is easy to set up in counterpoise to the Columbia. The Elwha is economically insignificant, produces little power that is easily replaceable, blocks a river that is embedded in relatively pristine habitat, and does not have a complex mix of constituents with a vested interest in keeping the two dams in place. These are legitimate points to make, but it is important to think historically. As White points out, "History does not go away." The fact of the matter is that when these removals were called for on the Elwha, such propositions were unprecedented and considered extreme measures—proposals that responsible adults like the owners of the mill and the dams could safely ignore as the shrieks and cries (or the religious recantations of sins) of extreme environmentalists.

Not only is the deed done, but it turns out that the path to restoration has been and will continue to be a complex one, using machinery, science, technical reports, experts, and natural methods in serious and informed efforts to "return the river to nature." These are not drum circle aficionados and Earth First! radicals rappelling the faces of dams. In fact, those seeking to return the Elwha to nature are respected fisheries and wildlife biologists of high stature in their field, tribal leaders, businessmen, and numerous members of federal, state, and local agencies. The plans to restore the river and its habitat, fisheries, shellfish, and wildlife are multidimensional, reflecting decades of experience, research, and debates.

What does this have to do with White's organic machine? First, the term as he uses it is applicable to not only the Columbia but to any dammed river performing labor for humans. The Columbia seems untouchable because of its centrality to the region's economy and the cheap, "clean" hydroelectricity its dams, particularly the Grand Coulee, provide for a multistate region. The sanctity of those dams seems even more untouchable when one considers the need to perpetuate and increase the use of hydroelectricity in order to reduce pollutants that drive global warming. To push the point a bit more, it might be that the sacrifice of the Columbia makes it possible to preserve the salmon in rivers where the dams are insignificant or where proposed dams would be of little value in terms of hydroelectric production. Regardless, as White should understand, and undoubtedly does, it is reckless to accept a dam as a permanent feature of a river or a society. History may not go away but dams clearly do.

SOME IMPLICATIONS OF ELWHA RESTORATION

The Elwha dams are being torn down and time's passage has provided an opportunity for Elwha advocates to carefully plan the restoration process and studies that will be conducted to evaluate the return of the salmon and the growing health of the watershed ecosystem.[62]

Assuming success over the long term, these studies will provide not only data that support other dam removal efforts across the nation, but also information on how to improve the restoration process to make it more ecologically productive and successful. If this is the case, then the delays in Elwha restoration may strengthen the environmental restoration movement. In fact, the Elwha River dams, their removal long delayed, may still prove to be the important transition in the environmental and river restoration movements that many assumed they would be back in the 1990s. These were the first high-head dam removals for environmental purposes in the United States. It is also the most costly river and fisheries restoration to this point, with a combined current estimated cost of approximately $300 million. Much of the expense arises from the need for extreme mitigation measures. Many dam removal projects (all low-head dams to date) have required little in terms of preparation and mitigation, in some cases a backhoe tearing a trench in the dam or cofferdam has represented the peak of the effort. On the Elwha, the cost of actual dam removal is a minority of the overall project price. Because the National Park Service decided to allow for natural erosion of stored sediment behind the dams, the necessary new water treatment plants plus flood protection and septic tank replacement downstream drive costs higher. While the Olympic National Park had held out the promise of jobs in restoration work as a strategy for building community support, it was decided that active sediment removal was too expensive and environmentally damaging. So for a few years the river will flush out high levels of sediment, and then begin to return to normal. Completion of such a complex and expensive restoration project, particularly if the salmon return in strong numbers, will provide a model and momentum for even larger and more complex river restoration projects. Dams that now seem untouchable may come under fire as salmon advocates demonstrate the legitimacy of restoration while applying the force of law and treaties in defense of salmon and Indian rights.[63]

When the legislation was passed in 1992 calling for restoration of the Elwha River and its fisheries, there was exultation and anticipation of the physical event of dam removal and salmon returns. A great deal of excitement also stemmed from the achievement of an unprecedented act, and the speedy timelines for dam removals. The reality of partisan politics and obstruction delayed the dam removals and changed the significance of dam removal on the Elwha River. However, it is possible that the delays have allowed for the development of a better restoration model, one that will best serve native Elwha stock and generate new knowledge and understanding of the process of river restoration that can be applied to other, similar projects.

UNDERSTANDING THE RIVER

The dams were not simply removed to allow fish to move upstream; the process of restoration is much more complicated than merely removing a barrier. The mountains of sediment behind the dams and the varying health of the native salmon stock preclude a casual restoration of this type, such as was done successfully on the Kennebec River in Maine. Restoring the fish to the river necessitates a complex, well-orchestrated system of recolonization, hatchery use, and introduction of fish to the river at different stages of life. It also requires placing fish at various spots in the river, both to maximize restoration and to avoid high mortality rates due to turbidity from the mountains of sediment flushed downstream.

To better understand the effectiveness of restoration, resource managers and scientists representing multiple agencies, as well as the Lower Elwha Klallam, organized and implemented a careful program of study to effectively evaluate and catalog the ecosystem prior to dam removal. This establishes a baseline for future studies and for understanding the consequences of dam removal. A series of conferences have been conducted to organize these studies and establish cooperation and consistency between researchers.[64]

The baseline studies are complex and rigorous and reveal a scientific zeal and sophistication about the potential physical results and scientific knowledge accruing from dam removal that could not have been foreseen when the legislation was originally passed. One might assume a great deal of excitement and interest on the part of the fisheries biologists in particular because their work is now not in service of continued mitigation, technological optimism, and other half-measures meant to sustain economic development over salmon health, but rather part of a real solution to the salmon crisis—representing a profound next step for fishery professionals and environmentalists alike.

In one article discussing the biological impacts of dam removal on salmon and their responses, the authors described the work done to evaluate woody debris in the lower Elwha. In their inventory, snags and logjams were identified, measured, tagged, and mapped with GPS. Specific information regarding width, length, type of tree, and orientation of the logjams and snags was collected and recorded.[65]

In order to effectively ascertain and evaluate existing salmonid populations, a number of methodologies were employed. Spawning ground surveys of the mainstem and side channels were conducted by foot and boat to locate and catalog active salmon redds. Locations were recorded via GPS and further details such as water depth and velocity, the size of gravel and cobble in the redd, the distance to woody debris, the type of habitat, and the distances to stream banks and pools were collected as well.[66]

In addition to this painstaking and thorough methodology, an innovative snorkel study, one of the longest on the North American continent, was conducted. Twenty-one fisheries biologists participated in the 42-mile survey, the approximate length of the river. Biologists from the National Park Service, United States Geological Survey, Lower Elwha Klallam tribe, National Oceanic and Atmospheric Administration, U.S. Fish and Wildlife Service, Peninsula College, and the Wild Salmon Center snorkeled the river. Conducted over a few days in August 2007, the swimmers recorded populations of bull and rainbow trout above the dams, and rainbow and bull trout as well as pink and chinook salmon in the lower Elwha.[67]

RETURN OF THE RIVER

Salmon and their access to the river certainly dominate most people's thinking about the Elwha, but there are other significant ecological issues that are not as obvious. With the interruption of sediment transport, the ecological impacts of the dams moved beyond the destruction of the salmon runs. For example, the loss of gravel and cobble from the river forced Port Angeles to spend millions of dollars over the years hauling rock to replenish and stabilize Ediz Hook. Where there used to be a wide estuary at the mouth of the Elwha, rich with clam beds critical to the Elwha economy, the beaches are almost entirely gone. The dams stopped the replenishing of the beaches and estuary. The blocking of sediment flow, resulting in "sediment starvation," has also caused the expansion of kelp beds and a reduction in eelgrass, with impacts on various species of fish, including salmon. Additionally, the coarsening of the beaches has damaged some species of clams and the Dungeness crab population.

Now that the dams are being removed, at least 18 million cubic meters of sediment formerly blocked by the dams are again flowing downstream, restoring the regular sediment transport of the Elwha River. It is anticipated that in the first five years after dam removal, 2 to 2.5 million cubic meters of sand and gravel and as much as 5 million cubic meters of sand silt will be transported down the lower Elwha River. Scientists are strongly interested in studying and understanding the processes by which the Elwha will restore its own hydrology and river geology, as well as the impacts on the nearshore environments discussed above. Extensive studies are already planned in order to better understand these changes. While dam removal is causing habitat change and improvement of the Elwha River ecosystem, other work needs to happen to make this restoration as complete as possible. Shoreline revetments, a dike separating estuaries from the Strait of Juan de Fuca, and a 3,300-meter bulkhead have all effectively armored the beach and limit the ability of sediment to restore the original beach conditions in the area just east of the river mouth. This is a reminder that dam removal is just one step, albeit a major step, in the complete restoration of the Elwha River ecosystem.[68]

RETURN OF THE SALMON

Understanding and implementing the return of salmon to the Elwha necessitates an understanding of the current state of the fisheries on the river and the difficulties the fish will face in colonizing the opened river. Removing the dams was the first step in a long, complex process. Variability in surviving genetic stock, weather, sediment flow, and river turbidity, as well as the ability of fish to migrate to different parts of the river ecosystem to spawn, are just some of the factors that fisheries biologists have to consider in reestablishing salmon runs throughout the entire Elwha River watershed.

It was believed that pink salmon had gone extinct on the river but apparently a few colonized the river or a small remnant population escaped notice; there is now a very small pink population. These salmon tend to spawn in large numbers, have high stray rates, and also maintain short residencies in their natal streams. Therefore, they should colonize the Elwha watershed fairly quickly. All salmon species have a certain percentage that stray from their home streams to new streams, with pinks having a stray rate as high as 34 percent in bad conditions. Colonization can occur quite quickly. In Alaska, streams exposed by retreating glaciers have been colonized by multiple salmon populations in mere decades. Faster natural colonization of one to five years has occurred on streams where culverts have been removed or fish ladders installed.[69] Pinks utilize a broad range of habitat, including flood plain channels. Also, their spawning period in summer and early fall is a time of lower water flow and they are therefore less likely to face the high turbidity than other salmon species will. Pink salmon, like chum, are not particularly good at overcoming barriers, so their spatial reach will be limited and they will remain in the lower parts of the Elwha. Because they spawn every two years and in very large numbers, they have the potential to produce a strong population quickly and may very well be the first sign of restoration success on the Elwha.

Like the pink, there is a small chum salmon population extant in the Elwha. They are the least able of Pacific Northwest salmonids to overcome physical barriers, and therefore have an even more limited range than the pink salmon. Moreover, their spawning period in late autumn and winter occirs at a time of higher water flow, which will mean more turbidity in the first few years of restoration, resulting in a higher mortality rate for chum salmon in that early stage.

Elwha River sockeye salmon present some interesting questions. The historical Elwha sockeye spawned on the shores of Lake Sutherland, which is connected to the Elwha by Indian Creek. Cut off completely from traditional spawning grounds, a small remnant population has barely managed to continue in the lower river. These could be remnants but are more likely strays. What is known is that with the dams down, the sockeye will colonize the lake. A resident kokanee salmon population in the lake may have originated from the original sockeye but that isn't known for certain. Non-native kokanee from Lake Whatcom were planted in Lake Sutherland from 1934 to 1964 but genetic tests show distinct subpopulations of native and non-native versions of this fish.[70]

Coho and chinook salmon seem to offer the most potential for large-scale recolonization of salmon. The chinook are the most magnificent of Pacific salmon in terms of their size and strength. Because of hatchery efforts over the 20th century, the river still hosts a small reproducing population, although there are questions whether the spring chinook, which produced the biggest kings, still exist.[71] These powerful fish are expected to do well in the restoration. Their size and strength, evolutionary adaptations to barriers in the river, allow them to overcome more obstacles than other salmon species. There were questions as to their ability to pass some significant barriers in the river—notably, Rica Canyon and Grand Canyon. In 1984, summer steelhead were fitted with tags and released above Glines Canyon Dam. The steelhead passed the canyons and proceeded far up the mainstem of the river, demonstrating beyond question the capacity of chinook to colonize the river far into the mountains. The Elwha kings also utilize floodplains for juvenile and adult life stages. Swimming, jumping, driving relentlessly upward and onward into the heart of the Olympics, they will occupy and colonize more mainstem and tributary miles than the other salmon species.[72]

Another important salmon on the river that has not garnered as much attention as the chinook is the coho, otherwise known as silver salmon. A historically strong species and important food source, the coho is valued generally because of the high quality of its flesh. The Lower Elwha Klallam director of river restoration, Robert Elofson, spoke in enthusiastic terms about the coho, anticipating that the recovery of this fish on the Elwha would be a real marker of success, and an exciting event. They are expected to be relatively successful because of larger numbers already existing in the lower river, and will likely take advantage of floodplains and tributaries such as Hayes, Lillian, Lost, and Goldie creeks. Steelhead trout will likely colonize such areas as well. Some problems are anticipated with stream turbidity; coho salmon and steelhead spawn in spring and winter and are likely to experience heavier loads of sediment before the river stabilizes.[73]

The restoration plan for the river prioritizes preserving existing native Elwha salmon while seeking a balance between production goals and creating as natural a restoration process as possible. In reality, this means a complex and "adaptive" restoration program that will make adjustments based on proven successes and failures. Because of the fear of damage to existing salmon stocks due to high turbidity of sediments washing downstream, particularly in the first five years of the restoration process, multiple hatcheries are preserving eggs and milt from native stock and will supplement the runs with hatchery planting on the river. Also, windows will be created for native spawning salmon, stopping dam destruction to limit sediment flow and turbidity that might hurt those fish. The construction of woody debris sites ahead of dam removal, along with plans for the reforestation of floodplains, the removal or alteration of dikes, and the acquisition of floodplains will enhance the Elwha River ecosystem and contribute to the success of the restoration project.[74]

While fishery biologists want to allow as much natural recolonization as possible, the pressure to show strong results in a 25- to 30-year timeframe and the worry about damage to existing salmon stocks mean that hatcheries will be used in a substantive manner. Under the current plan, sockeye salmon will not be planted in Lake Sutherland. Rather, the kokanee that exist there are expected to adapt an anadromous pattern and become sockeye. If that doesn't occur, it is expected that sockeye strays from other runs will colonize the river. The use of hatcheries for other fish will be done in a way that emphasizes variability within the species and watershed. They will be planted by truck, helicopter, and backpack, and the fish planted will reflect multiple stages within a juvenile smolt's lifespan. Hatcheries are no longer a panacea, a scientific, technological replacement for rivers. Rather, they serve a role within a broader, complex plan for bringing the salmon river back to life.[75]

It will likely be several years before it is clear what salmon have colonized the river successfully and which species have not. There will be variability in this success based on the species and spawning period, but other factors such as heavy rains, incidents of high turbidity, etc. may also have impacts. Once the flow of sediment has stabilized over the first decade after dam removal, the restoration of the salmon should move forward in a fairly straightforward manner. They will find their way up the Elwha and make it a fully functioning salmon river once again.[76]

As the salmon colonize the rivers, and fisheries employees plant parr (pre-smolt juvenile salmon) and smolt across the Elwha watershed, it is hard not to wonder at what kinds of numbers will return. The predictions for salmon population growth seem quite optimistic. Within 25 years, it is expected that the Elwha will produce 6,000 chinook, 12,000 coho, 40,000 chum, and approximately 250,000 pinks. If these numbers are accomplished by both human and salmon action, then the Elwha River will begin to resemble its historical self. This will be a monumental achievement of society finding its way back to a healthier relationship with nature and a healthy, salmon-rich Elwha River.

THE ELWHA IN THE GLOBAL WARMING ERA

Over the 20 years from the Elwha River Restoration Act in 1992 to the present, perception of the environmental importance of the Elwha River changed. The passage of time as well as the current and predicted impacts of climate change have re-elevated the importance of the Elwha River restoration in what will certainly become a desperate struggle to preserve as many Pacific Northwest salmon as possible over the next 50 years. With the numbers of salmon expected to populate the river, the meaning of the Elwha is shifting again as the river becomes central to the fight to preserve salmon.

An examination of the impact of global warming on Pacific Northwest salmon is horrifying and disheartening in the most objective sense. Equally nerve-wracking is the dominance of techno-optimistic solutions and a complete absence of discussions of conservation and sacrifice in Americans' discourse on this most fundamental issue. The impacts of global warming are manifold and ripple out across the greater salmon bio-region in numerous, complex, and not easily understood ways. A restored Elwha River with increasing runs of salmon, even as climate change impacts regional salmon populations, will make the Elwha a critical ecosystem in the broader efforts to protect and preserve salmon.

Salmon derive a wide range of benefits from their river habitats. Depending on species and size, they use small streams, large rivers, estuaries, and lakes for spawning, migration, and habitat. The optimal size of cobble and force of current flow for redds varies by species; generally, bigger fish can build their nests in bigger cobble and within heavier river flow. Besides spending varying amounts of time in natal streams, rivers, lakes, and estuaries before migrating to the ocean, different species also spawn at varying times of the year. These variations allow for full use of riparian ecosystems for salmon reproduction.

By multiplying this general variability, which exists within one river watershed, by all the various subspecies found in thousands of rivers and streams of the Pacific Northwest, one can envision a tableau of remarkable complexity based on millennia of evolution and adaptation. Global warming will wash away the foundations of this remarkable structure, creating instability and chaos for Pacific Northwest salmon for the next century, at least.

Climate change has already forced powerful ecological change with significant impacts on Northwest salmon. For example, snowpack in the Washington Cascades has been reduced by 30 to 60 percent in some areas—this after a regional temperature increase of 1.5 degrees Fahrenheit since 1920.[77] Rain is replacing snow in many cases during the winter, further lessening snowpack and altering stream hydrology. A recent study by the Climate Impacts Group estimates that by 2080 there will be no dominant snow basins left in the North Cascades of Washington State, which means none in Oregon or northern California either, and only 10 transient snow basins remaining in the North Cascades.[78] What will be the impact of climate change on Pacific Northwest salmon? Specific predictions are difficult and limited research has been conducted in this area. But there are general impacts that can be understood and explained in at least a limited fashion.

Taking a general approach, the warming of water is the fundamental problem, but in myriad ways. As noted, temperatures in the Northwest have increased 1.5 degrees Fahrenheit since 1920, slightly more than the global temperature increase. An average of multiple models of climate change estimates conservatively that temperatures will increase by at least 1.7 to 5 degrees Fahrenheit by 2080; the temperature rise could be dramatically higher. In fact, up to this point, actual temperatures and impacts have been increasing more quickly than earlier models predicted. Warmer water has several direct impacts on salmonids. These types of fish, which include salmon, steelhead, and trout, thrive in water temperatures ranging from 54 to 65 degrees Fahrenheit. Stress increases at temperatures over 65 degrees, disease increases dramatically at 69 to 71 degrees, and mortality occurs at 73 to 75 degrees, depending on the species. Specifically, temperatures of 73 to 75 degrees lead to massive fish kills.

In addition to weakened immune systems, disease, and death caused directly by temperature increase, there are other impacts to salmon that are not subtle but also not easily observed. For example, as thermal barriers increase, spawning salmon enter stretches of river and stream that are too warm as they move up to their natal sites. Upon hitting these water walls, salmon stop their movement to wait for the water to cool. Based on current models, those thermal barriers will increase and last for longer stretches of time. Thermal barriers in August, a key spawning period for many salmon species, are predicted to last 10 to 12 weeks on important salmon rivers like the Yakima, Columbia, Snake, and Tucannon, and the Lake Washington Ship Canal. If the warm water is still present when spawning begins, the salmon that are blocked begin seeking out redd sites on the downstream side of the barrier. The result is that these salmon will not return to their natal sites and a great deal of salmon habitat will go unused, diminishing both the salmon runs and the river ecosystem. For example, salmon on the Snake River blocked by downstream thermal barriers will be unable to use the thousands of square miles of relatively healthy habitat in Idaho and Oregon on federal lands, wilderness areas, and wild and scenic areas. Moreover, the salmon seeking new sites due to warm water will displace other salmon redds, both of their own and other species, destabilizing the whole system. The overall result is the reduction of salmon numbers on a particular river, multiplied hundreds or thousands of times across the region.

Another major impact of climate change is the dramatic alteration of the hydrology of salmon waters. Increased rain precipitation is replacing snow precipitation, turning snow-dominant basins into transient basins and transient basins into rain-dominant basins. Historically, glaciers have provided a steady supply of icy, clean water to salmon rivers and streams; those glacial tributaries to streams and rivers are quickly diminishing and disappearing, further disrupting the hydrology and water temperatures of regional rivers and streams. In the North Cascades, glaciers have lost 25 to 45 percent of their volume since 1985. Many glaciers have disappeared completely. Olympic Mountain glaciers are in widespread, rapid retreat. The Hoh Glacier has retreated 450 meters since 1990; Blue Glacier, 270 meters; and Humes Glacier, approximately 120 meters. The loss of water from glaciers compounds the problems arising from shifts in precipitation patterns—less winter snow and more winter rain, and earlier snowmelts.[79]

Consequently, a series of dramatic and overlapping changes will damage Northwest salmon runs. Over thousands of years salmon have evolved to a pattern of hydrological events that will now undergo rapid and dramatic transformation. For example, the smolts of many salmon species use the spring snowmelt and the full, fast-moving streams to be flushed quickly to the ocean as their physiology shifts from freshwater to saltwater. This set of events depends on a heavy winter snowpack. The diminishment of the snowpack threatens to unravel this complex system. The lack or reduction of spring snowmelt will reduce the stream flow, smolts will take longer to get to the ocean, and some will be stranded and killed in smaller streams. Also, the slower migration will increase their vulnerability to predators such as bass (an introduced species in the Northwest) that will thrive and expand their range as water temperatures increase. For smolts that don't migrate immediately, the reduced snowpack and lower streams in spring will mean lower waters over the course of the year, reducing the amount of available habitat, again rendering them more vulnerable to predators. Spawning salmon will face not only thermal barriers but also streams and rivers with lower water levels, or even dried-up waterways. This will make the spawning journey and reproductive process difficult or impossible, depending on local conditions.

One may be tempted to take refuge from these frightening predictions by reflecting on the abundance of healthy upstream habitat in the Pacific Northwest. Protected forests and habitat in the North Cascades and Olympic Peninsula of Washington, the coastal range of Oregon, and national forests and wilderness areas in Idaho seemingly must provide some balance to the problems presented above. However, studies indicate that these protected areas will not preserve healthy salmon habitat. One study modeling climate change and its impact on chinook salmon in the Snohomish River basin, on the western slope of the Cascade Mountains of Washington, projected a 20 to 40 percent decline in spawning numbers throughout the basin. The healthy, high mountain habitat would be particularly hard-hit by the variations in rainfall, snowfall, and snowmelt patterns.[80] Another study of tributary creeks to the Middle Fork of the Salmon River in Idaho that are located in healthy, protected habitat reinforces the prediction of losses from global warming. Warmer water temperatures slow the transition from parr to smolt, reduce predator avoidance, and limit growth. Also, lower water levels reduce habitat, thereby increasing competition for food while diminishing places for the smolts to hide to avoid predators.[81] The authors predict an approximate 50 percent juvenile mortality rate in this watershed. It is safe to say that other watersheds in western

Oregon, Washington, northern California, and British Columbia will experience similar reductions of salmon populations.[82]

The critical point is that these fish already spawn and survive as smolts in relatively healthy watersheds. These studies argue, based on multiple projection models, that even highly protected wilderness and national park lands, ecosystems so healthy that little can be done to improve them, will suffer under the impact of climate change. Hence, damaged and exploited habitat must be restored in order to mitigate the losses in healthy habitat. The impact of climate change on the overall region necessitates an even greater commitment to the reconstruction of nature, in order to give salmon the highest odds possible at all stages of their journeys as smolts and spawning adults.[83]

Pacific Northwest salmon advocates recognize that the nature of the debate over salmon has shifted with the multiple threats produced by climate change. First, the argument is no longer economics versus environment. Seemingly, this conflict pits environmental issues against each other. One problem for salmon advocates is that hydroelectric dams provide power without contributing greenhouse gases to the environment. This creates the conundrum of pitting two environmental issues against each other: clean energy or salmon? The lack of a functional land ethic in America allows for solutions aimed at human convenience to gain precedence over seemingly "idealistic" and "unrealistic" efforts to preserve and restore salmon. Second, techno-optimistic solutions and ideas continue to dominate the national discourse on climate change. The effort to preserve and restore salmon necessitates a consistent refrain that sacrifice, conservation, and other steps can preclude the necessity for dams or nuclear power plants. Essentially, the opportunity exists for salmon advocates to complicate the debate from one of "What can be done most easily to fix this pressing problem?" to one of examining the ethical system guiding Americans' interaction with and uses of nature. A continuous and intelligent discussion of the need to preserve and restore salmon as part of a solution to global warming will help make the discourse more intelligent and mature, and in the end, more successful.

It may be necessary to make strategic moves to restore and preserve salmon, while recognizing that some clean energy sources such as the dams on the Columbia River are probably off-limits. Waterways like the Elwha and the Rogue and Klamath rivers of Oregon and California become important in this respect. In the case of the Elwha, with a sharp decline from the glacier fields to the Strait of Juan de Fuca, a distance of only 45 miles, the river offers a pristine ecosystem and clean water for salmon and steelhead; while glaciers retreat on the Olympic Peninsula and elsewhere, a respectable reserve of ice and snowpack remains in this range. The opportunity exists to restore population numbers from today's approximately 5,000 salmon to tens of thousands within a decade or two, while also expanding the diversity of the river's salmon, in imitation of its historical productivity and biodiversity. The removal of the dams on the Elwha provides compensatory salmon habitat for areas that may become unsuitable because of global warming, or for rivers where dams must remain because they provide credible amounts of hydroelectricity. Salmon advocates would do well to develop a strategy that requires mitigation of small rivers with dams as part of any package to develop an already sacrificed river, or as part of any relicensing process for a seemingly sacrosanct hydroelectric dam. Restoration advocates on smaller rivers throughout the region need to argue for the importance of these rivers in offsetting the impacts of global warming, giving a new urgency to their efforts that is not contrived but very real. The days of monumental rhetoric, aesthetics, and continued dependence on techno-optimistic solutions are coming to an end. Where possible, rivers have to be restored as completely as possible if salmon are going to survive their next peril.

Salmon advocates are pushing a fight-on-all-fronts strategy, which offers an opportunity to propose a natural reconstruction argument. By attempting to help salmon in numerous ways and places, a healthy process of habitat and ecosystem linkage is taking place. In so doing, they make the case for other benefits besides salmon; for example, the recent call by marine biologists for better salmon efforts to benefit diminishing orca populations. Not only does this advance the discourse, it also helps generate more support and broaden the constituency for rivers and salmon. Making the case that salmon preservation and restoration benefits multiple species strengthens advocates' efforts.

Extending that point, salmon advocates need to link widespread, complex ecosystem improvements, with salmon as the linchpin, to economic benefits. The case needs to be driven home that an ethical system which includes a healthy relationship with nature can also provide jobs and sustainable economic growth. For example, restoration of salmon streams provides indirect jobs through tourism, sport and commercial fishing, and of course, restoration work itself.[84]

Another strategy is promoting salmon efforts as a jobs and stimulus package. Replanting tree corridors along rivers; building pumping stations and laying pipe for warm-water and low-water events; restoring estuaries in the lowlands of the coastal region; removing culverts and dams; rebuilding stream and river ecosystems—all provide jobs and benefit local economies. Moreover, building an educational component into these jobs, like the Civilian Conservation Corps (CCC) did with their restoration projects,[85] will not only recruit workers to these efforts but also help educate the broader public. Demonstration projects of stream restoration and returning salmon runs, like the demonstration projects of the CCC, could go a long way toward educating and building support as well as providing tangible evidence of the benefits of using the land ethic to reconstruct Americans' relationship with nature.

This all leads to the most important point—one that needs to be centered in the dialogue about salmon and climate change, and which is largely missing at this point: the still-imperative need to construct a new narrative about our relationship with nature that emphasizes the land ethic. Seventy years after Aldo Leopold's articulation of the land ethic, Americans still fall drastically short of that idea. The broad-based, fight-on-all-fronts strategy needs to be built around the argument of a re-envisioning of the relationship between human society and nature, with the centerpiece of that relationship being the land ethic.

The efforts to create salmon strongholds in Canada, the U.S., and Russia reflect many of the strategies stated above, and if achievable, offer a comprehensive approach to salmon preservation and restoration. The proposed Pacific Salmon Stronghold Conservation Act (2009) in the United States sought to set aside and protect the salmon ecosystems that are currently healthy and contain diverse populations. Although this bill failed to gain enough support to move forward, this approach holds great future promise. Canada is a little further down this path with the creation of its first salmon stronghold on the Harrison River of British Columbia. The importance of healthy national park ecosystems in the Pacific Northwest, with an increasing emphasis on habitat and species preservation over time, attains greater importance in the discussion of necessary steps for protecting salmon in the face of climate change. For example, the Hoh River, draining the western and rainforest side of the Olympic Mountains, is a very healthy ecosystem from its headwaters in Hoh Glacier to the point that it leaves the park. The river still hosts strong salmon and steelhead runs and a local partnership managed to set aside 7,000 acres of protected river habitat, stretching from the Pacific Ocean to the park boundary. This model of government and local action, focused on stronghold creation, holds a great deal of promise for salmon conservation in the face of climate change's devastating impacts. The other benefit is that these strongholds will extend and improve habitat for elk, bear, marbled murrelets, and numerous other species.[86]

The restored Elwha River could be a cornerstone and model in this effort to create and extend a land ethic while reconstructing nature. Or, the Elwha could serve another, less positive purpose. If, in fact, Americans fail to construct a better ethical system for our relationship with nature, refusing to make major moves to stop and reverse global warming and protect Northwest salmon stocks, then rivers like the Elwha, Klamath, Snohomish, and Rogue could well serve as ark rivers—uniquely healthy rivers that can preserve enough salmon stock to reintroduce species across the region when and if we get on the other side of the global warming crisis.

The history of the Elwha River from the early 19th century to the present shows an ever-changing relationship between human communities and the river, as well as corresponding changes in use. As society and its needs changed, the meaning of the Elwha River changed as well. Once the ecological and cultural heart of the Lower Elwha Klallam Indian community and a prodigious producer of magnificent salmon, the river was transformed and degraded by the construction of one dam, then another. A new industrial river was created in order to "spawn," sustain, and expand a thriving, industrial metropolis on the Olympic Peninsula.

By making the Elwha River an industrial river, the local boosters, capitalists, and leaders elided the river's original meaning. Their river use and practices, as well as the limitations of state conservationists' power, exacerbated the river's deterioration, inflicting great damage on downstream salmon in addition to the destruction of upstream salmon. Their destruction of the Elwha River as a salmon river, culturally and functionally, did not go uncontested. Local voices insisted that the Elwha remain at least partially a salmon river. Their continuing use of the lower river, their critiques of dam owners, and the pressure they placed on the Washington State Department of Fisheries swelled—until the 1970s and 1980s, when a major challenge arose and discussion over the river's meaning and therefore its uses changed once again. Not satisfied with this limited organic machine, fish biologists, environmentalists, and the Lower Elwha Klallam launched a fight to resurrect the Elwha to some version of its original health and productivity and restore the Elwha's meaning as a salmon river.

Insistence on recreating the Elwha as a salmon river—together with persistent, effective organizing and consensus building; a regional Northwest salmon crisis; and growing national environmental consciousness—led to the passage of the Elwha Restoration Act in 1992. Since then, the restoration and re-creation of this river has been hindered by political gamesmanship and lack of appropriations.

With the dams gone, the salmon will again find the river and begin swimming upstream. In the end, the salmon themselves will find the Elwha River and its watershed and begin the last stage of restoring it to a salmon river once again.

Even as the salmon reclaim creeks, estuaries, and the upper river itself, the meaning of the Elwha will likely begin to shift again, as climate change looms. At one time, the Elwha River was poised to become a landmark in American history and in American environmentalism. While the Elwha removals will remain important as the largest dams removed for fisheries restoration in American history, and, hopefully, for the successes of the restoration, the more important new meaning of the Elwha may derive from the impending climate crisis. Healthy river ecosystems like the Elwha will become exponentially more important if and when salmon stocks collapse throughout the region. They will serve as ark rivers as temperatures rise. The Elwha will invariably suffer like other rivers, but the relative pristine nature of its watershed and the variety of salmon on the river may enable it to preserve enough salmon for a day when temperatures decrease and salmon reintroduction can begin again on damaged rivers. It is hard to imagine a river having such significance and bearing such a burden, but the Elwha River has always been important to the communities living on and near its shores. As the salmon nose their way into the deep pools and thrash through the riffles, I look forward to seeing this both new and old Elwha become a salmon river once again.

Notes

INTRODUCTION

1. Steelhead trout and salmon are similar species with a couple of important differences. The key similarity is that steelhead and salmon both spend time in the ocean and travel upstream to spawn and reproduce. For the sake of simplicity, in this book I will use salmon inclusively for salmon and steelhead. Chapter 1 will cover some of their differences and similarities.

CHAPTER 1

1. My late father was a lifelong conservative and lover of nature. When I showed him the dam I had spent so much time studying (the Elwha Dam), he immediately recognized the crux of the problem, that so small and limited a dam could do so much damage. While the statement he made may sound presumptuous, that was not his style. He was just surprised by how small and antiquated the dam appeared and recognized how seemingly easy it would be to fix an environmental problem on this particular river.

2. Stewart T. Schultz, *The Northwest Coast: A Natural History* (Portland, OR: Timber Press, 1990), 13–15; Rowland W. Tabor, *Geology of Olympic National Park* (Seattle, WA: Pacific Northwest National Parks & Forests Association, 1987), 28–36; Bates McKee, *Cascadia: The Geologic Evolution of the Pacific Northwest* (New York: McGraw-Hill Book Company, 1972), 48–65, 154–72.

3. Salmon are genetically predisposed for colonization. A small percentage of salmon from each spawning group migrate to other streams. When the Olympic Mountains were a raw mound of rock and mud, with the streams beginning to cut their way through the sandstone and basalt, stray salmon from other rivers found streams such as the Elwha and colonized them.

4. Tabor, *Geology of Olympic National Park*, 41–44, 85–87; Tim McNulty, *Olympic National Park: A Natural History Guide* (New York: Houghton Mifflin Company, 1996), 57–58; Robert L. Wood, *Olympic Mountains Trail Guide: National Park and National Forest* (Seattle, WA: The Mountaineers, 1984), 8–9.

5. Wood, *Olympic Mountains Trail Guide*, 38; National Park Service, *The Elwha Report: Restoration of the Elwha River Ecosystem & Native Anadromous Fisheries* (Denver, CO: National Park Service, September 1993), introduction.

6. McNulty, *Olympic National Park*, 91.

7. Tabor, *Geology of Olympic National Park*, 86–87; National Park Service, *The Elwha Report*, introduction; Jerry F. Franklin and C. T. Dyrness, *Natural Vegetation of Oregon and Washington* (Corvallis, OR: Oregon State University Press, 1988), 94–95; Wood, *Olympic Mountains Trail Guide*, 40–44.

8. Smolting is a process in which the fry begin to physically change in preparation for their entry into a saltwater habitat. At this point they are referred to as smolts.

9. Turbidity refers to the amount of suspended sediments in the water.

10. Thomas P. Quinn, *The Behavior and Ecology of Pacific Salmon and Trout* (Seattle, WA: University of Washington Press, 2005).

11. Issues of water velocity, depth, and size of gravel and cobble vary by species and size within species.

12. Quinn, *The Behavior and Ecology of Pacific Salmon and Trout*, 114.

13. Ibid., 110–16.

14. Bruce Brown, *Mountain in the Clouds: A Search for the Wild Salmon* (New York: Collier Books, 1990), 77. I owe a great deal to this book. It helped me to really see the Olympic Peninsula, including the Elwha River, before I went to college and spent many of my weekends hiking the river trails of the range. Brown's story of the Elwha Dam captured my imagination.

15. Douglas Gantenbein, "Let the River Run: Demolishing Two Dams on the Olympic Peninsula Promises to Restore the Legendary Salmon of the Elwha River; Washington State: Olympic National Park," *National Parks* 11 (January 1997): 22.

16. Robert E. Bilby, Brian R. Fransen, and Peter A. Bisson, "Incorporation of Nitrogen and Carbon from Spawning Coho Salmon into the Trophic System of Small Streams: Evidence from Stable Isotopes," *Canadian Journal of Fisheries and Aquatic Sciences* 53, no. 1 (January 1996): 164–73; Gantenbein, "Let the River Run," 22.

17. Brown, *Mountain in the Clouds*, 62; McNulty, *Olympic National Park*, 106–8.

18. James G. Swan with an introduction by Norman H. Clark, *The Northwest Coast: Or, Three Years Residence in Washington Territory* (1857; reprinted Seattle, WA: University of Washington Press, 1977), v.

19. Ibid., 256.

20. Ibid., 274–75.

21. Ibid., 41.

22. Colleen Elizabeth Boyd, "Changer Is Coming: History, Identity, and the Land among the Lower Elwha Klallam Tribe of the North Olympic Peninsula," PhD diss., University of Washington, 2001, v (preface).

23. Wayne Suttles, *Coast Salish Essays* (Seattle, WA: University of Washington Press, 1987), 3–14; Carlos A. Schwantes, *The Pacific Northwest: An Interpretive History* (Lincoln, NE: University of Nebraska Press, 1989), 28–32.

24. Jamie Valadez, "Elwha Klallam" in *Native Peoples of the Olympic Peninsula*, ed. Jacilee Wray (Norman, OK: University of Oklahoma Press, 2002), 21.

25. Ibid.

26. George Pierre Castile, ed., *The Indians of Puget Sound: The Notebooks of Myron Eells* (Seattle, WA: University of Washington Press, 1985), 17, 18.

27. Ibid., 18.

28. Ibid.

29. Erna Gunther, "Klallam Ethnography," *University of Washington Publications in Anthropology*, vol. 1 (Seattle, WA: University of Washington Press, 1927), 183, 186.

30. Erna Gunther, *Ethnobotany of Western Washington: The Knowledge and Uses of Indigenous Plants by Native Americans* (Seattle, WA: University of Washington Press, 1945), 15–19.

31. Gunther, "Klallam Ethnography," 211.

32. Ibid., 212–13, 219–26; Keith Ervin, *Fragile Majesty: The Battle for North America's Last Great Forest* (Seattle, WA: The Mountaineers, 1989), 30.

33. Gunther, "Klallam Ethnography," 231.

34. Ibid., 171–314.

35. Ibid., 202.

36. Ibid., 205.

37. Ibid., 195, 196.

38. Ibid., 191–204; Suttles, "Variation in Habitat and Culture on the Northwest Coast," *Coast Salish Essays*, 26–44. While in this essay the author is not reporting specifically on the Klallam people, he is discussing tribes in the immediate area, 20 miles across the Strait of Juan de Fuca to the north, who were culturally very similar to the Klallam. This essay provides a valuable discussion of the use of resources within the ecosystem by the Coast Salish Indians.

39. Gunther, "Klallam Ethnography," 199.

40. Ibid., 199, 200.

41. Ibid.

42. Ibid.

43. National Park Service, *The Elwha Report*, 7; Gunther, "Klallam Ethnography," 198–200.

44. Gunther, "Klallam Ethnography," 200.

45. Ibid.

46. Ibid., 207, 208.

47. Boyd, "Changer Is Coming," 91, 92.

48. Gunther, "Klallam Ethnography," 203.

49. Ibid., 203, 204; J. Donald Hughes, *American Indian Ecology* (El Paso, TX: Texas Western Press, 1983), 23–48; Valadez, "Elwha Klallam," 22.

50. *San Francisco Bulletin*, January 18, 1860.

51. Gunther, "Klallam Ethnography," 202.

52. Ibid., 203.

53. Ibid., 233.

54. Ibid., 212, 213.

55. Ibid., 195.

56. Suttles, *Coast Salish Essays*, 25, 204.

57. Ibid., 204.

58. Ibid., 205.

59. Ibid.

60. Joseph Taylor, *Making Salmon: An Environmental History of the Northwest Fisheries Crisis* (Seattle, WA: University of Washington Press, 1999), 20.

61. Ibid., 27–37.

62. Lynda V. Mapes, *Breaking Ground: The Lower Elwha Klallam Tribe and the Unearthing of Tse-Whit-zen Village* (Seattle, WA: University of Washington Press, 2009), 40–47; a thorough description of losses to disease by Native Americans in the Puget Sound Region is provided in Richard White's *Land Use, Environment, and Social Change: The Shaping of Island County, Washington* (Seattle: University of Washington Press, 1980), 26–29. "Smallpox pushed into the interior of the continent well ahead of the Europeans, probably reaching Puget Sound in 1782 or 1783. When George Vancouver first sailed into Puget Sound in 1792, smallpox scars . . . were already borne by many . . . Near Port Discovery on the Olympic Peninsula, Vancouver described a deserted village 'capable of containing a hundred habitants,' but 'The habitations had now fallen into decay; their inside, as well as a small surrounding space that appeared to have been formerly occupied, were overrun with weed; amongst which were found several human skulls, and other bones, promiscuously scattered about.'"

63. Schwantes, *The Pacific Northwest*, 36, 37.

64. Community Development Block Grant Program Preapplication Narrative Statement, by The Lower Elwha Tribal Community, 1, 2, Box 15, Washington State Archives–Olympia (WSA); Robert H. Ruby and John A. Brown, *Indians of the Pacific Northwest* (Norman, OK: University of Oklahoma Press, 1981), 134, 135.

65. Boyd, "Changer Is Coming," 247.

66. Ibid., 251; Valadez, "Elwha Klallam," 25.

CHAPTER 2

1. *San Francisco Bulletin*, January 25, 1860.

2. Ruby El Hult, *The Untamed Olympics: The Story of a Peninsula* (Portland, OR: Binford & Mort, 1954), 90–92; Paul J. Martin and Peggy Brady, *Port Angeles, Washington: A History* (Port Angeles, WA: Peninsula Publishing, 1983), 9–11; *Dungeness Beacon* (Port Angeles, WA), July 29, 1892, August 19, 1892, September 2, 1892, September 16, 1892; *The Tribune-Times* (Port Angeles, WA), August 2, 1894, 3; August 16, 1894, 3; January 31, 1895, 3; August 2, 1895, 2; August 23, 1895, 3; *The Model Commonwealth* (Port Angeles, WA), June 18, 1886.

3. Schwantes, *The Pacific Northwest*, 159.

4. Murray Morgan, *The Last Wilderness* (Seattle, WA: University of Washington Press, 1976), 87.

5. Ibid.

6. Ibid., 87, 88.

7. Thomas T. Aldwell, *Conquering the Last Frontier* (Seattle, WA: Superior Publishing Company, 1950), 19–20.

8. The Lower Elwha Klallam use that term to refer to the non-Indians who migrated into the area.

9. Mapes, *Breaking Ground*, 62.

10. Aldwell, *Conquering the Last Frontier*, 18–20.

11. Hult, *Untamed Olympics*, 106, 107, 113–17; Martin and Brady, *Port Angeles, Washington*, 55.

12. Hult, *Untamed Olympics*, 114, 115.

13. Ibid., 106, 107, 113–17; *Dungeness Beacon* (Port Angeles, WA), February 3, 1893; *Tribune-Times* (Port Angeles, WA), July 26, 1894, 5; Martin and Brady, *Port Angeles, Washington*, 55; Aldwell, *Conquering the Last Frontier*, 19–20.

14. Aldwell, *Conquering the Last Frontier*, 26.

15. William Cronon employed these terms in *Nature's Metropolis*. Simply put, first nature is the landscape and resources available when Americans arrive and begin building a community. First nature specifically refers to a way of seeing and touting the natural benefits of a place. Fertile soil, minerals, good transportation routes such as rivers, lakes, ocean, and flat land, as well as salmon and other resources, are promoted as beneficial aspects of first nature. Second nature refers to the ways these early community builders transform the landscape to make it even more economically beneficial. Roads, railroads, canals, the lifting of towns from drainages, and dams are among the changes that transform first nature to second nature.

16. Aldwell, *Conquering the Last Frontier*, 68.

17. Ibid.

18. Ibid., 20; Hult, *Untamed Olympics*, 114–19; Martin and Brady, *Port Angeles, Washington*, 55.

19. "Scenic Wonders of the Picturesque Elwha River," *Seattle Post-Intelligencer*, December 1, 1901.

20. Ibid.

21. "Development News—Rural Electricity in the West," *Pacific Monthly* XXIV, no. 2 (August 1910): 222; "Development News—Immense Water Power of the Pacific Northwest," *Pacific Monthly* XXIII, no. 1 (January 1910): 104–5; Bruce Wolverton, "The Water Power of the Pacific Northwest," *Pacific Monthly* XI, no. 3 (March 1904): 155–69; Thomas P. Hughes, *Networks of Power: Electrification in Western Society, 1880–1930* (Baltimore, MD: The Johns Hopkins University Press, 1983), 129–39, 270–84.

22. Frederick H. Newell, "Part IV—Hydrography," in *United States Geological Survey 19th Annual Report 1897–98*.

23. Frederick H. Newell, "Part IV—Hydrography," in *United States Geological Survey 20th Annual Report 1898–99*.

24. Wolverton, "The Water Power of the Pacific Northwest," 169.

25. Clallam County Immigration Association, *Port Angeles, the Gate City of the Pacific Coast* (Port Angeles, WA: Clallam County Immigration Association, 1898), 46. Port Angeles civic leaders and boosters sought not only the extraction of resources for profit but also the creation of a major urban metropolis.

26. Ibid.

27. "Our Magnificent Waterpower," *The Democrat Leader* (Port Angeles, WA), January 11, 1895, 2.

28. Ibid., 80–83; "Industrial Power Franchise Granted," *Olympic Leader*, April 1, 1910; Hosey and Associates, unpublished report prepared by Hosey and Associates for the James River Corporation, "Response to Request for Additional Information of May 28, 1987: Elwha Project FERC No. 2683, Glines Project FERC No. 588," February 12, 1988, 28, 29.

29. Boyd, "Changer Is Coming," 253.

30. Ibid., 256.

31. Valadez, "Elwha Klallam," 23.

32. Boyd, "Changer Is Coming," 258.

33. Hult, *Untamed Olympics*, 190–93; "Elwha Power to Be Developed," *Port Angeles Tribune-Times*, February 11, 1910.

34. "The Elwha Water Power," *Olympic Leader*, February 11, 1910.

35. Aldwell, *Conquering the Last Frontier*, 83–85; Articles of Incorporation, Olympic Power & Development Company, Secretary of State's Records at the WSA; *Port Angeles Tribune-Times*, April 1, 1910, 1; April 8, 1910, 1; "Industrial Power Franchise Granted," *Olympic Leader*, April 1, 1910.

36. "Peninsula Opens Lively Campaign of Development," *Seattle Times*, March 12, 1911.

37. Ibid.

38. Aldwell, *Conquering the Last Frontier*, 85.

39. Ibid., 87–90; Articles of Incorporation, Olympic Power Company, Secretary of State's Records, WSA.

40. Hult, *Untamed Olympics*, 186.

41. Ibid., 184–90; Hosey and Associates, "Response to Request . . . ", 28.

42. William G. Robbins, *Hard Times in Paradise: Coos Bay, Oregon, 1850–1986* (Seattle, WA: University of Washington Press, 1988), 3.

43. Hult, *Untamed Olympics*, 192.

44. William G. Robbins, *Colony and Empire: The Capitalist Transformation of the American West* (Lawrence, KS: University Press of Kansas, 1994), 62.

45. *The Commonwealth*, December 28, 1888, 2; *Tribune-Times*, August 2, 1894, 3; "Prosperity Edition," *Tribune-Times*, May 15, 1914.

46. Duncan Hay, *Hydroelectric Development in the United States, 1880–1940* (Washington, D.C.: Edison Electric Institute, 1991), 100–103; "Western Hydroelectric Transmission Developments," *Journal of Electricity, Power and Gas*, 34, no. 23 (June 5, 1915): 444–47.

47. Jim Lichatowich, *Salmon Without Rivers: A History of the Pacific Salmon Crisis* (Washington, D.C.: Island Press, 1999), 76, 77.

48. Roderick Nash, *Wilderness and the American Mind* (New Haven, CT: Yale University Press, 1967), 24–25.

49. Richard White, *The Organic Machine: The Remaking of the Columbia River* (New York: Hill and Wang, 1995), 48.

50. "Fatal Accident at Elwha Power Plant," *Olympic Leader*, March 8, 1912, 1.

51. Ibid.

52. "Plunged to His Death," *Tribune-Times*, August 18, 1911.

53. "New Lighting Plan Complete," *Tribune-Times*, July 12, 1912, 1.

54. Ibid.

55. "Olympic Power Plant Turning Up," *Tribune-Times*, October 25, 1912, 1.

56. Thomas Aldwell to J. L. Houghteling, Jr. of Peabody, Houghteling & Co., April 23, 1912, 1. Thomas Aldwell Papers, Box 2, Folder 17, UWSC.

57. Thomas Aldwell to Alexander Smith of Peabody, Houghteling & Co., April 29, 1912, 1, 2. Aldwell Papers, Box 2, Folder 17, USWC.

58. Ibid.

59. Ibid., 1.

60. Charles M. Maib, "A Historical Note on the Elwha River Its Power Development and It's Industrial Diversion," (Olympia, WA: Washington Stream Improvement Division, State Department of Fisheries [no date]), 3. OLYM 429, Box 2, Folder 44, The Philip R.S. Johnson Elwha River Sources, Olympic National Park Cultural Resources Office Archives (ONPA).

61. Thomas Aldwell, to Alexander Smith of Peabody, Houghteling & Co., June 10, 1912, 2, 3 Aldwell Papers, Box 2, Folder 18, UWSC; Maib, "Historical Note on the Elwha River," 3, 4.

62. Thomas Aldwell to Alexander Smith of Peabody, Houghteling & Co., July 1, 1912, 1, 2. Aldwell Papers, Box 2, Folder 18, UWSC.

63. Thomas Aldwell to Alexander Smith of Peabody, Houghteling & Co., July 12, 1912, 1. Aldwell Papers, Box 2, Folder 18, UWSC.

64. Thomas Aldwell to J. L. Houghteling, Jr. of Peabody, Houghteling & Co., July 16, 1912, 1. Aldwell Papers, Box 2, Folder 18, UWSC

65. Ibid.

66. Aldwell, *Conquering the Last Frontier*, 91–107. "Olympic Power Company's Big Dam Blows Out Below," *Tribune-Times*, November 1, 1912, 1. The first published comment on the status of salmon blocked by the dams was published half a month following the blowout of the dam. "Following the breaking of the dam the salmon immediately took advantage of the breach and a number were seen in Little River and Indian Creek. These streams were favorite spawning rounds [*sic*] of the salmon in the past, but since construction work was commenced on the dams, two years ago, they have been entirely shut out as the company made no provision whatever for them to get by the dam." "News Items from Over the County," *Tribune-Times*, November 15, 1912, 3.

67. "Olympic Power Company's Big Dam Blows Out Below," *Tribune-Times*, November 1, 1912, 1.

68. Ibid.

69. Valadez, "Elwha Klallam," 28, 29.

70. "Olympic Power Company's Big Dam Blows Out Below," *Tribune-Times*, November 1, 1912, 1.

71. Quoted from Brian D. Winters and Patrick Crain, "Making the Case for Ecosystem Restoration by Dam Removal in the Elwha River, Washington," special issue, *Northwest Science* 82 (2008): 15.

72. Aldwell, *Conquering the Last Frontier*, 108–11; Maib, "Historical Note on the Elwha River," 5.

73. James H. Price, Secretary of State, *"Session Laws of the State of Washington, Session of 1893,"* Olympia, WA: O.C. White, State Printer, 1893.

74. J. W. Pike, Clallam County Game Warden, to John L. Riseland, Washington State Fish Commissioner, September 12, 1911, Elwha River File, Box 1010-38, WSA.

75. Ibid.

76. John Crawford, General Superintendent of Washington State Fish Hatcheries, to John L. Riseland, Washington State Fish Commissioner, October 23, 1911, Elwha River File, WSA.

77. John L. Riseland, Washington State Fish Commissioner, to Thomas Aldwell, January 11, 1912, Elwha River File, WSA.

78. "Capt. Riseland Succeeded in Office by Darwin," *The Bellingham Herald*, April 3, 1913, 1; Obituary, *The Bellingham Herald*, May 8, 1955, 3.

79. Several newspaper articles and editorials from the paper demonstrate its progressive tone and Darwin's concerns. "Personal Gain Is Back of B.B.I. Interest in Road," *American Reveille*, September 3, 1911, 1, 2; "People are Learning Truth: Fact Is Being Borne in on Voters That Equalizers Slipped Fish Trust Double Prize Package in Assessment," *American Reveille*, September 3, 1911, 1, 2. One editorial stated, "Throughout the centuries labor has been held to be menial and degrading. As education and civilization make headway it is coming more and more to be recognized as highly honorable. In truth, today the person who does not labor is despised or pitied, according to the viewpoint from which the question is approached. We believe that the Creator intended that every person should work, and that the unhappiest class today are those whose possession of great riches enable them to exist with it. It is the idle sons and daughters of the very wealthy whose names fill most of the scandal and suicide columns of the papers today." "Labor Day," *American Reveille*, September 3, 1911, 4. Another editorial, a week later, more unequivocally states the progressive philosophy: "Believing that every person of intelligence must appreciate that in order to perpetuate the principles of a Republican form of government it is necessary that the power be retained in the hands of the people, we shall favor men who believe in amending the city charter so as to place the power of the recall of unfaithful and inefficient public officers in the hands of the people" (*American Reveille*, September 10, 1911, 4); "Today's Election Busts the Trusts: Nominee of Special Interests Doomed to Defeat—Miller, People's Friend Will Lead at the Polls—Last Lies of Reptile Press Are Nailed," *American Reveille*, November 7, 1911, 1, 2; "Big Fish Trust Is Arrested for Violating Law: Pacific American Fisheries Will Be Prosecuted on Charge of Working Women More Than Eight Hours," *American Reveille*, November 7, 1911, 1, 2.

80. Iola I. Berg, *History of the Washington State Department of Fisheries, 1890–1967* (Olympia, WA: General Administration Building, 1968), 11; Brown, *Mountain in the Clouds*, 66–69; Lottie Roeder Roth, ed., *History of Whatcom County*, vol. 1 (Seattle, WA: Pioneer Historical Publishing Company, 1926), 586–87.

81. Clayton R. Koppes, "Efficiency/Equity/Esthetics: Towards a Reinterpretation of American Conservation," *Environmental Review* 11, no. 2 (Summer 1987): 128.

82. Richard Hofstadter, *The Age of Reform: From Bryan to F.D.R.* (New York: Alfred A. Knopf, 1955), 10.

83. Ibid., 144.

84. Koppes, "Efficiency/Equity/Esthetics," 129.

85. Gifford Pinchot, *Breaking New Ground* (Seattle, WA: University of Washington Press, 1947), 83.

86. Patricia Nelson Limerick, *The Legacy of Conquest: The Unbroken Past of the American West* (New York: W. W. Norton & Company, 1987), 299; Robert H. Wiebe, *The Search for Order: 1877–1920* (New York: Hill and Wang, 1967), 164–95; Donald Worster, *Nature's Economy: A History of Ecological Ideas* (New York: Cambridge University Press, 1977), 266–68.

87. L. H. Darwin, *Thirtieth and Thirty-first Annual Reports of the State Fish Commissioner to the Governor of the State of Washington, April 1, 1919, to March 31, 1921* (Olympia, WA: Frank M. Lamborn, 1921), 14.

88. Koppes, "Efficiency/Equity/Esthetics," 130.

89. Darwin, *Thirtieth and Thirty-first Annual Reports*, 15.

90. Samuel P. Hays, *Conservation and the Gospel of Efficiency: The Progressive Conservation Movement, 1890–1920* (Cambridge, MA: Harvard University Press, 1959), 265.

91. Darwin, *Thirtieth and Thirty-first Annual Reports*, 15.

92. Ibid.

93. Ibid.

94. Hays, *Conservation and the Gospel of Efficiency*, 265–75; Alfred Runte, *National Parks: The American Experience* (Lincoln, NE: University of Nebraska Press, 1979); Stephen Fox, *The American Conservation Movement: John Muir and His Legacy* (Madison, WI: University of Wisconsin Press, 1981); L. H. Darwin, *Twenty-fourth and Twenty-fifth Annual Reports of the State Fish Commissioner to the Governor of the State of Washington, April 1, 1913, to March 31, 1915* (Olympia, WA: Frank M. Lamborn, 1916), 14, 27.

95. L. H. Darwin, Washington State Fish Commissioner, to Thomas Aldwell, August 17, 1913, Elwha River File, WSA.

96. Ibid.; Brown, *Mountain in the Clouds*, 68.

97. L. H. Darwin to Thomas Aldwell, June 2, 1914, Elwha River File, WSA.

98. Ibid., June 3, 1914; several letters between Aldwell and Darwin through the month of June, Elwha River File, WSA; Virginia Egan, "Restoring the Elwha: Salmon, Dams and People on the Olympic Peninsula, A Case Study of Environmental Decision-Making" (PhD diss., Antioch University, 2007), 65.

99. Darwin, *Twenty-fourth and Twenty-fifth Annual Reports*, 101.

100. John N. Cobb, *Pacific Salmon Fisheries: Appendix III to the Report of U.S. Commissioner of Fisheries for 1916* (Washington, D.C.: Government Printing Office, 1917), 244.

101. Lichatowich, *Salmon Without Rivers*, 121; J. T. Brown, "A History of Fish Culture as Related to the Development of Fishery Programs," in *A Century of Fisheries in North America*, Norman G. Benson, ed., (Washington, D.C.: American Fisheries Society, 1970), 81–83.

102. Lichatowich, *Salmon Without Rivers*, 116.

103. Ibid., 118.

104. Ibid., 120–22; Brown, "A History of Fish Culture," 72–80.

105. Quoted from Paul E. Thompson, "The First Fifty Years: The Exciting Ones," in *A Century of Fisheries*, 5.

106. *Report of the Commissioners of Fisheries of the State of Maine, 1879*, 6.

107. Ibid.

108. Taylor, *Making Salmon*, 98.

109. Ibid., 75.

110. Ibid., 76.

111. They also introduced other numerous species around the nation, like smallmouth and largemouth bass, multiple varieties of carp, as well as brook and rainbow trout.

112. Taylor, *Making Salmon*, 82.

113. Arthur F. McEvoy, *The Fisherman's Problem: Ecology and Law in the California Fisheries, 1850–1980* (New York: Cambridge University Press, 1986), 104.

114. Ibid.

115. Ibid., 72, 73.

116. Ibid.

117. Lichatowich, *Salmon Without Rivers*, 113.

118. McEvoy, *The Fisherman's Problem*, 108.

119. Ibid., 113.

120. Taylor, *Making Salmon*, 89.

121. While some might condemn my seemingly ahistorical criticism of Stone, it must be pointed out that the only way he could have come to such a belief is by ignoring all evidence and local knowledge.

122. Bill M. Bakke and Joseph Cone, "Commentary," in *The Northwest Salmon Crisis: A Documentary History*, Joseph Cone and Sandy Ridlington, eds. (Corvallis, OR: Oregon State University Press, 1996), 47.

123. Bakke and Cone, "Commentary," 46, 47; Livingston Stone, "Explorations on the Columbia River," in *The Northwest Salmon Crisis*, 28, 29.

124. Lichatowich, *Salmon Without Rivers*, 141, 142.

125. Ibid.

126. Bakke and Cone, "Commentary," 48.

127. Taylor, *Making Salmon*, 89.

128. Lichatowich, *Salmon Without Rivers*, 149.

129. Ibid.

130. Ibid.

131. Ibid., 158.

132. L. H. Darwin to Governor Ernest Lister, September 8, 1915, Lister File, WSA.

133. Brown, *Mountain in the Clouds*, 71; L. H. Darwin to J. W. Pike, Clallam County Game Warden, May 20, 1914, Elwha River File, WSA; Darwin, *Twenty-eighth and Twenty-ninth Annual Reports of the State Fish Commissioner to the Governor of the State of Washington, April 1, 1917, to March 31, 1919*, 18, 19; Darwin, *Twenty-sixth and Twenty-seventh Annual Reports of the State Fish Commissioner to the Governor of the State of Washington*, 39.

134. Darwin, *Twenty-fourth and Twenty-fifth Annual Reports of the State Fish Commissioner to the Governor of the State of Washington, April 1, 1913, to March 31, 1915*, 112; Berg, *History of the Washington State Department of Fisheries*, 11.

135. Ibid., Introduction.

136. Darwin, *Thirtieth and Thirty-first Annual Reports of the State Fish Commissioner to the Governor of the State of Washington, April 1, 1919, to March 31, 1921*, 7.

137. Ibid., 7–9, 14–15.

138. Aldwell, *Conquering the Last Frontier*, 114–19; *Thirty-fourth and Thirty-fifth Annual Reports of State Supervisor of Fisheries for the Period from April 1, 1923, to March 31, 1925* (Olympia, WA: Jay Thomas, 1925), 23; Brian D. Winters and Patrick Crain, "Making the Case for Ecosystem Restoration": 15.

CHAPTER 3

1. Hosey and Associates, "Response to Request . . . ", 46–52.

2. Mapes, *Breaking Ground*, 70.

3. Ibid., 71, 72.

4. Ibid., 74.

5. Ernest M. Brannon, superintendent of the Dungeness Hatchery, to the Washington State Supervisor of Fisheries, November 3, 1930, 1.

6. Ibid., 1, 2.

7. "Elwha River Ecosystem Restoration Implementations, 1996," 29. In 1996 there was an estimated 17.7 million cubic yards of clay, silt, gravel, and sand behind the dams. Because almost all of the watershed is in protected national park land there is not the concern of buildup of toxics in the sediment that is a consideration in other dam removal and sediment removal efforts.

8. Ibid., 28.

9. Brannon, to the Washington State Supervisor of Fisheries, November 3, 1930, 2, 3.

10. Brannon, to the Washington State Supervisor of Fisheries, July 15, 1931.

11. Egan, "Restoring the Elwha, 74.

12. Ibid.

13. Robert Lundhahl, transcript from documentary film, *Unconquering the Last Frontier*, 2002, 11.

14. Brown, *Mountain in the Clouds*, 93.

15. E. M. Benn to Washington State Director of Fisheries B. M. Brennan, March 16, 1934.

16. Ibid.

17. Congressman Francis Pearson to B. M. Brennan, August 24, 1938.

18. Ibid.

19. B. M. Brennan to Congressman Francis Pearson, August 27, 1938, 1.

20. Ibid.

21. Ibid., 2.

22. Ibid.

23. Washington State Director of Fisheries Fred J. Foster to Lew R. Thompson, December 5, 1941.

24. Milo Moore to Charles A. Faussett, December 26, 1946.

25. Ibid.

26. North Olympic Peninsula Chapter of the Poggie Club to the Director of the Washington State Department of Fisheries, February 14, 1951, Elwha River File, WSA.

27. Ibid.

28. Ibid.

29. Ibid.

30. Ibid.

31. Robert C. Meigs, assistant chief, Fishery Management Division, Washington State Department of Game, to Fred M. Veatch, district manager, Water Resources Division, U.S. Geological Survey, March 22, 1951.

32. John M. Hurley, chief, Stream Improvement Division, Washington State Department of Game, to Fred M. Veatch, March 26, 1951.

33. Ibid.

34. Marc Reisner, *Cadillac Desert: The American West and Its Disappearing Water* (New York: Penguin Books, 1986).

35. Ibid., 158, 159.

36. Ibid.

37. Lichatowich, *Salmon Without Rivers*, 184.

38. Ibid.

39. Ibid., 184–86.

40. Lisa Mighetto and Wesley J. Ebel, *Saving the Salmon: A History of the U.S. Army Corps of Engineers' Efforts to Protect Anadromous Fish on the Columbia and Snake Rivers* (Seattle, WA: Historical Research Associates, Inc., 1994), 70, 71.

41. "Game, Fishery Interests Oppose Cowlitz Dam," *Kelsonian Tribune*, March 27, 1947.

42. "Cowlitz Dam Will Injure Salmon," *Astoria Budget*, May 10, 1947.

43. Cain Allen, "'They Called it Progress': Indians, Salmon, and the Industrialization of the Columbia River" (MA thesis, Portland State University, 2000), 25–28.

44. Ibid., 28.

45. Katrine Barber, "After Celilo Falls: The Dalles Dam, Indian Fishing Rights, And Federal Energy Policy on the Mid-Columbia River" (PhD diss., Washington State University, 1999), 95.

46. Ibid.

47. I. T. Bode, director of the Missouri Department of Conservation, to Senator Thomas C. Hennings, Jr., April 7, 1953. Unprocessed Missouri

Department of Conservation Files, Missouri State Archives, Jefferson City, Missouri, 2.

48. Aldo Leopold, *A Sand County Almanac: And Sketches Here and There* (New York: Oxford University Press, 1949).

49. "Flood Control Program," *Walla Walla Union Bulletin*, November 14, 1948, 4.

50. Ibid.

51. "Must Speed River Program," *Walla Walla Union Bulletin*, November 12, 1948, 4.

52. Anthony Netboy, *The Columbia River Salmon and Steelhead Trout: Their Fight for Survival* (Seattle, WA: University of Washington Press, 1980).

53. Ibid., 87, 88.

54. Ibid., 88.

55. Dam boosters predicted the dams would be economically self-supporting, would not destroy salmon runs, and would turn interior port towns like Lewiston into bustling metropolises—all highly inaccurate. Opponents predicted that the dams would wreak havoc on salmon and steelhead runs and that taxpayers would end up bearing the burden of supporting the dam and lock system.

56. Keith Petersen, *River of Life, Channel of Death: Fish and Dams on the Lower Snake* (Lewiston, ID: Confluence Press, 1995), 113.

57. *State of Washington Department of Fisheries Annual Report for 1949, Washington Public Documents 1950.* (Olympia, WA: State Printing Plant, 1952), 4; Petersen, *River of Life,* 113; Goble, "Salmon in the Columbia Basin," 247.

58. Taylor, *Making Salmon*, 232.

59. Telegram from Robert J. Schoettler, director, Washington State Department of Fisheries, to Congressman Clarence Cannon, June 30, 1952, Ice Harbor, Snake River Files, WSA; Statement to the Appropriations Sub-Committee of Army Civil Functions from the Washington State Department of Fisheries, the Oregon State Fish Commission, the Washington State Department of Game, and the Oregon State Game Commission, June 27, 1952, Ice Harbor, Snake River Files, WSA.

60. Petersen, *River of Life,* 116.

61. "Long Range Basin Plans Under Study," *Walla Walla Union Bulletin*, November 11, 1948, 1.

62. Petersen, *River of Life,* 117.

63. From a Department of the Interior Press Release, Boise, ID, June 13, 1947, quoted from Blaine Harden, *A River Lost: The Life and Death of the Columbia* (New York: W.W. Norton & Company, 1996).

64. Mighetto and Ebel, *Saving the Salmon,* 1.

65. "Long Range Basin Plans Under Study," 1.

66. Taylor, *Making Salmon,* 247.

67. Mighetto and Ebel, *Saving the Salmon,* 55.

68. Ibid.

69. Harden, *A River Lost,* 207.

70. Shad are not indigenous to the Pacific Northwest and were introduced by the USFC during its early days of gleeful fish planting across the nation.

The shad fishery now thrives on the Columbia River and some tributary rivers like the Willamette in Oregon.

71. Mighetto and Ebel, *Saving the Salmon*, 106–12.

72. The smolt of different salmon species spend varying amounts of time in their natal streams before heading downriver.

73. Once commonly called squawfish, these fish are now officially designated the northern pikeminnow. Squawfish is still more commonly employed in the vernacular.

74. "2011 Northern Pikeminnow Sport-Reward Program," www.pikeminnow.or/info.html. Accessed July 5, 2011; Mark Yuasa, "Northern Pikeminnow Bounty Program Raised on Columbia River for Angler to Cash In On," *Seattle Times Online*, http://seattletimes.newsource.com/html/reeltimenorthwest/2009577743_northern_pikeminnow_bounty_rai.html. Accessed July 5, 2011.

75. Don Hannula, "Saving Salmon: Behold a $400 Squawfish," *Seattle Times*, July 15, 1992, A12.

76. Ibid.; Mark Yuasa, "Outdoor Notebook: Squawfish Bounty Gets an Extension," *Seattle Times*, September 24, 2000, C22.

77. National Research Council, *Upstream: Salmon and Society in the Pacific Northwest* (Washington, D.C.: National Academy Press, 1996), 234, 240.

78. Ibid., 230.

79. Mighetto and Ebel, *Saving the Salmon*, 90.

80. National Research Council, *Upstream: Salmon and Society*, 231, 232.

81. U.S. Army Corps of Engineers, *To Save the Salmon*, November 1997.

82. Susan Foster, chairwoman of the Oregon Fish and Wildlife Commission, to Will Stelle, regional director of the National Marine Fisheries Service, October 21, 1997. www.amrivers.org. Ms. Foster wrote about the problems with smolt transport and homing instincts. "The increase in the number of strays into the Deschutes [River] corresponds directly to a significant increase in the numbers of steelhead transported (barged). Information suggests that it is likely that homing of some adult steelhead that are transported as juveniles is impaired."

83. Mighetto and Ebel, *Saving the Salmon*, 119–25.

84. Michael C. Blumm, "The Northwest's Hydroelectric Heritage," in *Northwest Lands, Northwest Peoples: Readings in Environmental History*, Dale Goble and Paul Hirt, eds. (Seattle, WA: University of Washington Press, 1999), 284.

85. Independent Scientific Advisory Board, "Response to the Questions of the Implementation Team Regarding Juvenile Salmon Transportation in the 1998 Season," February 27, 1998; U.S. Army Corps of Engineers Web site, http://www.nwp.usace.army.mil/.

86. Mighetto and Ebel, *Saving the Salmon*, 115.

87. Jonathan Brinckman, "Fish-Friendly Turbines," *The Oregonian*, March 8, 2000.

88. NOAA Fisheries Service, "Northwest Fisheries Science Center," www.nwfsc.noaa.gov/index.cfm. Accessed July 6, 2011.

89. C. Jeff Cederholm, Matt D. Kunze, Takeshi Murota, and Atuhiro Sibatani, "Pacific Salmon Carcasses: Essential Contributions of Nutrients and Energy for Aquatic and Terrestrial Ecosystems," *Fisheries* 24, no. 10 (October 1999): 6–9.

90. Ray Hilborn, "Confessions of a Reformed Hatchery Basher," *Fisheries* 24, no. 5 (May 1999): 30.

91. Ibid.

92. Ibid.

93. Lichatowich, *Salmon Without Rivers*, 199.

94. Ibid., 194.

95. Ibid.

96. Meffe, Gary K., "Techno-Arrogance and Halfway Technologies: Salmon Hatcheries," *The Northwest Salmon Crisis*, 136.

97. Ibid., 136, 137.

98. Ibid.

99. Ibid., 137.

100. Ibid.

101. Ibid., 235–37; James R. Karr, "Restoring Wild Salmon: We Must Do Better," *Illahee: Journal for the Northwest Environment* 10 (Winter 1994): 318. This article spells out the numerous reasons for maintaining native salmon and steelhead stocks. "Native stocks are needed and will be needed in the future to (1) maintain natural genetic diversity within and among fish stocks needed to respond to major ecological and climatic changes, (2) provide the basis for re-establishing natural stocks where opportunities occur, (3) optimize natural production in streams, (4) support natural ecosystem function, (5) re-establish genetic variability in existing hatchery stocks, and (6) provide the basis for new hatchery stocks. While much progress has been made in artificially producing these fish, artificial production in itself cannot sustain them, and may contribute to the decline of native populations." Willa Nehlsen, Jack E. William, and James A. Lichatowich, "Pacific Salmon at the Crossroads: Stocks at Risk from California, Oregon, Idaho, and Washington," *Fisheries* 16 (March–April 1991): 4.

102. The Independent Scientific Group (Richard N. Williams, Peter A. Bisson, Daniel L. Bottom, Lyle D. Calvin, Charles C. Coutant, Michael W. Erho, Jr., Christopher A. Frissell, James A. Lichatowich, William J. Liss, Willis E. McConnaha, Phillip R. Mundy, Jack A. Stanford, and Richard R. Whitney), "Scientific Issues in the Restoration of Salmonid Fishes in the Columbia River," *Fisheries* 24, no. 3 (March 1999): 10.

103. R.A. Porsch, *Port Angeles Evening News*, October 6, 1949 (Letter to Editor), OLYM 429, Box 1, Folder 23, ONPA.

104. Ibid.

105. Willard K. Largo to Milo Bell, September 5, 1956, OLYM 429, Box 1, Folder 23, ONPA.

106. W. H. Gwynn to Milo Bell, September 4, 1956, OLYM 429, Box 1, Folder 23, ONPA.

107. Milo Bell to W. H. Gwynn and Willard K. Largo, September 5 and 11, 1956, OLYM 429, Box 1, Folder 23, ONPA.

108. State of Washington Department of Fisheries Management and Research Division, "Elwha River Fisheries Studies," November 1971, 5.

109. Ibid., summary.

110. Ibid., 12.

111. Winters and Crain, "Making the Case for Ecosystem Restoration," 16; interview with Robert Elofson, September 27, 2010.

CHAPTER 4

1. Brown, *Mountain in the Clouds*, 26.

2. Ibid.

3. Egan, "Restoring the Elwha," 113, 114.

4. "Olympic National Park Proposed Elwha Dams' Mitigation," Unpublished Paper, March 18, 1985, 1. Rick Rutz Papers, Box 3, UWSC.

5. Ibid.

6. Ibid.

7. Egan, "Restoring the Elwha," 114.

8. Ibid., 112–14.

9. Ibid., 115, 116.

10. Daishowa America purchased the mill in 1998.

11. Egan, "Restoring the Elwha," 117.

12. Sandi Doughton, "Dam Removal Prescribed for Ill Elwha," *Tacoma News Tribune*, September 3, 1991.

13. Comptroller General of the United States to Congressman John D. Dingell, October 20, 1992, 5. Al Swift Papers, Box 572, Niles 3, File 5, WWUARC.

14. Lower Elwha Tribal Council to Governor Booth Gardner, July 29, 1989. Elwha River Files, WSA.

15. Larry Swisher, "Tear Down the Dams? It's No Longer Such a Radical Idea," *Lewiston Morning Tribune*, July 13, 1992, A5.

16. "A Step Closer," *Seattle Times*, May 11, 1992, A10.

17. Ibid.

18. Friends of the Earth, *Elwha River Restoration Brochure*, 1993.

19. "An Upstream Battle," *Friends of the Earth*, September 1991, 6–9.

20. Don Hannula, "Return of the Giant Kings of the Elwha?" *Seattle Times*, April 25, 1990, A6.

21. John Muir, *My First Summer in the Sierra* (New York: Penguin Books, 1987), 190.

22. Roderick Nash, *Wilderness and the American Mind* (New Haven, CT: Yale University Press, 1967), 44–66; Max Oelschlager, *The Idea of Wilderness* (New Haven, CT: Yale University Press, 1991).

23. Willett Kempton, James S. Boster, and Jennifer A. Hartley, *Environmental Values in American Culture* (Cambridge, MA: The MIT Press, 1995), 94.

24. Letter from Janet Heineck, September 18, 1990. Elwha River File, WSA.

25. Letter from the Olympic Rivers Council, January 9, 1990. Elwha River File, WSA.

26. Letter from Dr. Helen James, January 8, 1990. Elwha River File, WSA.

27. Alfred Runte, *National Parks: The American Experience* (Lincoln, NE: University of Nebraska Press, 1987).

28. Muir, *My First Summer in the Sierra*, 14.

29. Nash, *Wilderness and the American Mind*, 69.

30. Ibid.

31. Petition to FERC on Project Nos. 588 and 2683 by Conservation Group Intervenors, March 25, 1988. Rick Rutz Papers, Box 2, UWSC.

32. Egan, "Restoring the Elwha," 130–32.

33. Ibid., 132, 133.

34. Congressman John Dingell to Congressman Al Swift, June 12, 1989. Elwha River File, Box 2, Folder 89, WSA.

35. Ibid.

36. Congressman John Dingell to Comptroller General Charles A. Bowsher, June 12, 1989, 1, 2. Elwha River File, Box 2, Folder 89, WSA.

37. Ibid.

38. Congressman John Dingell to Secretary of the Interior Manuel Lujan, Jr. and FERC Chairman Martha O. Hesse, June 12, 1989, 1. Elwha River File, Box 2 Folder 89, WSA.

39. Ibid.

40. Egan, "Restoring the Elwha," 149, 150.

41. Ibid., 151, 152.

42. Ibid.

43. Jim Baker, to Rick Rutz, September 1990. Rick Rutz Papers, Box 4, UWSC.

44. Jim Baker "Elwha Update: BPA Position Brings Dam Removal Closer," *Washington Wildfire* (January–February 1991): 23. Rick Rutz Papers, Box 4, UWSC.

45. Ibid.

46. Egan, "Restoring the Elwha," 155, 156.

47. "Notes on Elwha Dams, December 1991 and January 1992." Al Swift Papers, Box 573, Niles Folder 4, File 3, WWUARC.

48. Ibid.

49. Eric Niles to Al Swift, internal memorandum, March 26, 1992. Al Swift Papers, Box 72, Folder 3, File 6, WWUARC.

50. Jim Baker to Congressman Al Swift, September 11, 1990. Rick Rutz Papers, Box 4, UWSC.

51. Associated Press, "Elwha Fish Need Dams Destroyed, Agency Reports," *Tacoma News Tribune*, May 28, 1994, A8.

52. Ibid.

53. Ibid.

54. Brooke M. Drury, "Olympic Peninsula Resource—Fishing and Tourism Would Benefit," *Seattle Times* (Letter to Editor), April 16, 1995, B7.

55. "Gorton Should Support Removal of Elwha Dams," *Seattle Times*, March 21, 1996, B6.

56. Ibid.

57. Ironically, only a few years later environmentalists launched an attack on the lower Snake River dams. As the editorial writer noted, the economic interests supporting the dams would block any effort to remove those dams, a point that has been borne out by events so far.

58. Jim Simon, "Babbitt Gets Closer Look at Elwha Dams—Secretary of Interior to Work with Gorton on Funds for Removal," *Seattle Times*, August 7, 1997, A15.

59. Excellent discussion and analysis of this conflict is provided by William Dietrich, *The Final Forest: The Battle for the Last Great Trees of the Pacific Northwest* (New York: Penguin Books, 1992) and Brent S. Steel, *Public Lands Management in the West: Citizens, Interest Groups, and Values* (Westport, CT: Praeger, 1997).

60. Letter from Larry Ward, April 25, 1990. Elwha River Files, WSA.

61. "GOP Likely to Ax Dams' Destruction; Elwha Fish-Run Plan Would Be Expensive," *Tacoma News Tribune*, November 18, 1994, B7.

62. Ibid.

63. Ibid.; "Negotiating a Yes from Gorton on Elwha Dams," *Seattle Times*, August 11, 1997, B4; "Gorton Should Support Removal of Elwha Dams," *Seattle Times*, March 21, 1996, B6; "Senator Gorton Is Wrong to Flip-Flop on Elwha," *Seattle Times*, August 18, 1994, B8; Slade Gorton, "A More Sensible Option for Elwha Dams," *Seattle Times*, July 31, 1996, B5; Robert T. Nelson, "Gorton Voted for Law He's Fighting—He Now Wants Elwha Dam Saved," *Seattle Times*, August 16, 1994, B1.

64. Egan, "Restoring the Elwha," 169, 170.

65. Ibid., 171.

66. Notes on Elwha Dams meeting, January 25, 1994. Set of notes taken by an advocate of restoration at a local meeting opposed to Elwha restoration. OLYM-429, Box 3, Folder 10, ONPA.

67. Ibid.

68. Ibid., 3.

69. Ibid.

70. Egan, "Restoring the Elwha," 171, 172.

71. Ibid., 172, 173.

72. Les Blumenthal, "President Has Much Riding on the Fate of 2 Elwha River Dams," *Tacoma News Tribune*, March 24, 1996, G5; "Senator Gorton is Wrong to Flip-Flop on Elwha," B8; Kim Murphy, "Clinton Plan Calls for Removing 2 Dams to Restore Salmon Runs," *Los Angeles Times*, March 20, 1996, A12.

73. Associated Press, "Removal of Elwha Dams Urged; Next Move Is President's," *Tacoma News Tribune*, November 15, 1996, B6; "Welcome Prod on Elwha," *Seattle Times*, May 7, 1996, B4; "Gorton Should Support Removal of Elwha Dams," B6; Associated Press, "White to Push Removal of Dams," *The Columbian*, May 6, 1996, A2; Les Blumenthal, "White Airs Ideas on How to Fund Destruction of Elwha Dams," *Tacoma News Tribune*, May 15, 1996, A16.

74. "Negotiating a Yes from Gorton on Elwha Dams," B4; Simon, "Babbitt Gets Closer Look at Elwha Dams," A15.

75. Simon, "Babbitt Gets Closer Look at Elwha Dams," A15.

76. Dean Mosiman, "Group Alters Dam Opinion," *Peninsula Daily News*, May 8, 1996; Elwha Citizens Advisory Committee, "The Elwha River and Our Community's Future: Recommendations of the Elwha Citizens Advisory Committee" (unpublished report, April 30, 1996).

77. Elwha Citizens Advisory Committee, "The Elwha River and Our Community's Future," 5, 6.

78. William R. Lowry, *Dam Politics: Restoring America's Rivers* (Washington, D.C.: Georgetown University Press, 2003), 148.

79. Rich Landers, "Going with the Flow: Plan to Dismantle Two Outdated Dams will Allow Salmon to Swim Free Again," *Spokane Spokesman Review*, March 1, 1998, G1, 2.

CONCLUSION

1. They were removed in September, 2011, almost 20 years after the passage of the Elwha Restoration Act.

2. American Rivers Web site, accessed September 22, 2003, http://www.amrivers.org/

3. David Hart, D. Johnson, Thomas E. Bushaw-Newton, "Dam Removal: Challenges and Opportunities for Ecological Research and River Restoration," *Bioscience* 52, no. 8 (August 2002).

4. Steve Grant, "Freeing Maine River Signals Trend; Dam's End," *Hartford Courant*, July 1, 1999, A1.

5. Ibid.

6. Stephen Brooke interview; Blaine Harden, "U.S. Orders Dam Destroyed; For First Time, Fish Habitat Takes Priority over a Hydroelectric Dam," *Washington Post*, November 26, 1997, A1; "With Industry, Sewage Plans, Citizens Play Role," *Kennebec Journal*, March 22, 1990; Kenneth Z. Chutchian, "Kennebec Fish Stage a Comeback: But Dioxin Still Poses a Problem," *Kennebec Journal*, March 22, 1990.

7. George Manlove, "Removal of Dam Would Alter Face of River," *Kennebec Journal*, March 22, 1990, 8, 9.

8. Brooke interview.

9. M. O'Donnell, N. Gray, G. Wippelhauser, and P. Christman, *Kennebec River Diadromous Fish Restoration: Annual Progress Report—2000* (Augusta, ME: Maine Department of Marine Resources, 2000), 8.

10. Ibid.; Thomas Squiers interview.

11. Terri Stanley, "Fish Passage to Be Installed at Augusta Dam," *Kennebec Journal*, May 5, 1988.

12. Brooke interview.

13. Kim Leighton, "Coalition Ready to Apply for Control of Edwards Dam," *Kennebec Journal*, March 3, 1989.

14. Brooke interview.

15. Ibid.

16. Leighton, "Coalition Ready to Apply for Control of Edwards Dam."

17. Ibid.; "Dam Management Defended," *Kennebec Journal*, October 7, 1989.

18. Harden, "U.S. Orders Maine Dam Destroyed."

19. Ken Brack, "Augusta Takes on Big Brother for Dam," *Kennebec Journal*, March 19, 1990, 1, 8.

20. Ken Brack, "State Explains Its Dam Plan: Local Legislators Unhappy over Eminent Domain Proposal," *Kennebec Journal*, March 16, 1990, 1, 12; Ken Brack, "Augusta Takes on Big Brother for Dam," 1, 8; Ken Brack, "Dam Issue Gets Closer Look," *Kennebec Journal*, March 23, 1990, 1, 12.

21. George Manlove, "Removal of Dam Would Alter Face of River," *Kennebec Journal*, March 22, 1990, 8, 9.

22. Lucy Hood, "D.C. Group Explains Support of Plan to Breach Edwards Dam," *Kennebec Journal*, March 22, 1990.

23. "Maine Asks U.S. to Deny License to Dam Owners," *New York Times*, October 17, 1990, A21.

24. Brooke interview.

25. Ibid.

26. Dave Cheever, "City Dissatisfied; Plans Appeal after a Review," *Kennebec Journal*, November 26, 1997, 1.

27. Ned Porter, "Shortnose Sturgeon at Center of Debate on Damming Rivers," *Bangor Daily News*, September 15, 1994.

28. Evan Richert interview.

29. Ibid.

30. Ibid.

31. Carey Goldberg, "Fish Are Victorious over Dams as U.S. Agency Orders Shutdown," *New York Times*, November 26, 1997, A16.

32. Peter J. Howe, "U.S. Ends Maine Dam's License as Environment Gets the Nod," *Boston Globe*, November 26, 1997, A1.

33. Ibid.

34. Betsy Carpenter, "Conservationists Are Challenging the Utility of Old Dams," *U.S. News and World Report*, October 16, 1989, 90.

35. Dave Cheever, "Coalition Crows at Federal Decision," *Kennebec Journal*, November 26, 1997, 1.

36. Ibid.

37. Ibid.

38. "Dam Ruling Blow to Industry," *London Financial Times*, November 27, 1997, 3.

39. Ellen Jovin, "Edwards Dam: A Watershed Decision for Hydropower," *Electrical World* 212, no. 3 (March 1998): 44.

40. *Bangor Daily News*, December 31, 1997.

41. Dave Cheever, "More Join in Edwards Appeal," *Kennebec Journal*, January 5, 1998, 1.

42. Ibid.

43. Dave Cheever, "Senators Protest Lack of Reprieve for Edwards Owners," *Kennebec Journal*, February 9, 1998, 1.

44. Richert interview.

45. Dave Cheever, "Coalition Crows at Federal Decision," 1.

46. Dave Cheever interview.

47. Dave Cheever, "Edwards Removal OK'd: City Signs Agreement with State, Manufacturing Company," *Kennebec Journal*, May 9, 1998, 1; Dave

Cheever, "Augusta Approves Pact on Old Dam; The City Agrees to Let the State Take Possession and Dismantle the Edwards Dam," *Portland Press Herald*, May 5, 1998, 1B; Brooke interview.

48. Brooke interview; Richert interview; John McPhee, *The Founding Fish* (New York: Farrar, Straus and Giroux, 2002), 77.

49. Maine Department of Marine Resources, *Annual Report 2001*, January 2002, 22; "Stripers Caught above Edwards Dam," *Fly Fisherman*, 31, 2 (February 2000): 26; Dan McGillvray, "River's Rebirth Surprises Even Most Ardent Supporters," *Kennebec Journal*, June 30, 2000, A1.

50. Lowry, *Dam Politics*, 65–67.

51. Patrik Jonsson, "The Unsung Tale of a River's Restoration," *Christian Science Monitor* 93, 45 (January 30, 2001); Lowry, *Dam Politics*, 72.

52. Traci Watson, "Dam Removal May Help River Restoration," *USA Today*, June 30, 1999, A3; Grossman, *Watershed*, 44.

53. Grossman, *Watershed*, 68.

54. David Hart, Thomas E. Johnson, Karen L. Bushaw-Newton, Richard J. Horowitz, Angela T. Bednarek, Donald F. Charles, Daniel A. Kreeger, David J. Velinsky, "Dam Removal: Challenges and Opportunities for Ecological Research and River Restoration," *Bioscience* 52, no. 8 (August 2002): 674.

55. Andrew Murr and Sharon Begley, "A River Runs Through It, Tearing Down the Water Walls," *Newsweek*, July 12, 1999, 46.

56. Beth Daley, "US Aid May Preserve Huge Maine Tract," *Boston Globe*, December 23, 2007, B1.

57. Editorial, *Kennebec Journal*, January 4, 2008.

58. "PGE Starts Marmot Dam Removal," August 14, 2007; PGE Web site, www.portlandgeneral.com/community_and_env/hydropower_and_fish/sandy/default.aspx. Accessed July 23, 2009.

59. "Rogue River Dam Removal Starts Phase Two," *Northwest Construction* 12, no. 7 (July 1, 2009).

60. Sandy Bauers, "Let That River Flow," *The Philadelphia Inquirer*, June 4, 2007, C1.

61. Richard White, *The Organic Machine: The Remaking of the Columbia River* (New York: Hill and Wang, 1995), 112.

62. When I suggested to Robert Elofson that an unanticipated benefit of the delays was the ability to more carefully plan the restoration and the scientific studies, he was dubious and made the point that if the dams had been taken out in reasonable time, by 2010 there would have been approximately eight years of a dam-free Elwha with salmon making runs up the river already.

63. "Environment—Decommissioning Dams—Costs and Trends," *Water Power & Dam Construction*, February 28, 2009.

64. Jeffery Duda, Jerry E. Freilich, and Edward G. Schreiner, "Baseline Studies in the Elwha River Ecosystem Prior to Dam Removal: Introduction to the Special Issue," special issue, *Northwest Science* 82 (2008): 9.

65. George R. Pess, Michael L. McHenry, Timothy J. Beechie, and Jeremy Davies, "Biological Impacts of the Elwha River Dams and Potential

Salmonid Responses to Dam Removal," special issue, *Northwest Science* 82 (2008): 76.

66. Ibid.

67. USGS press release, "Biologist-Divers Complete 42-Mile Snorkel Survey of Elwha River," September 21, 2007.

68. J. Anne Shaffer, Patrick Crain, Brian Winter, Michael L. McHenry, Cathy Lear, and Timothy J. Randle, "Nearshore Restoration of the Elwha River Through Removal of the Elwha and Glines Canyon Dams: An Overview," special issue, *Northwest Science* 82 (2008): 48–52.

69. Brian D. Winter and Patrick Crain, "Making the Case for Ecosystem Restoration," 21; Pess et al., "Biological Impacts of the Elwha River Dams," 81.

70. Winter and Crain, "Making the Case for Ecosystem Restoration," 21.

71. Ibid., 20.

72. Ibid., 19, 20; Pess et al., "Biological Impacts of the Elwha River Dams," 84.

73. Elofson interview; Pess et al., "Biological Impacts of the Elwha River Dams," 84–86.

74. L. Ward, P. Crain, B. Freymond, M. McHenry, D. Morrill, G. Pess, R. Peters, J. A. Shaffer, B. Winter, and B. Wunderlich, "Elwha River Fish Restoration Plan—Developed Pursuant to the Elwha River Ecosystem and Fisheries Restoration, Act, Public Law 102-495" (Washington, D.C.: U.S. Department of Commerce, 2008), x, xiii, 7, 10, 14.

75. Ibid., xi, xii, 10.

76. Ibid., xiii.

77. Jim Martin and Patty Glick, *A Great Wave Rising: Solutions for Columbia and Snake River Salmon in the Age of Global Warming*, 9. Informational brochure produced at LightinTheRiver.org. Accessed July 28, 2009.

78. The Climate Impacts Group, M. McGuire Elsner, J. Littell, and L. Whitely Binder, eds., *The Washington Climate Change Impacts Assessment: Evaluating Washington's Future in a Changing Climate* (Seattle, WA: University of Washington, 2009), 217.

79. Mauri Pelto, "North Cascades Glacier Climate Impact Project," Glacier Home Page, accessed April 8, 2011, www.nichols.edu/departments/glacier/mb.htm; Pelto, "Elwha River: Impact of Ongoing Glacier Retreat," Glacier Home Page, accessed April 9, 2011, www.nichols.edu/departments/glacier/elwha%20fact%20sheet.pdf

80. James Battin, Matthew W. Wiley, Mary H. Ruckelshaus, Richard N. Palmer, Elizabeth Korb, Krista K. Bartz, and Hiroo Imaki, "Projected Impacts of Climate Change on Salmon Habitat Restoration," *Proceedings of the National Academy of Sciences* 104, 16 (April 17, 2007): 6721.

81. Lisa G. Crozier, Richard W. Zabel, and Alan F. Hamlet, "Predicting Differential Effects of Climate Change at the Population Level with Life-Cycle Models of Spring Chinook Salmon," *Global Change Biology* 14 (2008): 237.

82. Ibid., 244.

83. Battin et al., "Projected Impacts of Climate Change."

84. Lester R. Brown, *Plan B 3.0: Mobilizing to Save Civilization* (New York: W.W. Norton & Company, 2008), 165.

85. Neil Maher, *Nature's New Deal: The Civilian Conservation Corps and the Roots of the American Environmental Movement* (New York, NY: Oxford University Press, 2008).

86. "Senate Hearing on Stronghold Legislation," Spring 2010. Wild Salmon Center Web site, http://www.wildsalmoncenter.org/press/wsc_news_spring_2010.php#Hoh. Accessed March 14, 2011.

Bibliography

MANUSCRIPT SOURCES

University of Washington Special Collections (UWSC)
    Thomas Aldwell Papers
    John N. Cobb Papers
    Polly Dyer Papers
    Rick Rutz Papers
Olympic National Park Cultural Resources Office Archives (ONPA)
    The Philip R. S. Johnson Elwha River Sources
Washington State Archives–Olympia (WSA)
    Elwha River File
    Snake River File
Western Washington University Archives & Record Center (WWUARC)
    Al Swift Papers

GOVERNMENT DOCUMENTS

Cobb, John N. *Pacific Salmon Fisheries: Appendix III to the Report of U.S. Commissioner of Fisheries for 1916.* Washington, D.C.: GPO, 1917.

Hearing Before the Committee on Energy and Natural Resources, United States Senate, on S. 2527. Washington, D.C.: GPO, 1992.

Joint Hearing Before the Subcommittee of Energy and Power of the Committee on Energy and Commerce on H.R. 4844. Washington, D.C.: GPO, 1992.

Maib, Charles W. "A Historical Note on the Elwha River Its Power Development and It's Industrial Diversion," Washington State Department of Fisheries, no date.

National Park Service. *The Elwha Report: Restoration of the Elwha River Ecosystem & Native Anadromous Fisheries.* Denver: National Park Service, 1993.

———. *The Elwha River Report.* Denver: National Park Service, 1994.

Squiers, Thomas S., and Malcolm Smith. *Distribution and Abundance of Shortnose and Atlantic Sturgeon in the Kennebec River Estuary.* Augusta, ME: Department of Marine Resources, 1979.

State of Washington Department of Fisheries Annual Report for 1949. Olympia, WA: State Printing Plant, 1952.

Twenty-fourth and Twenty-fifth Annual Reports of the State Fish Commissioner to the Governor of the State of Washington, April 1, 1913, to March 31, 1915. Olympia: Frank M. Lamborn, 1916.

Twenty-sixth and Twenty-seventh Annual Reports of the State Fish Commissioner to the Governor of the State of Washington. Olympia: Frank M. Lamborn, 1918.

Twenty-eighth and Twenty-ninth Annual Reports of the State Fish Commissioner to the Governor of the State of Washington, April 1, 1917, to March 31, 1919. Olympia: Frank M. Lamborn, 1920.

Thirtieth and Thirty-first Annual Reports of the State Fish Commissioner to the Governor of the State of Washington, April 1, 1919, to March 31, 1921. Olympia: Frank M. Lamborn, 1921.

Thirty-fourth and Thirty-fifth Annual Reports of State Supervisor of Fisheries for the Period from April 1, 1923, to March 31, 1925. Olympia: Jay Thomas, 1925.

Ward, L., P. Crain, B. Freymond, M. McHenry, D. Morrill, G. Pess, R. Peters, J. A. Shaffer, B. Winter, and B. Wunderlich. Elwha River Fish Restoration Plan—Developed Pursuant to the Elwha River Ecosystem and Fisheries Restoration Act, Public Law 102-495. Washington, D.C.: U.S. Department of Commerce, 2008.

NEWSPAPERS

Astoria (OR) Budget
Augusta (ME) Kennebec Journal
Bangor (ME) Daily News
Bellingham (WA) American Reveille
Bellingham (WA) Herald
Boston Globe
Hartford (CT) Courant
Kelsonian Tribune (Kelso, WA)
Lewiston (ID) Morning Tribune
London Financial Times
Los Angeles Times
New York Times
Oregonian (Portland, OR)
Philadelphia Inquirer
Port Angeles (WA) Democratic Leader
Port Angeles (WA) Dungeness Beacon
Port Angeles (WA) Model Commonwealth
Port Angeles (WA) Olympic Leader
Port Angeles (WA) Peninsula Daily News
Port Angeles (WA) Tribune-Times
Portland (ME) Press-Herald
San Francisco Bulletin
Seattle Post-Intelligencer
Seattle Times
Spokane (WA) Spokesman Review
Tacoma (WA) News Tribune
Walla Walla (WA) Union Bulletin
Washington Post

PUBLISHED PRIMARY SOURCES

Aldwell, Thomas. *Conquering the Last Frontier.* Seattle, WA: Superior Publishing Company, 1950.

Clallam County Immigration Association. *Port Angeles, the Gate City of the Pacific Coast.* Port Angeles, WA: Clallam County Immigration Association, 1898.

Gunther, Erna. "Klallam Ethnography." *University of Washington Publications in Anthropology, Volume I.* Seattle, WA: University of Washington Press, 1927.

————. *Ethnobotany of Western Washington: The Knowledge and Uses of Indigenous Plants by Native Americans.* Seattle, WA: University of Washington Press, 1945.

Muir, John. *My First Summer in the Sierra.* New York: Penguin Books, 1987.

Roth, Lottie Roeder. *History of Whatcom County, Volume 1.* Seattle, WA: Pioneer Historical Publishing Company, 1926.

INTERVIEWS

Stephen Brooke, January 7, 2002.

Dave Cheever, January 8, 2002.

Robert Elofson, September 27, 2010.

Greg Ponte, January 7, 2002.

Evan Richert, January 8, 2002.

Thomas Squiers, January 6, 2002.

Interviews were conducted by the author, and are in his possession.

SECONDARY SOURCES

Abbott, Carl. *Boosters and Businessmen: Popular Economic Thought and Urban Growth in the Antebellum Middle West.* Westport, CT: Greenwood Press, 1981.

Benson, Norman G., ed. *A Century of Fisheries in North America.* Washington, D.C.: American Fisheries Society, Special Publication No. 7, 1970.

Berg, Iola. *History of the Washington State Department of Fisheries, 1890–1967.* Olympia, WA: General Administration Building, 1968.

Bilby, Robert E., Brian R. Fransen, and Peter A. Bisson. "Incorporation of Nitrogen and Carbon from Spawning Coho Salmon into the Trophic System of Small Streams: Evidence from Stable Isotopes." *Canadian Journal of Fisheries and Aquatic Sciences* 53 (January 1996).

Blumm, Michael C. "The Northwest's Hydroelectric Heritage." In *Northwest Lands, Northwest Peoples: Readings in Environmental History,* ed. Paul Hirt and Dale Goble. Seattle, WA: University of Washington Press, 1999.

Brown, Bruce. *Mountain in the Clouds: A Search for the Wild Salmon.* New York: Collier Books, 1990.

Brown, J. T. "A History of Fish Culture as Related to the Development of Fishery Programs." In *A Century of Fisheries in North America,* edited by Norman G. Benson. Washington, D.C.: American Fisheries Society, 1970.

Brown, Lester R. *Plan B 3.0: Mobilizing to Save Civilization.* New York: W.W. Norton & Company, 2008.

Castile, George Pierre. *The Indians of Puget Sound: The Notebooks of Myron Eells.* Seattle: University of Washington Press, 1985.

Cederholm, Jeff C., Matt D. Kunze, and Atuhiro Sibatani. "Pacific Salmon Carcasses: Essential Contributions of Nutrients and Energy for Aquatic and Terrestrial Ecosystems." *Fisheries* 24 (October 1999).

Cone, Joseph, and Sandy Ridlington. *The Northwest Salmon Crisis: A Documentary History.* Corvallis: Oregon State University Press, 1996.

Cronon, William. *Changes in the Land: Indians, Colonists, and the Ecology of New England.* New York: Hill and Wang, 1983.

Crosby, Alfred W. *The Columbian Exchange: Biological and Cultural Consequences of 1492.* Westport, CT: Greenwood Press, 1972.

Dodds, Gordon B. *The Salmon King of Oregon: R. D. Hume and the Pacific Fisheries.* Chapel Hill: University of North Carolina Press, 1959.

Duda, Jeffery J., Jerry E. Freilich, and Edward G. Schreiner. "Baseline Studies in the Elwha River Ecosystem Prior to Dam Removal: Introduction to the Special Issue." Special issue, *Northwest Science* 82 (2008).

Ervin, Keith. *Fragile Majesty: The Battle for North America's Last Great Forest.* Seattle, WA: The Mountaineers, 1989.

Fisher, E. P. "The Rights of Fisheries and Ecosystems." *Fisheries* 20 (April 1995).

Fox, Stephen. *The American Conservation Movement: John Muir and His Legacy.* Madison: University of Wisconsin Press, 1981.

Franklin, J., and C. T. Dyrness. *Natural Vegetation of Oregon and Washington.* Corvallis: Oregon State University Press, 1988.

Goble, Dale. "Salmon in the Columbia Basin: From Abundance to Extinction." In *Northwest Lands, Northwest Peoples: Readings in Environmental History*, ed. Paul Hirt and Dale Goble. Seattle: University of Washington Press, 1999.

Gottlieb, Robert. *Forcing the Spring: The Transformation of the American Environmental Movement.* Washington, D.C.: Island Press, 1993.

Grossman, Elizabeth. *Watershed: The Undamming of America.* New York: Counterpoint, 2002.

Harden, Blaine. *A River Lost: The Life and Death of the Columbia.* New York: W.W. Norton & Company, 1996.

Hart, David, Thomas E. Johnson, Karen L. Bushaw-Newton, Richard J. Horowitz, Angela T. Bednarek, Donald F. Charles, Daniel A. Kreeger, David J. Velinsky. "Dam Removal: Challenges and Opportunities for Ecological Research and River Restoration." *Bioscience* 52, No. 8 (August 2002).

Harvey, Mark. *A Symbol of Wilderness: Echo Park and the American Conservation Movement.* Seattle: University of Washington Press, 1994.

Hay, Duncan. *Hydroelectric Development in the United States, 1880–1940.* Washington, D.C.: Edison Electric Institute, 1991.

Hays, Samuel P. *Conservation and the Gospel of Efficiency: The Progressive Conservation Movement, 1890–1920.* Cambridge, MA: Harvard University Press, 1959.

———. *Beauty, Health, and Permanence: Environmental Politics in the United States, 1955–1985.* New York: Cambridge University Press, 1987.

Hilborn, Ray. "Confessions of a Reformed Hatchery Basher." *Fisheries* 24 (May 1999).

Hirt, Paul. *A Conspiracy of Optimism: Management of the National Forests Since World War II.* Lincoln: University of Nebraska Press, 1994.

———, and Dale Goble. *Northwest Lands, Northwest Peoples: Readings in Environmental History.* Seattle: University of Washington Press, 1999.

Hofstadter, Richard. *The Age of Reform: From Bryan to F.D.R.* New York: Alfred A. Knopf, 1955.

Hosey and Associates. "Response to Request for Additional Information of May 28, 1987: Elwha Project FERC No. 2683, Glines Project FERC No. 588." Unpublished report prepared for the James River Corporation. February 12, 1988.

Hughes, J. Donald. *American Indian Ecology.* El Paso: Texas Western Press, 1983.

Hughes, Thomas P. *Networks of Power: Electrification in Western Society, 1880–1930.* Baltimore, MD: The Johns Hopkins University Press, 1983.

Hult, Ruby El. *The Untamed Olympics: The Story of a Peninsula.* Portland, OR: Binford & Mort, 1954.

The Independent Scientific Group (Richard N. Williams, Peter A. Bisson, Daniel L. Bottom, Lyle D. Calvin, Charles C. Coutant, Michael W. Erho, Jr., Christopher A. Frissell, James A. Lichatowich, William J. Liss, Willis E. McConnaha, Phillip R. Mundy, Jack A. Stanford, and Richard R. Whitney). "Scientific Issues in the Restoration of Salmonid Fisheries in the Columbia River." *Fisheries* 24 (March 1999).

Judd, Richard W. *Common Lands, Common People: The Origins of Conservation in Northern New England.* Cambridge, MA: Harvard University Press, 1997.

Karr, James R. "Restoring Wild Salmon: We Must Do Better." *Illahee* 10 (Winter 1994).

Kempton, Willett, James S. Boster, and Jennifer A. Hartley. *Environmental Values in American Culture.* Cambridge, MA: The MIT Press, 1995.

Leopold, Aldo. *A Sand County Almanac: And Sketches Here and There.* New York: Oxford University Press, 1949.

Lichatowich, Jim. *Salmon Without Rivers: A History of the Pacific Salmon Crisis.* Washington, D.C.: Island Press, 1999.

Limerick, Patricia Nelson. *The Legacy of Conquest: The Unbroken Past of the American West.* New York: W.W. Norton & Company, 1987.

Lowry, William R. *Dam Politics: Restoring America's Rivers.* Washington, D.C.: Georgetown University Press, 2003.

Maher, Neil. *Nature's New Deal: The Civilian Conservation Corps and the Roots of the American Environmental Movement.* New York: Oxford University Press, 2008.

Mapes, Lynda V. *Breaking Ground: The Lower Elwha Klallam Tribe and the Unearthing of Tse-whit-zen Village.* Seattle: University of Washington Press, 2009.

Martin, Paul, and Peggy Brady. *Port Angeles, Washington: A History.* Port Angeles, WA: Peninsula Publishing, 1983.

McCallum, John, and Lorraine Wilcox Ross. *Port Angeles, U.S.A.: Centennial Edition 1862–1962.* Seattle, WA: Wood and Reber, Inc., 1961.

McEvoy, Arthur F. *The Fisherman's Problem: Ecology and Law in the California Fisheries, 1850–1980.* New York: Cambridge University Press, 1986.

McKee, Bates. *Cascadia: The Geologic Evolution of the Pacific Northwest.* New York: McGraw-Hill Book Company, 1972.

McNulty, Tim. *Olympic National Park: A Natural History Guide.* New York, NY: Houghton Mifflin Company, 1996.

McPhee, John. *The Founding Fish.* New York: Farrar, Straus, and Giroux, 2002.

Mighetto, Lisa, and Wesley J. Ebel. *Saving the Salmon: A History of the U.S. Army Corps of Engineers' Efforts to Protect Anadromous Fish on the Columbia and Snake Rivers.* Seattle, WA: Historical Research Associates, 1994.

Miller, Char, and Hal Rothman, eds. *Out of the Woods: Essays in Environmental History.* Pittsburgh, PA: University of Pittsburgh Press, 1997.

Nash, Roderick. *Wilderness and the American Mind.* New Haven, CT: Yale University Press, 1967.

———. *The Rights of Nature: A History of Environmental Ethics.* Madison: University of Wisconsin Press, 1989.

National Research Council. *Upstream: Salmon and Society in the Pacific Northwest.* Washington, D.C.: National Academy Press, 1996.

Nehlsen, Willa, Jack E. Williams, and James A. Lichatowich. "Pacific Salmon at the Crossroads: Stocks at Risk from California, Oregon, Idaho, and Washington." *Fisheries* 16, no. 2 (March–April 1991).

Netboy, Anthony. *The Columbia River Salmon and Steelhead Trout: Their Fight for Survival.* Seattle, WA: University of Washington Press, 1980.

Oelschlager, Max. *The Idea of Wilderness: From Prehistory to the Age of Ecology.* New Haven, CT: Yale University Press, 1991.

Pess, George R., Michael L. McHenry, Timothy J. Beechie, and Jeremy Davies. "Biological Impacts of the Elwha River Dams and Potential Salmonid Responses to Dam Removal." Special issue, *Northwest Science* 82 (2008).

Petersen, Keith C. *River of Life, Channel of Death: Fish and Dams on the Lower Snake.* Lewiston, ID: Confluence Press, 1995. (Reprinted 2001, Corvallis, OR: Oregon State University Press.)

Pinchot, Gifford. *Breaking New Ground.* Seattle: University of Washington Press, 1947.

Quinn, Thomas P. *The Behavior and Ecology of Pacific Salmon and Trout.* Seattle: University of Washington Press, 2005.

Reisner, Marc. *Cadillac Desert: The American West and Its Disappearing Water.* New York: Penguin Books, 1986.

Robbins, William G. *Hard Times in Paradise: Coos Bay, Oregon, 1850–1986.* Seattle: University of Washington Press, 1988.

———. *Colony and Empire: The Capitalist Transformation of the American West.* Lawrence: University Press of Kansas, 1994.

Ruby, Robert H., and John A. Brown. *Indians of the Pacific Northwest.* Norman: University of Oklahoma Press, 1981.

Runte, Alfred. *National Parks: The American Experience.* Lincoln: University of Nebraska Press, 1987.

Schultz, Stewart T. *The Northwest Coast: A Natural History.* Portland, OR: Timber Press, 1990.

Schwantes, Carlos A. *The Pacific Northwest: An Interpretive History.* Lincoln: University of Nebraska Press, 1989.

Sellers, Charles. *The Market Revolution: Jacksonian America, 1815–1846.* New York: Oxford University Press, 1991.

Shaffer, J. Anne, Patrick Crain, Brian Winter, Michael L. McHenry, Cathy Lear, and Timothy J. Randle. "Nearshore Restoration of the Elwha River Through Removal of the Elwha and Glines Canyon Dams: An Overview." Special issue, *Northwest Science* 82 (2008).

Stewart, H. *Indian Fishing: Early Methods on the Northwest Coast.* Seattle: University of Washington Press, 1977.

Suttles, Wayne. *Coast Salish Essays.* Seattle: University of Washington Press, 1987.

Tabor, Roland. *Geology of Olympic National Park.* Seattle, WA: Pacific Northwest National Parks & Forests Association, 1987.

Taylor, Joseph E. *Making Salmon: An Environmental History of the Northwest Fisheries Crisis.* Seattle: University of Washington Press, 1999.

Thomas, John L. *A Country in the Mind: Wallace Stegner, Bernard DeVoto, History and the American Land.* New York: Routledge, 2000.

White, Richard. *The Organic Machine: The Remaking of the Columbia River.* New York: Hill and Wang, 1995.

———. *Land Use, Environment, and Social Change: The Shaping of Island County, Washington.* Seattle: University of Washington Press, 1980.

Winter, Brian D., and Patrick Crain. "Making the Case for Ecosystem Restoration by Dam Removal in the Elwha River, Washington." Special issue, *Northwest Science* 82 (2008).

Wood, Robert. *Olympic Mountains Trail Guide: National Park and National Forest.* Seattle, WA: The Mountaineers, 1984.

Worster, Donald. *Nature's Economy: A History of Ecological Ideas.* New York: Cambridge University Press, 1977.

———. *The Ends of the Earth: Perspectives on Modern Environmental History.* New York: Cambridge University Press, 1988.

Wray, Jacilee, ed. *Native Peoples of the Olympic Peninsula.* Norman: University of Oklahoma Press, 2002.

Wunderlich, Robert C., Brian D. Winter, and John H. Meyer. "Restoration of the Elwha River Ecosystem." *Fisheries* 19, no. 8 (August 1994).

THESES AND DISSERTATIONS

Allen, Cain. "'They Called it Progress': Indians, Salmon, and the Industrialization of the Columbia River." MA thesis, Portland State University, 2000.

Barber, Katrine. "After Celilo Falls: The Dalles Dam, Indian Fishing Rights, and Federal Energy Policy on the Mid-Columbia River." PhD diss., Washington State University, 1999.

Boyd, Colleen Elizabeth. "Changer Is Coming: History, Identity, and the Land among the Lower Elwha Klallam Tribe of the North Olympic Peninsula." PhD diss., University of Washington, 2001.

Egan, Virginia G. "Restoring the Elwha: Salmon, Dams, and People on the Olympic Peninsula. A Case Study of Environmental Decision Making." PhD diss., Antioch University New England, 2007.

Index